Matrix Methods in Data Mining and Pattern Recognition

Fundamentals of Algorithms

Editor-in-Chief: Nicholas J. Higham, University of Manchester

The SIAM series on Fundamentals of Algorithms is a collection of short user-oriented books on state-of-the-art numerical methods. Written by experts, the books provide readers with sufficient knowledge to choose an appropriate method for an application and to understand the method's strengths and limitations. The books cover a range of topics drawn from numerical analysis and scientific computing. The intended audiences are researchers and practitioners using the methods and upper level undergraduates in mathematics, engineering, and computational science.

Books in this series not only provide the mathematical background for a method or class of methods used in solving a specific problem but also explain how the method can be developed into an algorithm and translated into software. The books describe the range of applicability of a method and give guidance on troubleshooting solvers and interpreting results. The theory is presented at a level accessible to the practitioner. MATLAB® software is the preferred language for codes presented since it can be used across a wide variety of platforms and is an excellent environment for prototyping, testing, and problem solving.

The series is intended to provide guides to numerical algorithms that are readily accessible, contain practical advice not easily found elsewhere, and include understandable codes that implement the algorithms.

Series Volumes

Lars Eldén

Linköping University
Linköping, Sweden

Matrix Methods in Data Mining and Pattern Recognition

Society for Industrial and Applied Mathematics
Philadelphia

Figures 6.2, 10.1, 10.7, 10.9, 10.11, 11.1, and 11.3 are from L. Eldén, Numerical linear algebra in data mining, *Acta Numer.*, 15:327–384, 2006. Reprinted with the permission of Cambridge University Press.

Figures 14.1, 14.3, and 14.4 were constructed by the author from images appearing in P. N. Belhumeur, J. P. Hespanha, and D. J. Kriegman, Eigenfaces vs. fisherfaces: Recognition using class specific linear projection, *IEEE Trans. Pattern Anal. Mach. Intell.*, 19:711–720, 1997.

Library of Congress Cataloging-in-Publication Data

Eldén, Lars, 1944-
    Matrix methods in data mining and pattern recognition / Lars Eldén.
        p. cm. — (Fundamentals of algorithms ; 04)
    Includes bibliographical references and index.
    ISBN 978-0-898716-26-9 (pbk. : alk. paper)
    1. Data mining. 2. Pattern recognition systems—Mathematical models. 3. Algebras, Linear. I. Title.

QA76.9.D343E52 2007
05.74—dc20
                                             2006041348

Partial royalties from the sale of this book are placed in a fund to help students attend SIAM meetings and other SIAM-related activities. This fund is administered by SIAM, and qualified individuals are encouraged to write directly to SIAM for guidelines.

Contents

Preface

The first version of this book was a set of lecture notes for a graduate course on data mining and applications in science and technology organized by the Swedish National Graduate School in Scientific Computing (NGSSC). Since then the material has been used and further developed for an undergraduate course on numerical algorithms for data mining and IT at Linköping University. This is a second course in scientific computing for computer science students.

The book is intended primarily for undergraduate students who have previously taken an introductory scientific computing/numerical analysis course. It may also be useful for early graduate students in various data mining and pattern recognition areas who need an introduction to linear algebra techniques.

The purpose of the book is to demonstrate that there are several very powerful numerical linear algebra techniques for solving problems in different areas of data mining and pattern recognition. To achieve this goal, it is necessary to present material that goes beyond what is normally covered in a first course in scientific computing (numerical analysis) at a Swedish university. On the other hand, since the book is application oriented, it is not possible to give a comprehensive treatment of the mathematical and numerical aspects of the linear algebra algorithms used.

The book has three parts. After a short introduction to a couple of areas of data mining and pattern recognition, linear algebra concepts and matrix decompositions are presented. I hope that this is enough for the student to use matrix decompositions in problem-solving environments such as MATLAB®. Some mathematical proofs are given, but the emphasis is on the existence and properties of the matrix decompositions rather than on how they are computed. In Part II, the linear algebra techniques are applied to data mining problems. Naturally, the data mining and pattern recognition repertoire is quite limited: I have chosen problem areas that are well suited for linear algebra techniques. In order to use intelligently the powerful software for computing matrix decompositions available in MATLAB, etc., some understanding of the underlying algorithms is necessary. A very short introduction to eigenvalue and singular value algorithms is given in Part III.

I have not had the ambition to write a book of recipes: "given a certain problem, here is an algorithm for its solution." That would be difficult, as the area is far too diverse to give clear-cut and simple solutions. Instead, my intention has been to give the student a set of tools that may be tried as they are but, more likely, that will need to be modified to be useful for a particular application. Some of the methods in the book are described using MATLAB scripts. They should not be considered as serious algorithms but rather as pseudocodes given for illustration purposes.

A collection of exercises and computer assignments are available at the book's Web page: www.siam.org/books/fa04.

The support from NGSSC for producing the original lecture notes is gratefully acknowledged. The lecture notes have been used by a couple of colleagues. Thanks are due to Gene Golub and Saara Hyvönen for helpful comments. Several of my own students have helped me to improve the presentation by pointing out inconsistencies and asking questions. I am indebted to Berkant Savas for letting me use results from his master's thesis in Chapter 10. Three anonymous referees read earlier versions of the book and made suggestions for improvements. Finally, I would like to thank Nick Higham, series editor at SIAM, for carefully reading the manuscript. His thoughtful advice helped me improve the contents and the presentation considerably.

Lars Eldén
Linköping, October 2006

Part I

Linear Algebra Concepts and Matrix Decompositions

Chapter 1

Vectors and Matrices in Data Mining and Pattern Recognition

1.1 Data Mining and Pattern Recognition

In modern society, huge amounts of data are collected and stored in computers so that useful information can later be extracted. Often it is not known at the time of collection what data will later be requested, and therefore the database is not designed to distill any particular information, but rather it is, to a large extent, unstructured. The science of extracting useful information from large data sets is usually referred to as "data mining," sometimes with the addition of "knowledge discovery."

Pattern recognition is often considered to be a technique separate from data mining, but its definition is related: "the act of taking in raw data and making an action based on the 'category' of the pattern" [31]. In this book we will not emphasize the differences between the concepts.

There are numerous application areas for data mining, ranging from e-business [10, 69] to bioinformatics [6], from scientific applications such as the classification of volcanos on Venus [21] to information retrieval [3] and Internet search engines [11].

Data mining is a truly interdisciplinary science, in which techniques from computer science, statistics and data analysis, linear algebra, and optimization are used, often in a rather eclectic manner. Due to the practical importance of the applications, there are now numerous books and surveys in the area [24, 25, 31, 35, 45, 46, 47, 49, 108].

It is not an exaggeration to state that everyday life is filled with situations in which we depend, often unknowingly, on advanced mathematical methods for data mining. Methods such as linear algebra and data analysis are basic ingredients in many data mining techniques. This book gives an introduction to the mathematical and numerical methods and their use in data mining and pattern recognition.

3

1.2 Vectors and Matrices

The following examples illustrate the use of vectors and matrices in data mining. These examples present the main data mining areas discussed in the book, and they will be described in more detail in Part II.

In many applications a matrix is just a rectangular array of data, and the elements are scalar, real numbers:

$$A = \begin{pmatrix} a_{11} & a_{12} & \cdots & a_{1n} \\ a_{21} & a_{22} & \cdots & a_{2n} \\ \vdots & \vdots & & \vdots \\ a_{m1} & a_{m2} & \cdots & a_{mn} \end{pmatrix} \in \mathbb{R}^{m \times n}.$$

To treat the data by mathematical methods, some mathematical structure must be added. In the simplest case, the columns of the matrix are considered as vectors in $\mathbb{R}^m$.

Example 1.1. *Term-document matrices* are used in *information retrieval*. Consider the following selection of five documents.[1] Key words, which we call *terms*, are marked in boldface.[2]

Document 1:   The **Google**™ **matrix** P is a model of the **Internet**.
Document 2: P_{ij} is nonzero if there is a **link** from **Web page** j to i.
Document 3:   The **Google matrix** is used to **rank** all **Web pages**.
Document 4:   The **ranking** is done by solving a **matrix eigenvalue** problem.
Document 5:   **England** dropped out of the top 10 in the **FIFA ranking**.

If we count the frequency of terms in each document we get the following result:

Term	Doc 1	Doc 2	Doc 3	Doc 4	Doc 5
eigenvalue	0	0	0	1	0
England	0	0	0	0	1
FIFA	0	0	0	0	1
Google	1	0	1	0	0
Internet	1	0	0	0	0
link	0	1	0	0	0
matrix	1	0	1	1	0
page	0	1	1	0	0
rank	0	0	1	1	1
Web	0	1	1	0	0

---

[1] In Document 5, FIFA is the Fédération Internationale de Football Association. This document is clearly concerned with football (soccer). The document is a newspaper headline from 2005. After the 2006 World Cup, England came back into the top 10.

[2] To avoid making the example too large, we have ignored some words that would normally be considered as terms (key words). Note also that only the stem of the word is significant: "ranking" is considered the same as "rank."

Thus each document is represented by a vector, or a point, in $\mathbb{R}^{10}$, and we can organize all documents into a term-document matrix:

$$A = \begin{pmatrix} 0 & 0 & 0 & 1 & 0 \\ 0 & 0 & 0 & 0 & 1 \\ 0 & 0 & 0 & 0 & 1 \\ 1 & 0 & 1 & 0 & 0 \\ 1 & 0 & 0 & 0 & 0 \\ 0 & 1 & 0 & 0 & 0 \\ 1 & 0 & 1 & 1 & 0 \\ 0 & 1 & 1 & 0 & 0 \\ 0 & 0 & 1 & 1 & 1 \\ 0 & 1 & 1 & 0 & 0 \end{pmatrix}.$$

Now assume that we want to find all documents that are relevant to the query **"ranking of Web pages."** This is represented by a *query* vector, constructed in a way analogous to the term-document matrix:

$$q = \begin{pmatrix} 0 \\ 0 \\ 0 \\ 0 \\ 0 \\ 0 \\ 0 \\ 1 \\ 1 \\ 1 \end{pmatrix} \in \mathbb{R}^{10}.$$

Thus the query itself is considered as a document. The information retrieval task can now be formulated as a mathematical problem: *find the columns of A that are close to the vector q*. To solve this problem we must use some distance measure in $\mathbb{R}^{10}$.

In the information retrieval application it is common that the dimension m is large, of the order 10^6, say. Also, as most of the documents contain only a small fraction of the terms, most of the elements in the matrix are equal to zero. Such a matrix is called *sparse*.

Some methods for information retrieval use linear algebra techniques (e.g., singular value decomposition (SVD)) for data compression and retrieval enhancement. Vector space methods for information retrieval are presented in Chapter 11.   ■

Often it is useful to consider the matrix not just as an array of numbers, or as a set of vectors, but also as a linear operator. Denote the columns of A

$$a_{.j} = \begin{pmatrix} a_{1j} \\ a_{2j} \\ \vdots \\ a_{mj} \end{pmatrix}, \qquad j = 1, 2, \ldots, n,$$

and write

$$A = \begin{pmatrix} a_{.1} & a_{.2} & \cdots & a_{.n} \end{pmatrix}.$$

Then the linear transformation is defined

$$y = Ax = \begin{pmatrix} a_{.1} & a_{.2} & \cdots & a_{.n} \end{pmatrix} \begin{pmatrix} x_1 \\ x_2 \\ \vdots \\ x_n \end{pmatrix} = \sum_{j=1}^{n} x_j a_{.j}.$$

Example 1.2. The classification of handwritten digits is a model problem in *pattern recognition*. Here vectors are used to represent digits. The image of one digit is a 16×16 matrix of numbers, representing gray scale. It can also be represented as a vector in $\mathbb{R}^{256}$, by stacking the columns of the matrix. A set of n digits (handwritten 3's, say) can then be represented by a matrix $A \in \mathbb{R}^{256 \times n}$, and the columns of A span a subspace of $\mathbb{R}^{256}$. We can compute an approximate basis of this subspace using the SVD $A = U\Sigma V^T$. Three basis vectors of the "3-subspace" are illustrated in Figure 1.1.

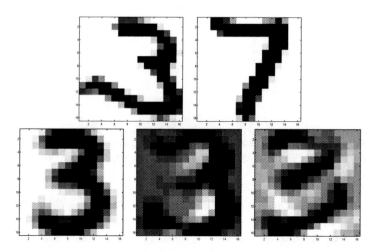

Figure 1.1. *Handwritten digits from the U.S. Postal Service database* [47], *and basis vectors for 3's (bottom).*

Let b be a vector representing an unknown digit. We now want to classify (automatically, by computer) the unknown digit as one of the digits 0–9. Given a set of approximate basis vectors for 3's, $u_1, u_2, \ldots, u_k$, we can determine whether b is a 3 by checking if there is a linear combination of the basis vectors, $\sum_{j=1}^{k} x_j u_j$, such that

$$b - \sum_{j=1}^{k} x_j u_j$$

is small. Thus, here we compute the coordinates of b in the basis $\{u_j\}_{j=1}^k$.

In Chapter 10 we discuss methods for classification of handwritten digits.   ■

The very idea of data mining is to extract useful information from large, often unstructured, sets of data. Therefore it is necessary that the methods used are efficient and often specially designed for large problems. In some data mining applications huge matrices occur.

Example 1.3. The task of extracting information from all Web pages available on the Internet is done by *search engines*. The core of the Google search engine is a matrix computation, probably the largest that is performed routinely [71]. The Google matrix P is of the order billions, i.e., close to the total number of Web pages on the Internet. The matrix is constructed based on the link structure of the Web, and element P_{ij} is nonzero if there is a link from Web page j to i.

The following small link graph illustrates a set of Web pages with outlinks and inlinks:

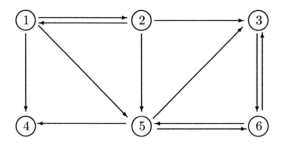

A corresponding *link graph matrix* is constructed so that the columns and rows represent Web pages and the nonzero elements in column j denote outlinks from Web page j. Here the matrix becomes

$$P = \begin{pmatrix} 0 & \frac{1}{3} & 0 & 0 & 0 & 0 \\ \frac{1}{3} & 0 & 0 & 0 & 0 & 0 \\ 0 & \frac{1}{3} & 0 & 0 & \frac{1}{3} & \frac{1}{2} \\ \frac{1}{3} & 0 & 0 & 0 & \frac{1}{3} & 0 \\ \frac{1}{3} & \frac{1}{3} & 0 & 0 & 0 & \frac{1}{2} \\ 0 & 0 & 1 & 0 & \frac{1}{3} & 0 \end{pmatrix}.$$

For a search engine to be useful, it must use a measure of quality of the Web pages. The Google matrix is used to rank all the pages. The ranking is done by solving an *eigenvalue problem* for P; see Chapter 12.   ■

1.3   Purpose of the Book

The present book is meant to be not primarily a textbook in numerical linear algebra but rather an application-oriented introduction to some techniques in modern linear algebra, with the emphasis on data mining and pattern recognition. It depends heavily on the availability of an easy-to-use programming environment that implements the algorithms that we will present. Thus, instead of describing in detail the algorithms, we will give enough mathematical theory and numerical background information so that a reader can understand and use the powerful software that is embedded in a package like MATLAB [68].

For a more comprehensive presentation of numerical and algorithmic aspects of the matrix decompositions used in this book, see any of the recent textbooks [29, 42, 50, 92, 93, 97]. The solution of linear systems and eigenvalue problems for large and sparse systems is discussed at length in [4, 5]. For those who want to study the detailed implementation of numerical linear algebra algorithms, software in Fortran, C, and C++ is available for free via the Internet [1].

It will be assumed that the reader has studied introductory courses in linear algebra and scientific computing (numerical analysis). Familiarity with the basics of a matrix-oriented programming language like MATLAB should help one to follow the presentation.

1.4   Programming Environments

In this book we use MATLAB [68] to demonstrate the concepts and the algorithms. Our codes are not to be considered as software; instead they are intended to demonstrate the basic principles, and we have emphasized simplicity rather than efficiency and robustness. *The codes should be used only for small experiments and never for production computations.*

Even if we are using MATLAB, we want to emphasize that any programming environment that implements modern matrix computations can be used, e.g., Mathematica® [112] or a statistics package.

1.5   Floating Point Computations

1.5.1   Flop Counts

The execution times of different algorithms can sometimes be compared by counting the number of *floating point operations*, i.e., arithmetic operations with floating point numbers. In this book we follow the standard procedure [42] and count each operation separately, and we use the term *flop* for one operation. Thus the statement y=y+a*x, where the variables are scalars, counts as two flops.

It is customary to count only the highest-order term(s). We emphasize that flop counts are often very crude measures of efficiency and computing time and can even be misleading under certain circumstances. On modern computers, which invariably have memory hierarchies, the data access patterns are very important. Thus there are situations in which the execution times of algorithms with the same flop counts can vary by an order of magnitude.

1.5.2 Floating Point Rounding Errors

Error analysis of the algorithms will not be a major part of the book, but we will cite a few results without proofs. We will assume that the computations are done under the *IEEE floating point standard* [2] and, accordingly, that the following model is valid.

A real number x, in general, cannot be represented exactly in a floating point system. Let $fl[x]$ be the floating point number representing x. Then

$$fl[x] = x(1 + \epsilon) \tag{1.1}$$

for some ϵ, satisfying $|\epsilon| \leq \mu$, where μ is the *unit round-off* of the floating point system. From (1.1) we see that the *relative error* in the floating point representation of any real number x satisfies

$$\left| \frac{fl[x] - x}{x} \right| \leq \mu.$$

In IEEE double precision arithmetic (which is the standard floating point format in MATLAB), the unit round-off satisfies $\mu \approx 10^{-16}$. In IEEE single precision we have $\mu \approx 10^{-7}$.

Let $fl[x \odot y]$ be the result of a floating point arithmetic operation, where $\odot$ denotes any of $+$, $-$, $*$, and $/$. Then, provided that $x \odot y \neq 0$,

$$\left| \frac{x \odot y - fl[x \odot y]}{x \odot y} \right| \leq \mu \tag{1.2}$$

or, equivalently,

$$fl[x \odot y] = (x \odot y)(1 + \epsilon) \tag{1.3}$$

for some ϵ, satisfying $|\epsilon| \leq \mu$, where μ is the unit round-off of the floating point system.

When we estimate the error in the *result* of a computation in floating point arithmetic as in (1.2) we can think of it as a *forward error*. Alternatively, we can rewrite (1.3) as

$$fl[x \odot y] = (x + e) \odot (y + f)$$

for some numbers e and f that satisfy

$$|e| \leq \mu|x|, \quad |f| \leq \mu|y|.$$

In other words, $fl[x \odot y]$ is the *exact* result of the operation on *slightly perturbed data*. This is an example of *backward error analysis*.

The smallest and largest positive real numbers that can be represented in IEEE double precision are 10^{-308} and 10^{308}, approximately (corresponding for negative numbers). If a computation gives as a result a floating point number of magnitude

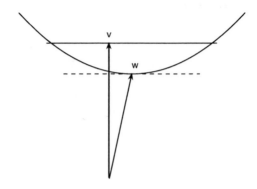

Figure 1.2. *Vectors in the GJK algorithm.*

smaller than 10^{-308}, then a floating point exception called *underflow* occurs. Similarly, the computation of a floating point number of magnitude larger than 10^{308} results in *overflow*.

Example 1.4 (floating point computations in computer graphics). The detection of a collision between two three-dimensional objects is a standard problem in the application of graphics to computer games, animation, and simulation [101]. Earlier fixed point arithmetic was used for computer graphics, but such computations now are routinely done in floating point arithmetic. An important subproblem in this area is the computation of the point on a convex body that is closest to the origin. This problem can be solved by the Gilbert–Johnson–Keerthi (GJK) algorithm, which is iterative. The algorithm uses the stopping criterion

$$S(v, w) = v^T v - v^T w \le \epsilon^2$$

for the iterations, where the vectors are illustrated in Figure 1.2. As the solution is approached the vectors are very close. In [101, pp. 142–145] there is a description of the numerical difficulties that can occur when the computation of $S(v, w)$ is done in floating point arithmetic. Here we give a short explanation of the computation in the case when v and w are scalar, $s = v^2 - vw$, which exhibits exactly the same problems as in the case of vectors.

Assume that the data are inexact (they are the results of previous computations; in any case they suffer from representation errors (1.1)),

$$\bar{v} = v(1 + \epsilon_v), \quad \bar{w} = w(1 + \epsilon_w),$$

where ϵ_v and ϵ_w are relatively small, often of the order of magnitude of μ. From (1.2) we see that each arithmetic operation incurs a relative error (1.3), so that

$$fl[v^2 - vw] = (v^2(1 + \epsilon_v)^2(1 + \epsilon_1) - vw(1 + \epsilon_v)(1 + \epsilon_w)(1 + \epsilon_2))(1 + \epsilon_3)$$
$$= (v^2 - vw) + v^2(2\epsilon_v + \epsilon_1 + \epsilon_3) - vw(\epsilon_v + \epsilon_w + \epsilon_2 + \epsilon_3) + O(\mu^2),$$

where we have assumed that $|\epsilon_i| \leq \mu$. The relative error in the computed quantity can be estimated by

$$\left| \frac{fl[v^2 - vw] - (v^2 - vw)}{(v^2 - vw)} \right| \leq \frac{v^2(2|\epsilon_v| + 2\mu) + |vw|(|\epsilon_v| + |\epsilon_w| + 2\mu) + O(\mu^2)}{|v^2 - vw|}.$$

We see that if v and w are large, and close, then the relative error may be large. For instance, with $v = 100$ and $w = 99.999$ we get

$$\left| \frac{fl[v^2 - vw] - (v^2 - vw)}{(v^2 - vw)} \right| \leq 10^5((2|\epsilon_v| + 2\mu) + (|\epsilon_v| + |\epsilon_w| + 2\mu) + O(\mu^2)).$$

If the computations are performed in IEEE single precision, which is common in computer graphics applications, then the relative error in $fl[v^2 - vw]$ may be so large that the termination criterion is never satisfied, and the iteration will never stop. In the GJK algorithm there are also other cases, besides that described above, when floating point rounding errors can cause the termination criterion to be unreliable, and special care must be taken; see [101]. ∎

The problem that occurs in the preceding example is called *cancellation*: when we subtract two almost equal numbers with errors, the result has fewer significant digits, and the relative error is larger. For more details on the IEEE standard and rounding errors in floating point computations, see, e.g., [34, Chapter 2]. Extensive rounding error analyses of linear algebra algorithms are given in [50].

1.6   Notation and Conventions

We will consider vectors and matrices with real components. Usually vectors will be denoted by lowercase italic Roman letters and matrices by uppercase italic Roman or Greek letters:

$$x \in \mathbb{R}^n, \quad A = (a_{ij}) \in \mathbb{R}^{m \times n}.$$

Tensors, i.e., arrays of real numbers with three or more indices, will be denoted by a calligraphic font. For example,

$$\mathcal{S} = (s_{ijk}) \in \mathbb{R}^{n_1 \times n_2 \times n_3}.$$

We will use $\mathbb{R}^m$ to denote the vector space of dimension m over the real field and $\mathbb{R}^{m \times n}$ for the space of $m \times n$ matrices.

The notation

$$e_i = \begin{pmatrix} 0 \\ \vdots \\ 0 \\ 1 \\ 0 \\ \vdots \\ 0 \end{pmatrix},$$

where the 1 is in position i, is used for the "canonical" unit vectors. Often the dimension is apparent from the context.

The identity matrix is denoted I. Sometimes we emphasize the dimension and use I_k for the $k \times k$ identity matrix. The notation $\mathrm{diag}(d_1, \ldots, d_n)$ denotes a diagonal matrix. For instance, $I = \mathrm{diag}(1, 1, \ldots, 1)$.

Chapter 2

Vectors and Matrices

We will assume that the basic notions of linear algebra are known to the reader. For completeness, some will be recapitulated here.

2.1 Matrix-Vector Multiplication

How basic operations in linear algebra are defined is important, since it influences one's mental images of the abstract notions. Sometimes one is led to thinking that the operations should be done in a certain order, when instead the *definition as such* imposes no ordering.[3] Let A be an $m \times n$ matrix. Consider the definition of matrix-vector multiplication:

$$y = Ax, \qquad y_i = \sum_{j=1}^{n} a_{ij} x_j, \quad i = 1, \ldots, m. \tag{2.1}$$

Symbolically one can illustrate the definition

$$\begin{pmatrix} \times \\ \times \\ \times \\ \times \end{pmatrix} = \begin{pmatrix} \leftarrow & - & - & \rightarrow \\ \leftarrow & - & - & \rightarrow \\ \leftarrow & - & - & \rightarrow \\ \leftarrow & - & - & \rightarrow \end{pmatrix} \begin{pmatrix} \uparrow \\ | \\ | \\ \downarrow \end{pmatrix}. \tag{2.2}$$

It is obvious that the computation of the different components of the vector y are completely independent of each other and can be done in any order. However, the definition may lead one to think that the matrix should be accessed rowwise, as illustrated in (2.2) and in the following MATLAB code:

---

[3] It is important to be aware that on modern computers, which invariably have memory hierarchies, the order in which operations are performed is often critical for the performance. However, we will not pursue this aspect here.

```
for i=1:m
  y(i)=0;
  for j=1:n
    y(i)=y(i)+A(i,j)*x(j);
  end
end
```

Alternatively, we can write the operation in the following way. Let $a_{.j}$ be a column vector of A. Then we can write

$$y = Ax = \begin{pmatrix} a_{.1} & a_{.2} & \cdots & a_{.n} \end{pmatrix} \begin{pmatrix} x_1 \\ x_2 \\ \vdots \\ x_n \end{pmatrix} = \sum_{j=1}^{n} x_j a_{.j}.$$

This can be illustrated symbolically:

$$\begin{pmatrix} \uparrow \\ | \\ | \\ \downarrow \end{pmatrix} = \begin{pmatrix} \uparrow & \uparrow & \uparrow & \uparrow \\ | & | & | & | \\ | & | & | & | \\ \downarrow & \downarrow & \downarrow & \downarrow \end{pmatrix} \begin{pmatrix} \times \\ \times \\ \times \\ \times \end{pmatrix}. \tag{2.3}$$

Here the vectors are accessed columnwise. In MATLAB, this version can be written[4]

```
for i=1:m
    y(i)=0;
end
for j=1:n
    for i=1:m
        y(i)=y(i)+A(i,j)*x(j);
    end
end
```

or, equivalently, using the vector operations of MATLAB,

```
y(1:m)=0;
for j=1:n
    y(1:m)=y(1:m)+A(1:m,j)*x(j);
end
```

Thus the two ways of performing the matrix-vector multiplication correspond to changing the order of the loops in the code. This way of writing also emphasizes the view of the column vectors of A as *basis vectors* and the components of x as *coordinates* with respect to the basis.

---

[4]In the terminology of LAPACK [1] this is the SAXPY version of matrix-vector multiplication. SAXPY is an acronym from the Basic Linear Algebra Subroutine (BLAS) library.

2.2   Matrix-Matrix Multiplication

Matrix multiplication can be done in several ways, each representing a different access pattern for the matrices. Let $A \in \mathbb{R}^{m \times k}$ and $B \in \mathbb{R}^{k \times n}$. The definition of matrix multiplication is

$$\mathbb{R}^{m \times n} \ni C = AB = (c_{ij}),$$

$$c_{ij} = \sum_{s=1}^{k} a_{is}b_{sj}, \quad i = 1, \ldots, m, \quad j = 1, \ldots, n. \tag{2.4}$$

In a comparison to the definition of matrix-vector multiplication (2.1), we see that in matrix multiplication *each column vector in B is multiplied by A.*

We can formulate (2.4) as a matrix multiplication code

```
for i=1:m
  for j=1:n
    for s=1:k
      C(i,j)=C(i,j)+A(i,s)*B(s,j)
    end
  end
end
```

This is an inner product version of matrix multiplication, which is emphasized in the following equivalent code:

```
for i=1:m
  for j=1:n
    C(i,j)=A(i,1:k)*B(1:k,j)
  end
end
```

It is immediately seen that the the loop variables can be permuted in $3! = 6$ different ways, and we can write a *generic matrix multiplication code*:

```
for ...
  for ...
    for ...
      C(i,j)=C(i,j)+A(i,s)*B(s,j)
    end
  end
end
```

A column-oriented (or SAXPY) version is given in

```
for j=1:n
  for s=1:k
    C(1:m,j)=C(1:m,j)+A(1:m,s)*B(s,j)
  end
end
```

The matrix A is accessed by columns and B by scalars. This access pattern can be illustrated as

$$
\begin{pmatrix} & \Big\updownarrow & \\ & & \end{pmatrix} = \begin{pmatrix} \Big\updownarrow & \Big\updownarrow & \Big\updownarrow & \Big\updownarrow \end{pmatrix} \begin{pmatrix} & \times & \\ & \times & \\ & \times & \\ & \times & \end{pmatrix}
$$

In another permutation we let the s-loop be the outermost:

```
for s=1:k
  for j=1:n
    C(1:m,j)=C(1:m,j)+A(1:m,s)*B(s,j)
  end
end
```

This can be illustrated as follows. Let $a_{.k}$ denote the column vectors of A and let $b_{k.}^T$ denote the row vectors of B. Then matrix multiplication can be written as

$$
C = AB = \begin{pmatrix} a_{.1} & a_{.2} & \cdots & a_{.k} \end{pmatrix} \begin{pmatrix} b_{1.}^T \\ b_{2.}^T \\ \vdots \\ b_{k.}^T \end{pmatrix} = \sum_{s=1}^{k} a_{.s} b_{s.}^T . \tag{2.5}
$$

This is the *outer product* form of matrix multiplication. Remember that the outer product follows the standard definition of matrix multiplication: let x and y be column vectors in $\mathbb{R}^m$ and $\mathbb{R}^n$, respectively; then

$$
xy^T = \begin{pmatrix} x_1 \\ x_2 \\ \vdots \\ x_m \end{pmatrix} \begin{pmatrix} y_1 & y_2 & \cdots & y_n \end{pmatrix} = \begin{pmatrix} x_1 y_1 & x_1 y_2 & \cdots & x_1 y_n \\ x_2 y_1 & x_2 y_2 & \cdots & x_2 y_n \\ \vdots & \vdots & & \vdots \\ x_m y_1 & x_m y_2 & \cdots & x_m y_n \end{pmatrix}
$$

$$
= \begin{pmatrix} y_1 x & y_2 x & \cdots & y_n x \end{pmatrix} = \begin{pmatrix} x_1 y^T \\ x_2 y^T \\ \vdots \\ x_m y^T \end{pmatrix} .
$$

Writing the matrix $C = AB$ in the outer product form (2.5) can be considered as an *expansion* of C in terms of simple matrices $a_{.s} b_{s.}^T$. We will later see that such matrices have *rank* equal to 1.

2.3 Inner Product and Vector Norms

In this section we will discuss briefly how to measure the "size" of a vector. The most common vector norms are

$$\| x \|_1 = \sum_{i=1}^{n} |x_i|, \quad \text{1-norm,}$$

$$\| x \|_2 = \sqrt{\sum_{i=1}^{n} x_i^2}, \quad \text{Euclidean norm (2-norm),}$$

$$\| x \|_\infty = \max_{1 \le i \le n} |x_i|, \quad \text{max-norm.}$$

The Euclidean vector norm is the generalization of the standard Euclidean distance in $\mathbb{R}^3$ to $\mathbb{R}^n$. All three norms defined here are special cases of the p-norm:

$$\| x \|_p = \left(\sum_{i=1}^{n} |x_i|^p \right)^{1/p}.$$

Associated with the Euclidean vector norm is the *inner product* between two vectors x and y in $\mathbb{R}^n$, which is defined

$$(x, y) = x^T y.$$

Generally, a *vector norm* is a mapping $\mathbb{R}^n \to \mathbb{R}$ with the properties

$$\| x \| \ge 0 \text{ for all } x,$$
$$\| x \| = 0 \text{ if and only if } x = 0,$$
$$\| \alpha x \| = |\alpha| \| x \|, \ \alpha \in \mathbb{R},$$
$$\| x + y \| \le \| x \| + \| y \|, \text{ the triangle inequality.}$$

With norms we can introduce the concepts of continuity and error in approximations of vectors. Let $\bar{x}$ be an approximation of the vector x. Then for any given vector norm, we define the *absolute error*

$$\| \delta x \| = \| \bar{x} - x \|$$

and the *relative error* (assuming that $x \ne 0$)

$$\frac{\| \delta x \|}{\| x \|} = \frac{\| \bar{x} - x \|}{\| x \|}.$$

In a finite dimensional vector space all vector norms are equivalent in the sense that for any two norms $\| \cdot \|_\alpha$ and $\| \cdot \|_\beta$ there exist constants m and M such that

$$m \| x \|_\alpha \le \| x \|_\beta \le M \| x \|_\alpha, \tag{2.6}$$

where m and M do not depend on x. For example, with $x \in \mathbb{R}^n$,

$$\| x \|_2 \leq \| x \|_1 \leq \sqrt{n} \| x \|_2.$$

This equivalence implies that if a sequence of vectors $(x_i)_{i=1}^{\infty}$ converges to x^* in one norm,

$$\lim_{i \to \infty} \| x_i - x^* \| = 0,$$

then it converges to the same limit in all norms.

In data mining applications it is common to use the *cosine of the angle* between two vectors as a distance measure:

$$\cos \theta(x, y) = \frac{x^T y}{\| x \|_2 \| y \|_2}.$$

With this measure two vectors are close if the cosine is close to one. Similarly, x and y are *orthogonal* if the angle between them is $\pi/2$, i.e., $x^T y = 0$.

2.4   Matrix Norms

For any vector norm we can define a corresponding *operator norm*. Let $\| \cdot \|$ be a vector norm. The corresponding *matrix norm* is defined as

$$\| A \| = \sup_{x \neq 0} \frac{\| Ax \|}{\| x \|}.$$

One can show that such a matrix norm satisfies (for $\alpha \in \mathbb{R}$)

$$\| A \| \geq 0 \text{ for all } A,$$
$$\| A \| = 0 \text{ if and only if } A = 0,$$
$$\| \alpha A \| = |\alpha| \| A \|, \ \alpha \in \mathbb{R},$$
$$\| A + B \| \leq \| A \| + \| B \|, \text{ the triangle inequality.}$$

For a matrix norm defined as above the following fundamental inequalities hold.

Proposition 2.1. *Let* $\| \cdot \|$ *denote a vector norm and the corresponding matrix norm. Then*

$$\| Ax \| \leq \| A \| \| x \|,$$
$$\| AB \| \leq \| A \| \| B \|.$$

Proof. From the definition we have

$$\frac{\| Ax \|}{\| x \|} \leq \| A \|$$

on system
a not in
inventory
but can't
zz it
(barcode
same in
book &
on Aleph.)

LIVERPOOL JOHN MOORES UNIVERSITY

No: ....

Self Collection of holds

Last 6 digits of barcode no. located on the bottom of your University card

Please issue the item at the self service machine before you leave this area.

for all $x \neq 0$, which gives the first inequality. The second is proved by using the first twice for $\| ABx \|$. □

One can show that the 2-*norm* satisfies

$$\| A \|_2 = \left(\max_{1 \leq i \leq n} \lambda_i(A^T A) \right)^{1/2},$$

i.e., the square root of the largest eigenvalue of the matrix $A^T A$. Thus it is a comparatively heavy computation to obtain $\| A \|_2$ for a given matrix (of medium or large dimensions). It is considerably easier to compute the *matrix infinity norm* (for $A \in \mathbb{R}^{m \times n}$),

$$\| A \|_\infty = \max_{1 \leq i \leq m} \sum_{j=1}^{n} |a_{ij}|,$$

and the *matrix 1-norm*

$$\| A \|_1 = \max_{1 \leq j \leq n} \sum_{i=1}^{m} |a_{ij}|.$$

In Section 6.1 we will see that the 2-norm of a matrix has an explicit expression in terms of the singular values of A.

Let $A \in \mathbb{R}^{m \times n}$. In some cases we will treat the matrix not as a linear operator but rather as a point in a space of dimension mn, i.e., $\mathbb{R}^{mn}$. Then we can use the *Frobenius* matrix norm, which is defined by

$$\| A \|_F = \sqrt{\sum_{i=1}^{m} \sum_{j=1}^{n} a_{ij}^2}. \tag{2.7}$$

Sometimes it is practical to write the Frobenius norm in the equivalent form

$$\| A \|_F^2 = \text{tr}(A^T A), \tag{2.8}$$

where the *trace* of a matrix $B \in \mathbb{R}^{n \times n}$ is the sum of its diagonal elements,

$$\text{tr}(B) = \sum_{i=1}^{n} b_{ii}.$$

The Frobenius norm does not correspond to a vector norm, so it is not an operator norm in that sense. This norm has the advantage that it is easier to compute than the 2-norm. The Frobenius *matrix norm* is actually closely related to the Euclidean *vector norm* in the sense that it is the Euclidean vector norm on the (linear space) of matrices $\mathbb{R}^{m \times n}$, when the matrices are identified with elements in $\mathbb{R}^{mn}$.

2.5   Linear Independence: Bases

Given a set of vectors $(v_j)_{j=1}^n$ in $\mathbb{R}^m$, $m \geq n$, consider the set of linear combinations

$$\mathrm{span}(v_1, v_2, \ldots, v_n) = \left\{ y \mid y = \sum_{j=1}^n \alpha_j v_j \right\}$$

for arbitrary coefficients α_j. The vectors $(v_j)_{j=1}^n$ are called *linearly independent* when

$$\textstyle\sum_{j=1}^n \alpha_j v_j = 0 \text{ if and only if } \alpha_j = 0 \text{ for } j = 1, 2, \ldots, n.$$

A set of m linearly independent vectors in $\mathbb{R}^m$ is called a *basis* in $\mathbb{R}^m$: any vector in $\mathbb{R}^m$ can be expressed as a linear combination of the basis vectors.

Proposition 2.2. *Assume that the vectors $(v_j)_{j=1}^n$ are linearly dependent. Then some v_k can be written as linear combinations of the rest, $v_k = \sum_{j \neq k} \beta_j v_j$.*

Proof. There exist coefficients α_j with some $\alpha_k \neq 0$ such that

$$\sum_{j=1}^n \alpha_j v_j = 0.$$

Take an $\alpha_k \neq 0$ and write

$$\alpha_k v_k = \sum_{j \neq k} -\alpha_j v_j,$$

which is the same as

$$v_k = \sum_{j \neq k} \beta_j v_j$$

with $\beta_j = -\alpha_j / \alpha_k$.   ☐

If we have a set of linearly dependent vectors, then we can keep a linearly independent subset and express the rest in terms of the linearly independent ones. Thus we can consider the number of linearly independent vectors as a measure of the information contents of the set and compress the set accordingly: take the linearly independent vectors as representatives (basis vectors) for the set, and compute the coordinates of the rest in terms of the basis. However, in real applications we seldom have *exactly linearly dependent vectors* but rather *almost linearly dependent vectors*. It turns out that for such a *data reduction procedure* to be practical and numerically stable, we need the basis vectors to be not only linearly independent but orthogonal. We will come back to this in Chapter 4.

2.6   The Rank of a Matrix

The *rank* of a matrix is defined as the maximum number of linearly independent column vectors. It is a standard result in linear algebra that the number of linearly independent column vectors is equal to the number of linearly independent row vectors.

We will see later that any matrix can be represented as an expansion of rank-1 matrices.

Proposition 2.3. *An outer product matrix xy^T, where x and y are vectors in $\mathbb{R}^n$, has rank 1.*

Proof.

$$xy^T = \begin{pmatrix} y_1 x & y_2 x & \cdots & y_n x \end{pmatrix} = \begin{pmatrix} x_1 y^T \\ x_2 y^T \\ \vdots \\ x_n y^T \end{pmatrix}.$$

Thus, all the columns (rows) of xy^T are linearly dependent. $\square$

A square matrix $A \in \mathbb{R}^{n \times n}$ with rank n is called *nonsingular* and has an *inverse* A^{-1} satisfying

$$AA^{-1} = A^{-1}A = I.$$

If we multiply linearly independent vectors by a nonsingular matrix, then the vectors remain linearly independent.

Proposition 2.4. *Assume that the vectors $v_1, \ldots, v_p$ are linearly independent. Then for any nonsingular matrix T, the vectors $Tv_1, \ldots, Tv_p$ are linearly independent.*

Proof. Obviously $\sum_{j=1}^p \alpha_j v_j = 0$ if and only if $\sum_{j=1}^p \alpha_j T v_j = 0$ (since we can multiply any of the equations by T or T^{-1}). Therefore the statement follows. $\square$

Chapter 3

Linear Systems and Least Squares

In this chapter we briefly review some facts about the solution of linear systems of equations,

$$Ax = b, \tag{3.1}$$

where $A \in \mathbb{R}^{n \times n}$ is square and nonsingular. The linear system (3.1) can be solved using *Gaussian elimination* with *partial pivoting*, which is equivalent to factorizing the matrix as a product of triangular matrices.

We will also consider *overdetermined linear systems*, where the matrix $A \in \mathbb{R}^{m \times n}$ is *rectangular* with $m > n$, and their solution using the least squares method. As we are giving the results only as background, we mostly state them without proofs. For thorough presentations of the theory of matrix decompositions for solving linear systems of equations, see, e.g., [42, 92].

Before discussing matrix decompositions, we state the basic result concerning conditions for the existence of a unique solution of (3.1).

Proposition 3.1. *Let $A \in \mathbb{R}^{n \times n}$ and assume that A is nonsingular. Then for any right-hand-side b, the linear system $Ax = b$ has a unique solution.*

Proof. The result is an immediate consequence of the fact that the column vectors of a nonsingular matrix are linearly independent. □

3.1 LU Decomposition

Gaussian elimination can be conveniently described using *Gauss transformations*, and these transformations are the key elements in the equivalence between Gaussian elimination and LU decomposition. More details on Gauss transformations can be found in any textbook in numerical linear algebra; see, e.g., [42, p. 94]. In Gaussian elimination with partial pivoting, the reordering of the rows is accomplished by *permutation matrices*, which are identity matrices with the rows reordered; see, e.g., [42, Section 3.4.1].

Consider an $n \times n$ matrix A. In the first step of Gaussian elimination with partial pivoting, we reorder the rows of the matrix so that the element of largest magnitude in the first column is moved to the $(1, 1)$ position. This is equivalent to multiplying A from the left by a permutation matrix P_1. The elimination, i.e., the zeroing of the elements in the first column below the diagonal, is then performed by multiplying

$$A^{(1)} := L_1^{-1} P_1 A, \tag{3.2}$$

where L_1 is a Gauss transformation

$$L_1 = \begin{pmatrix} 1 & 0 \\ m_1 & I \end{pmatrix}, \qquad m_1 = \begin{pmatrix} m_{21} \\ m_{31} \\ \vdots \\ m_{n1} \end{pmatrix}.$$

The result of the first step of Gaussian elimination with partial pivoting is

$$A^{(1)} = \begin{pmatrix} a'_{11} & a'_{12} & \cdots & a'_{1n} \\ 0 & a^{(1)}_{22} & \cdots & a^{(1)}_{2n} \\ \vdots & & & \\ 0 & a^{(1)}_{n2} & \cdots & a^{(1)}_{nn} \end{pmatrix}.$$

The Gaussian elimination algorithm then proceeds by zeroing the elements of the second column below the main diagonal (after moving the largest element to the diagonal position), and so on.

From (3.2) we see that the first step of Gaussian elimination with partial pivoting can be expressed as a matrix factorization. This is also true of the complete procedure.

Theorem 3.2 (LU decomposition). *Any nonsingular $n \times n$ matrix A can be decomposed into*

$$PA = LU,$$

where P is a permutation matrix, L is a lower triangular matrix with ones on the main diagonal, and U is an upper triangular matrix.

Proof (sketch). The theorem can be proved by induction. From (3.2) we have

$$P_1 A = L_1 A^{(1)}.$$

Define the $(n - 1) \times (n - 1)$ matrix

$$B = \begin{pmatrix} a^{(1)}_{22} & \cdots & a^{(1)}_{2n} \\ \vdots & & \\ a^{(1)}_{n2} & \cdots & a^{(1)}_{nn} \end{pmatrix}.$$

By an induction assumption, B can be decomposed into

$$P_B B = L_B U_B,$$

and we then see that $PA = LU$, where

$$U = \begin{pmatrix} a'_{11} & a_2^T \\ 0 & U_B \end{pmatrix}, \qquad L = \begin{pmatrix} 1 & 0 \\ P_B m_1 & L_B \end{pmatrix}, \qquad P = \begin{pmatrix} 1 & 0 \\ 0 & P_B \end{pmatrix} P_1,$$

and $a_2^T = (a'_{12} \, a'_{13} \, \ldots \, a'_{1n})$. $\square$

It is easy to show that the amount of work for computing the LU decomposition is $2n^3/3$ flops, approximately. In the kth step of Gaussian elimination, one operates on an $(n-k+1) \times (n-k+1)$ submatrix, and for each element in that submatrix one multiplication and one addition are performed. Thus the total number of flops is

$$2 \sum_{k=1}^{n-1} (n-k+1)^2 \approx \frac{2n^3}{3},$$

approximately.

3.2   Symmetric, Positive Definite Matrices

The LU decomposition of a symmetric, positive definite matrix A can always be computed without pivoting. In addition, it is possible to take advantage of symmetry so that the decomposition becomes symmetric, too, and requires half as much work as in the general case.

Theorem 3.3 (LDL^T decomposition). *Any symmetric, positive definite matrix A has a decomposition*

$$A = LDL^T,$$

where L is lower triangular with ones on the main diagonal and D is a diagonal matrix with positive diagonal elements.

Example 3.4. The positive definite matrix

$$A = \begin{pmatrix} 8 & 4 & 2 \\ 4 & 6 & 0 \\ 2 & 0 & 3 \end{pmatrix}$$

has the LU decomposition

$$A = LU = \begin{pmatrix} 1 & 0 & 0 \\ 0.5 & 1 & 0 \\ 0.25 & -0.25 & 1 \end{pmatrix} \begin{pmatrix} 8 & 4 & 2 \\ 0 & 4 & -1 \\ 0 & 0 & 2.25 \end{pmatrix}$$

and the LDL^T decomposition

$$A = LDL^T, \quad D = \begin{pmatrix} 8 & 0 & 0 \\ 0 & 4 & 0 \\ 0 & 0 & 2.25 \end{pmatrix}. \quad \blacksquare$$

The diagonal elements in D are positive, and therefore we can put

$$D^{1/2} = \begin{pmatrix} \sqrt{d_1} & & & \\ & \sqrt{d_2} & & \\ & & \ddots & \\ & & & \sqrt{d_n} \end{pmatrix},$$

and then we get

$$A = LDL^T = (LD^{1/2})(D^{1/2}L^T) = U^T U,$$

where U is an upper triangular matrix. This variant of the LDL^T decomposition is called the *Cholesky decomposition*.

Since A is symmetric, it is only necessary to store the main diagonal and the elements above it, $n(n + 1)/2$ matrix elements in all. Exactly the same amount of storage is needed for the LDL^T and the Cholesky decompositions. It is also seen that since only half as many elements as in the ordinary LU decomposition need to be computed, the amount of work is also halved—approximately $n^3/3$ flops. When the LDL^T decomposition is computed, it is not necessary to first compute the LU decomposition, but the elements in L and D can be computed directly.

3.3   Perturbation Theory and Condition Number

The *condition number* of a nonsingular matrix A is defined as

$$\kappa(A) = \|A\| \, \|A^{-1}\|,$$

where $\| \cdot \|$ denotes any operator norm. If we use a particular matrix norm, e.g., the 2-norm, then we write

$$\kappa_2(A) = \|A\|_2 \, \|A^{-1}\|_2. \tag{3.3}$$

The condition number is used to quantify how much the solution of a linear system $Ax = b$ can change, when the matrix and the right-hand side are perturbed by a small amount.

Theorem 3.5. *Assume that A is nonsingular and that*

$$\|\delta A\| \, \|A^{-1}\| = r < 1.$$

Then the matrix $A + \delta A$ is nonsingular, and

$$\|(A + \delta A)^{-1}\| \leq \frac{\|A^{-1}\|}{1 - r}.$$

The solution of the perturbed system

$$(A + \delta A)y = b + \delta b$$

satisfies

$$\frac{\|y - x\|}{\|x\|} \leq \frac{\kappa(A)}{1 - r} \left(\frac{\|\delta A\|}{\|A\|} + \frac{\|\delta b\|}{\|b\|} \right).$$

For a proof, see, for instance, [42, Theorem 2.7.2] or [50, Theorem 7.2]

A matrix with a large condition number is said to be *ill-conditioned*. Theorem 3.5 shows that a linear system with an ill-conditioned matrix is sensitive to perturbations in the data (i.e., the matrix and the right-hand side).

3.4 Rounding Errors in Gaussian Elimination

From Section 1.5.2, on rounding errors in floating point arithmetic, we know that any real number (representable in the floating point system) is represented with a relative error not exceeding the unit round-off μ. This fact can also be stated

$$fl[x] = x(1 + \epsilon), \qquad |\epsilon| \leq \mu.$$

When representing the elements of a matrix A and a vector b in the floating point system, there arise errors:

$$fl[a_{ij}] = a_{ij}(1 + \epsilon_{ij}), \qquad |\epsilon_{ij}| \leq \mu,$$

and analogously for b. Therefore, we can write

$$fl[A] = A + \delta A, \qquad fl[b] = b + \delta b,$$

where

$$\|\delta A\|_\infty \leq \mu \|A\|_\infty, \qquad \|\delta b\|_\infty \leq \mu \|b\|_\infty.$$

If, for the moment, we assume that no further rounding errors arise during the solution of the system $Ax = b$, we see that $\widehat{x}$ satisfies

$$(A + \delta A)\widehat{x} = b + \delta b.$$

This is an example of *backward error analysis*: the computed solution $\widehat{x}$ is the *exact solution of a perturbed problem.*

Using perturbation theory, we can estimate the error in $\widehat{x}$. From Theorem 3.5 we get

$$\frac{\|\widehat{x} - x\|_\infty}{\|x\|_\infty} \leq \frac{\kappa_\infty(A)}{1 - r} 2\mu$$

(provided that $r = \mu\kappa_\infty(A) < 1$).

We can also analyze how rounding errors in Gaussian elimination affect the result. The following theorem holds. (For detailed error analyses of Gaussian elimination, see [50, Chapter 9] or [42, Chapters 3.3, 3.4].)

Theorem 3.6. *Assume that we use a floating point system with unit round-off μ. Let $\widehat{L}$ and $\widehat{R}$ be the triangular factors obtained from Gaussian elimination with partial pivoting, applied to the matrix A. Further, assume that $\widehat{x}$ is computed using forward and back substitution:*

$$\widehat{L}\widehat{y} = Pb, \quad \widehat{R}\widehat{x} = \widehat{y}.$$

Then $\widehat{x}$ is the exact solution of a system

$$(A + \delta A)\widehat{x} = b,$$

where

$$\|\delta A\|_\infty \leq k(n)g_n\mu\|A\|_\infty, \qquad g_n = \frac{\max_{i,j,k} |\widehat{a}_{ij}^{(k)}|}{\max_{i,j} |a_{ij}|},$$

$k(n)$ is a third-degree polynomial in n, and $\widehat{a}_{ij}^{(k)}$ are the elements computed in step $k - 1$ of the elimination procedure.

We observe that g_n depends on the growth of the matrix elements during the Gaussian elimination and not explicitly on the magnitude of the multipliers. g_n can be computed, and in this way an *a posteriori* estimate of the rounding errors can be obtained.

A priori (in advance), one can show that $g_n \leq 2^{n-1}$, and matrices can be constructed where in fact the element growth is that serious (note that $g_{31} = 2^{30} \approx 10^9$). In practice, however, g_n is seldom larger than 8 in Gaussian elimination with partial pivoting.

It is important to note that there are classes of matrices for which there is no element growth during Gaussian elimination, i.e., $g_n = 1$, even if no pivoting is done. This is true, e.g., if A is symmetric and positive definite.

In almost all cases, the estimate in the theorem is much too pessimistic with regard to the third-degree polynomial $k(n)$. In order to have equality, all rounding errors must be maximally large, and their accumulated effect must be maximally unfavorable.

We want to emphasize that the main objective of this type of a priori error analysis is not to give error estimates for the solution of linear systems but rather to expose potential instabilities of algorithms and provide a basis for comparing different algorithms. Thus, Theorem 3.6 demonstrates the main weakness of Gauss transformations as compared to the orthogonal transformations that we will introduce in Chapter 4: they can cause a large growth of the matrix elements, which, in turn, induces rounding errors.

3.5 Banded Matrices

In many situations, e.g., boundary value problems for ordinary and partial differential equations, matrices arise where a large proportion of the elements are equal to zero. If the nonzero elements are concentrated around the main diagonal, then the matrix is called a band matrix. More precisely, a matrix A is said to be a *band matrix* if there are natural numbers p and q such that

$$a_{ij} = 0 \ \text{ if } \ j - i > p \ \text{ or } \ i - j > q.$$

Example 3.7. Let $q = 2$, $p = 1$. Let A be a band matrix of dimension 6:

$$A = \begin{pmatrix} a_{11} & a_{12} & 0 & 0 & 0 & 0 \\ a_{21} & a_{22} & a_{23} & 0 & 0 & 0 \\ a_{31} & a_{32} & a_{33} & a_{34} & 0 & 0 \\ 0 & a_{42} & a_{43} & a_{44} & a_{45} & 0 \\ 0 & 0 & a_{53} & a_{54} & a_{55} & a_{56} \\ 0 & 0 & 0 & a_{64} & a_{65} & a_{66} \end{pmatrix}. \quad \blacksquare$$

$w = q + p + 1$ is called the *bandwidth* of the matrix. From the example, we see that w is the maximal number of nonzero elements in any row of A.

When storing a band matrix, we do not store the elements outside the band. Likewise, when linear systems of equations are solved, one can take advantage of the band structure to reduce the number of operations.

We first consider the case $p = q = 1$. Such a band matrix is called *tridiagonal*. Let

$$A = \begin{pmatrix} \alpha_1 & \beta_1 & & & & \\ \gamma_2 & \alpha_2 & \beta_2 & & & \\ & \gamma_3 & \alpha_3 & \beta_3 & & \\ & & \ddots & \ddots & \ddots & \\ & & & \gamma_{n-1} & \alpha_{n-1} & \beta_{n-1} \\ & & & & \gamma_n & \alpha_n \end{pmatrix}.$$

The matrix can be stored in three vectors. In the solution of a tridiagonal system $Ax = b$, it is easy to utilize the structure; we first assume that A is diagonally dominant, so that no pivoting is needed.

```
% LU Decomposition of a Tridiagonal Matrix.
for k=1:n-1
  gamma(k+1)=gamma(k+1)/alpha(k);
  alpha(k+1)=alpha(k+1)*beta(k);
end
% Forward Substitution for the Solution of Ly = b.
y(1)=b(1);
for k=2:n
  y(k)=b(k)-gamma(k)*y(k-1);
end
% Back Substitution for the Solution of Ux = y.
x(n)=y(n)/alpha(n);
for k=n-1:-1:1
  x(k)=(y(k)-beta(k)*x(k+1))/alpha(k);
end
```

The number of operations (multiplications and additions) is approximately $3n$, and the number of divisions is $2n$.

In Gaussian elimination *with partial pivoting*, the band width of the upper triangular matrix increases. If A has band width $w = q + p + 1$ (q diagonals under the main diagonal and p over), then, with partial pivoting, the factor U will have band width $w_U = p + q + 1$. It is easy to see that no new nonzero elements will be created in L.

The factors L and U in the LU decomposition of a band matrix A are band matrices.

Example 3.8. Let

$$
A = \begin{pmatrix}
4 & 2 & & & \\
2 & 5 & 2 & & \\
& 2 & 5 & 2 & \\
& & 2 & 5 & 2 \\
& & & 2 & 5
\end{pmatrix}.
$$

A has the Cholesky decomposition $A = U^T U$, where

$$
U = \begin{pmatrix}
2 & 1 & & & \\
& 2 & 1 & & \\
& & 2 & 1 & \\
& & & 2 & 1 \\
& & & & 2
\end{pmatrix}.
$$

The inverse is

$$
A^{-1} = \frac{1}{2^{10}} \begin{pmatrix}
341 & -170 & 84 & -40 & 16 \\
-170 & 340 & -168 & 80 & -32 \\
84 & -168 & 336 & -160 & 64 \\
-40 & 80 & -160 & 320 & -128 \\
16 & -32 & 64 & -128 & 256
\end{pmatrix},
$$

which is dense.   ∎

It turns out that the inverse of a band matrix is usually a dense matrix. Therefore, in most cases the inverse of a band matrix should not be computed explicitly.

3.6   The Least Squares Problem

In this section we will introduce the least squares method and the solution of the linear least squares problem using the normal equations. Other methods for solving the least squares problem, based on orthogonal transformations, will be presented in Chapters 5 and 6. We will also give a perturbation result for the least squares problem in Section 6.6. For an extensive treatment of modern numerical methods for linear least squares problem, see [14].

Example 3.9. Assume that we want to determine the elasticity properties of a spring by attaching different weights to it and measuring its length. From Hooke's law we know that the length l depends on the force F according to

$$e + \kappa F = l,$$

where e and κ are constants to be determined.[5] Assume that we have performed an experiment and obtained the following data:

F	1	2	3	4	5
l	7.97	10.2	14.2	16.0	21.2

The data are illustrated in Figure 3.1. As the measurements are subject to error we want to use all the data in order to minimize the influence of the errors. Thus we are lead to a system with more data than unknowns, an *overdetermined system*,

$$e + \kappa 1 = 7.97,$$
$$e + \kappa 2 = 10.2,$$
$$e + \kappa 3 = 14.2,$$
$$e + \kappa 4 = 16.0,$$
$$e + \kappa 5 = 21.2,$$

or, in matrix form,

$$\begin{pmatrix} 1 & 1 \\ 1 & 2 \\ 1 & 3 \\ 1 & 4 \\ 1 & 5 \end{pmatrix} \begin{pmatrix} e \\ \kappa \end{pmatrix} = \begin{pmatrix} 7.97 \\ 10.2 \\ 14.2 \\ 16.0 \\ 21.2 \end{pmatrix}.$$

We will determine an approximation of the elasticity constant of the spring using the least squares method. ∎

---

[5] In Hooke's law the *spring constant* is $1/\kappa$.

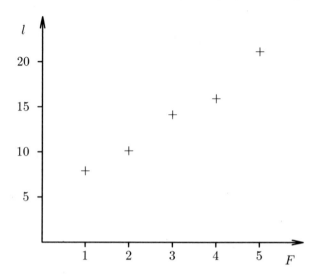

Figure 3.1. *Measured data in spring experiment.*

Let $A \in \mathbb{R}^{m \times n}$, $m > n$. The system

$$Ax = b$$

is called *overdetermined*: it has more equations than unknowns. In general such a system has no solution. This can be seen geometrically by letting $m = 3$ and $n = 2$, i.e., we consider two vectors $a_{.1}$ and $a_{.2}$ in $\mathbb{R}^3$. We want to find a linear combination of the vectors such that

$$x_1 a_{.1} + x_2 a_{.2} = b.$$

In Figure 3.2 we see that usually such a problem has no solution. The two vectors span a plane, and if the right-hand side b is not in the plane, then there is no linear combination of $a_{.1}$ and $a_{.2}$ such that $x_1 a_{.1} + x_2 a_{.2} = b$.

In this situation one obvious alternative to "solving the linear system" is to make the vector $r = b - x_1 a_{.1} - x_2 a_{.2} = b - Ax$ as small as possible. $b - Ax$ is called the *residual vector* and is illustrated in Figure 3.2.

The solution of the problem depends on how we measure the length of the residual vector. In the *least squares method* we use the standard Euclidean distance. Thus we want to find a vector $x \in \mathbb{R}^n$ that solves the minimization problem

$$\min_x \| b - Ax \|_2. \tag{3.4}$$

As the unknown x occurs linearly in (3.4), this is also referred to as the *linear least squares problem*.

In the example we know immediately from our knowledge of distances in $\mathbb{R}^3$ that the distance between the tip of the vector b and the plane is minimized if we choose the linear combination of vectors in the plane in such a way that the residual

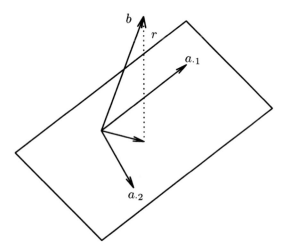

Figure 3.2. *The least squares problem, $m = 3$ and $n = 2$. The residual vector $b - Ax$ is dotted.*

vector is orthogonal to the plane. Since the columns of the matrix A span the plane, we see that we get the solution by *making r orthogonal to the columns of A. This geometric intuition is valid also in the general case:

$$r^T a_{\cdot j} = 0, \qquad j = 1, 2, \ldots, n.$$

(See the definition of orthogonality in Section 2.3.) Equivalently, we can write

$$r^T \begin{pmatrix} a_{\cdot 1} & a_{\cdot 2} & \cdots & a_{\cdot n} \end{pmatrix} = r^T A = 0.$$

Then, using $r = b - Ax$, we get the *normal equations* (the name is now obvious)

$$A^T A x = A^T b$$

for determining the coefficients in x.

Theorem 3.10. *If the column vectors of A are linearly independent, then the normal equations*

$$A^T A x = A^T b$$

are nonsingular and have a unique solution.

Proof. We first show that $A^T A$ is positive definite. Let x be an arbitrary nonzero vector. Then, from the definition of linear independence, we have $Ax \neq 0$. With $y = Ax$, we then have

$$x^T A^T A x = y^T y = \sum_{i=1}^{n} y_i^2 > 0,$$

which is equivalent to $A^T A$ being positive definite. Therefore, $A^T A$ is nonsingular, and the normal equations have a unique solution, which we denote $\widehat{x}$.

Then, we show that $\widehat{x}$ is the solution of the least squares problem, i.e., $\|\widehat{r}\|_2 \leq \|r\|_2$ for all $r = b - Ax$. We can write

$$r = b - A\widehat{x} + A(\widehat{x} - x) = \widehat{r} + A(\widehat{x} - x)$$

and

$$\|r\|_2^2 = r^T r = (\widehat{r} + A(\widehat{x} - x))^T (\widehat{r} + A(\widehat{x} - x))$$
$$= \widehat{r}^T \widehat{r} + \widehat{r}^T A(\widehat{x} - x) + (\widehat{x} - x)^T A^T \widehat{r} + (\widehat{x} - x)^T A^T A(\widehat{x} - x).$$

Since $A^T \widehat{r} = 0$, the two terms in the middle are equal to zero, and we get

$$\|r\|_2^2 = \widehat{r}^T \widehat{r} + (\widehat{x} - x)^T A^T A(\widehat{x} - x) = \|\widehat{r}\|_2^2 + \|A(\widehat{x} - x)\|_2^2 \geq \|\widehat{r}\|_2^2,$$

which was to be proved.   □

Example 3.11. We can now solve the example given at the beginning of Section 3.6. We have

$$\begin{pmatrix} 1 & 1 \\ 1 & 2 \\ 1 & 3 \\ 1 & 4 \\ 1 & 5 \end{pmatrix} \begin{pmatrix} e \\ \kappa \end{pmatrix} = \begin{pmatrix} 7.97 \\ 10.2 \\ 14.2 \\ 16.0 \\ 21.2 \end{pmatrix}.$$

Using MATLAB we then get

```
>> C=A'*A              % Normal equations

C =   5      15
      15     55

>> x=C\(A'*b)

x = 4.2360
    3.2260  ■
```

Solving the linear least squares problems using the normal equations has two significant drawbacks:

1. Forming $A^T A$ can lead to loss of information.

2. The condition number $A^T A$ is the square of that of A:

$$\kappa(A^T A) = (\kappa(A))^2.$$

We illustrate these points in a couple of examples.

Example 3.12. Let ϵ be small, and define the matrix

$$A = \begin{pmatrix} 1 & 1 \\ \epsilon & 0 \\ 0 & \epsilon \end{pmatrix}.$$

It follows that

$$A^T A = \begin{pmatrix} 1+\epsilon^2 & 1 \\ 1 & 1+\epsilon^2 \end{pmatrix}.$$

If ϵ is so small that the floating point representation of $1+\epsilon^2$ satisfies $fl[1+\epsilon^2] = 1$, then in floating point arithmetic the normal equations become singular. Thus vital information that is present in A is lost in forming $A^T A$. ∎

The condition number of a rectangular matrix A is defined using the singular value decomposition of A. We will state a result on the conditioning of the least squares problem in Section 6.6.

Example 3.13. We compute the condition number of the matrix in Example 3.9 using MATLAB:

```
A =  1      1
     1      2
     1      3
     1      4
     1      5

cond(A) = 8.3657

cond(A'*A) = 69.9857
```

Then we assume that we have a linear model

$$l(x) = c_0 + c_1 x$$

with data vector $x = (101\,102\,103\,104\,105)^T$. This gives a data matrix with large condition number:

```
A =  1     101
     1     102
     1     103
     1     104
     1     105

cond(A) = 7.5038e+03

cond(A'*A) = 5.6307e+07
```

If instead we use the model

$$l(x) = b_0 + b_1(x - 103),$$

the corresponding normal equations become diagonal and much better conditioned (demonstrate this).   ∎

It occurs quite often that one has a sequence of least squares problems with the same matrix,

$$\min_{x_i} \| A x_i - b_i \|_2, \qquad i = 1, 2, \ldots, p,$$

with solutions

$$x_i = (A^T A)^{-1} A^T b_i, \qquad i = 1, 2, \ldots, p.$$

Defining $X = \begin{pmatrix} x_1 & x_2 & \ldots & x_p \end{pmatrix}$ and $X = \begin{pmatrix} b_1 & b_2 & \ldots & b_p \end{pmatrix}$ we can write this in matrix form

$$\min_{X} \| A X - B \|_F \tag{3.5}$$

with the solution

$$X = (A^T A)^{-1} A^T B.$$

This follows from the identity

$$\| A X - B \|_F^2 = \sum_{i=1}^{p} \| A x_i - b_i \|_2^2$$

and the fact that the p subproblems in (3.5) are independent.

Chapter 4

Orthogonality

Even if the Gaussian elimination procedure for solving linear systems of equations and normal equations is a standard algorithm with widespread use in numerous applications, it is not sufficient in situations when one needs to separate the most important information from less important information ("noise"). The typical linear algebra formulation of "data quality" is to quantify the concept of "good and bad basis vectors"; loosely speaking, good basis vectors are those that are "very linearly independent," i.e., close to orthogonal. In the same vein, vectors that are almost linearly dependent are bad basis vectors. In this chapter we will introduce some theory and algorithms for computations with orthogonal vectors. A more complete quantification of the "quality" of a set of vectors is given in Chapter 6.

Example 4.1. In Example 3.13 we saw that an unsuitable choice of basis vectors in the least squares problem led to ill-conditioned normal equations. Along similar lines, define the two matrices

$$
A = \begin{pmatrix} 1 & 1.05 \\ 1 & 1 \\ 1 & 0.95 \end{pmatrix}, \qquad B = \begin{pmatrix} 1 & 1/\sqrt{2} \\ 1 & 0 \\ 1 & -1/\sqrt{2} \end{pmatrix},
$$

whose columns are plotted in Figure 4.1. It can be shown that the column vectors of the two matrices span the same plane in $\mathbb{R}^3$. From the figure it is clear that the columns of B, which are orthogonal, determine the plane much better than the columns of A, which are quite close. ∎

From several points of view, it is advantageous to use orthogonal vectors as basis vectors in a vector space. In this chapter we will list some important properties of orthogonal sets of vectors and orthogonal matrices. We assume that the vectors are in $\mathbb{R}^m$ with $m \geq n$.

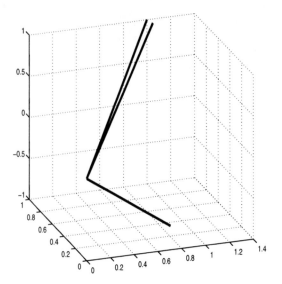

Figure 4.1. *Three vectors spanning a plane in* $\mathbb{R}^3$.

4.1   Orthogonal Vectors and Matrices

We first recall that two nonzero vectors x and y are called *orthogonal* if $x^T y = 0$ (i.e., $\cos\theta(x,y) = 0$).

Proposition 4.2. *Let q_j, $j = 1, 2, \ldots, n$, be orthogonal, i.e., $q_i^T q_j = 0$, $i \neq j$. Then they are linearly independent.*

Proof. Assume they are linearly dependent. Then from Proposition 2.2 there exists a q_k such that

$$q_k = \sum_{j \neq k} \alpha_j q_j.$$

Multiplying this equation by q_k^T we get

$$q_k^T q_k = \sum_{j \neq k} \alpha_j q_k^T q_j = 0,$$

since the vectors are orthogonal. This is a contradiction.   □

Let the set of orthogonal vectors q_j, $j = 1, 2, \ldots, m$, in $\mathbb{R}^m$ be normalized,

$$\|q_j\|_2 = 1.$$

Then they are called *orthonormal*, and they constitute an *orthonormal basis* in $\mathbb{R}^m$.
   A square matrix

$$Q = \begin{pmatrix} q_1 & q_2 & \cdots & q_m \end{pmatrix} \in \mathbb{R}^{m \times m}$$

whose columns are orthonormal is called an *orthogonal matrix*. Orthogonal matrices satisfy a number of important properties that we list in a sequence of propositions.

Proposition 4.3. *An orthogonal matrix Q satisfies $Q^T Q = I$.*

Proof.

$$Q^T Q = \begin{pmatrix} q_1 & q_2 & \cdots & q_m \end{pmatrix}^T \begin{pmatrix} q_1 & q_2 & \cdots & q_m \end{pmatrix} = \begin{pmatrix} q_1^T \\ q_2^T \\ \cdots \\ q_m^T \end{pmatrix} \begin{pmatrix} q_1 & q_2 & \cdots & q_m \end{pmatrix}$$

$$= \begin{pmatrix} q_1^T q_1 & q_1^T q_2 & \cdots & q_1^T q_m \\ q_2^T q_1 & q_2^T q_2 & \cdots & q_2^T q_m \\ \vdots & \vdots & & \vdots \\ q_m^T q_1 & q_m^T q_2 & \cdots & q_m^T q_m \end{pmatrix} = \begin{pmatrix} 1 & 0 & \cdots & 0 \\ 0 & 1 & \cdots & 0 \\ \vdots & \vdots & & \vdots \\ 0 & 0 & \cdots & 1 \end{pmatrix},$$

due to orthonormality. ☐

The orthogonality of its columns implies that an orthogonal matrix has full rank, and it is trivial to find the inverse.

Proposition 4.4. *An orthogonal matrix $Q \in \mathbb{R}^{m \times m}$ has rank m, and, since $Q^T Q = I$, its inverse is equal to $Q^{-1} = Q^T$.*

Proposition 4.5. *The rows of an orthogonal matrix are orthogonal, i.e., $QQ^T = I$.*

Proof. Let x be an arbitrary vector. We shall show that $QQ^T x = x$. Given x there is a uniquely determined vector y, such that $Qy = x$, since Q^{-1} exists. Then

$$QQ^T x = QQ^T Qy = Qy = x.$$

Since x is arbitrary, it follows that $QQ^T = I$. ☐

Proposition 4.6. *The product of two orthogonal matrices is orthogonal.*

Proof. Let Q and P be orthogonal, and put $X = PQ$. Then

$$X^T X = (PQ)^T PQ = Q^T P^T PQ = Q^T Q = I. \qquad ☐$$

Any orthonormal basis of a subspace of $\mathbb{R}^m$ can be enlarged to an orthonormal basis of the whole space. The next proposition shows this in matrix terms.

Proposition 4.7. *Given a matrix $Q_1 \in \mathbb{R}^{m \times k}$, with orthonormal columns, there exists a matrix $Q_2 \in \mathbb{R}^{m \times (m-k)}$ such that $Q = (Q_1 \, Q_2)$ is an orthogonal matrix.*

This proposition is a standard result in linear algebra. We will later demonstrate how Q can be computed.

One of the most important properties of orthogonal matrices is that they preserve the length of a vector.

Proposition 4.8. *The Euclidean length of a vector is invariant under an orthogonal transformation Q.*

Proof. $\|Qx\|_2^2 = (Qx)^T Qx = x^T Q^T Qx = x^T x = \|x\|_2^2.$ $\square$

Also the corresponding matrix norm and the Frobenius norm are *invariant under orthogonal transformations.*

Proposition 4.9. *Let $U \in \mathbb{R}^{m \times m}$ and $V \in \mathbb{R}^{n \times n}$ be orthogonal. Then for any $A \in \mathbb{R}^{m \times n}$,*

$$\| UAV \|_2 = \| A \|_2,$$
$$\| UAV \|_F = \| A \|_F.$$

Proof. The first equality is easily proved using Proposition 4.8. The second is proved using the alternative expression (2.8) for the Frobenius norm and the identity $\mathrm{tr}(BC) = \mathrm{tr}(CB)$. $\square$

4.2   Elementary Orthogonal Matrices

We will use elementary orthogonal matrices to reduce matrices to compact form. For instance, we will transform a matrix $A \in \mathbb{R}^{m \times n}$, $m \geq n$, to triangular form.

4.2.1   Plane Rotations

A 2×2 plane rotation matrix[6]

$$G = \begin{pmatrix} c & s \\ -s & c \end{pmatrix}, \qquad c^2 + s^2 = 1,$$

is orthogonal. Multiplication of a vector x by G rotates the vector in a clockwise direction by an angle θ, where $c = \cos\theta$. A plane rotation can be used to zero the second element of a vector x by choosing $c = x_1 / \sqrt{x_1^2 + x_2^2}$ and $s = x_2 / \sqrt{x_1^2 + x_2^2}$:

$$\frac{1}{\sqrt{x_1^2 + x_2^2}} \begin{pmatrix} x_1 & x_2 \\ -x_2 & x_1 \end{pmatrix} \begin{pmatrix} x_1 \\ x_2 \end{pmatrix} = \begin{pmatrix} \sqrt{x_1^2 + x_2^2} \\ 0 \end{pmatrix}.$$

By embedding a two-dimensional rotation in a larger unit matrix, one can manipulate vectors and matrices of arbitrary dimension.

---

[6]In the numerical literature, plane rotations are often called Givens rotations, after Wallace Givens, who used them for eigenvalue computations around 1960. However, they had been used long before that by Jacobi, also for eigenvalue computations.

Example 4.10. We can choose c and s in

$$G = \begin{pmatrix} 1 & 0 & 0 & 0 \\ 0 & c & 0 & s \\ 0 & 0 & 1 & 0 \\ 0 & -s & 0 & c \end{pmatrix}$$

so that we zero element 4 in a vector $x \in \mathbb{R}^4$ *by a rotation in plane* $(2, 4)$. Execution of the MATLAB script

```
x=[1;2;3;4];
sq=sqrt(x(2)^2+x(4)^2);
c=x(2)/sq; s=x(4)/sq;
G=[1 0 0 0; 0 c 0 s; 0 0 1 0; 0 -s 0 c];
y=G*x
```

gives the result

```
y = 1.0000
    4.4721
    3.0000
        0   ∎
```

Using a sequence of plane rotations, we can now transform an arbitrary vector to a multiple of a unit vector. This can be done in several ways. We demonstrate one in the following example.

Example 4.11. Given a vector $x \in \mathbb{R}^4$, we transform it to κe_1. First, by a rotation G_3 in the plane $(3, 4)$ we zero the last element:

$$\begin{pmatrix} 1 & 0 & 0 & 0 \\ 0 & 1 & 0 & 0 \\ 0 & 0 & c_1 & s_1 \\ 0 & 0 & -s_1 & c_1 \end{pmatrix} \begin{pmatrix} \times \\ \times \\ \times \\ \times \end{pmatrix} = \begin{pmatrix} \times \\ \times \\ * \\ 0 \end{pmatrix}.$$

Then, by a rotation G_2 in the plane $(2, 3)$ we zero the element in position 3:

$$\begin{pmatrix} 1 & 0 & 0 & 0 \\ 0 & c_2 & s_2 & 0 \\ 0 & -s_2 & c_2 & 0 \\ 0 & 0 & 0 & 1 \end{pmatrix} \begin{pmatrix} \times \\ \times \\ \times \\ 0 \end{pmatrix} = \begin{pmatrix} \times \\ * \\ 0 \\ 0 \end{pmatrix}.$$

Finally, the second element is annihilated by a rotation G_1:

$$\begin{pmatrix} c_3 & s_3 & 0 & 0 \\ -s_3 & c_3 & 0 & 0 \\ 0 & 0 & 1 & 0 \\ 0 & 0 & 0 & 1 \end{pmatrix} \begin{pmatrix} \times \\ \times \\ 0 \\ 0 \end{pmatrix} = \begin{pmatrix} \kappa \\ 0 \\ 0 \\ 0 \end{pmatrix}.$$

According to Proposition 4.8 the Euclidean length is preserved, and therefore we know that $\kappa = \|x\|_2$.

We summarize the transformations. We have

$$\kappa e_1 = G_1(G_2(G_3 x)) = (G_1 G_2 G_3)x.$$

Since the product of orthogonal matrices is orthogonal (Proposition 4.6) the matrix $P = G_1 G_2 G_3$ is orthogonal, and the overall result is $Px = \kappa e_1$. ∎

Plane rotations are very flexible and can be used efficiently for problems with a sparsity structure, e.g., band matrices. On the other hand, for dense matrices they require more flops than Householder transformations; see Section 4.3.

Example 4.12. In the MATLAB example earlier in this section we explicitly embedded the 2×2 in a matrix of larger dimension. This is a waste of operations, since the computer execution of the code does not take into account the fact that only two rows of the matrix are changed. Instead the whole matrix multiplication is performed, which requires $2n^3$ flops in the case of matrices of dimension n. The following two MATLAB functions illustrate how the rotation should be implemented to save operations (and storage):

```
function [c,s]=rot(x,y);
  % Construct a plane rotation that zeros the second
  % component in the vector [x;y]' (x and y are scalars)
  sq=sqrt(x^2 + y^2);
  c=x/sq; s=y/sq;

function X=approt(c,s,i,j,X);
  % Apply a plane (plane) rotation in plane (i,j)
  % to a matrix X
  X([i,j],:)=[c s; -s c]*X([i,j],:);
```

The following script reduces the vector x to a multiple of the standard basis vector e_1:

```
x=[1;2;3;4];
for i=3:-1:1
  [c,s]=rot(x(i),x(i+1));
  x=approt(c,s,i,i+1,x);
end

>> x = 5.4772
            0
            0
            0
```

After the reduction the first component of x is equal to $\|x\|_2$. ∎

4.2.2   Householder Transformations

Let $v \neq 0$ be an arbitrary vector, and put

$$P = I - \frac{2}{v^T v} v v^T;$$

P is symmetric and orthogonal (verify this by a simple computation!). Such matrices are called *reflection matrices* or *Householder transformations*. Let x and y be given vectors of the same length, $\|x\|_2 = \|y\|_2$, and ask the question, "Can we determine a Householder transformation P such that $Px = y$?"

The equation $Px = y$ can be written

$$x - \frac{2 v^T x}{v^T v} v = y,$$

which is of the form $\beta v = x - y$. Since v enters P in such a way that a factor β cancels, we can choose $\beta = 1$. With $v = x - y$ we get

$$v^T v = x^T x + y^T y - 2 x^T y = 2(x^T x - x^T y),$$

since $x^T x = y^T y$. Further,

$$v^T x = x^T x - y^T x = \frac{1}{2} v^T v.$$

Therefore we have

$$Px = x - \frac{2 v^T x}{v^T v} v = x - v = y,$$

as we wanted. In matrix computations we often want to zero elements in a vector and we now choose $y = \kappa e_1$, where $\kappa = \pm\|x\|_2$, and $e_1^T = \begin{pmatrix} 1 & 0 & \cdots & 0 \end{pmatrix}$. The vector v should be taken equal to

$$v = x - \kappa e_1.$$

In order to avoid cancellation (i.e., the subtraction of two close floating point numbers), we choose $\text{sign}(\kappa) = -\text{sign}(x_1)$. Now that we have computed v, we can simplify and write

$$P = I - \frac{2}{v^T v} v v^T = I - 2 u u^T, \qquad u = \frac{1}{\|v\|_2} v.$$

Thus the Householder vector u has length 1. The computation of the Householder vector can be implemented in the following MATLAB code:

```
function u=househ(x)
  % Compute the Householder vector u such that
  % (I - 2 u * u')x = k*e_1, where
  % |k| is equal to the euclidean norm of x
  % and e_1 is the first unit vector
  n=length(x);      % Number of components in x
  kap=norm(x); v=zeros(n,1);
  v(1)=x(1)+sign(x(1))*kap;
  v(2:n)=x(2:n);
  u=(1/norm(v))*v;
```

In most cases one should avoid forming the Householder matrix P explicitly, since it can be represented much more compactly by the vector u. Multiplication by P should be done according to $Px = x - (2u^Tx)u$, where the matrix-vector multiplication requires $4n$ flops (instead of $O(n^2)$ if P were formed explicitly). The matrix multiplication PX is done

$$PX = A - 2u(u^T X). \tag{4.1}$$

Multiplication by a Householder transformation is implemented in the following code:

```
function Y=apphouse(u,X);
  % Multiply the matrix X by a Householder matrix
  % Y = (I - 2 * u * u') * X
  Y=X-2*u*(u'*X);
```

Example 4.13. The first three elements of the vector $x = \begin{pmatrix} 1 & 2 & 3 & 4 \end{pmatrix}^T$ are zeroed by the following sequence of MATLAB statements:

```
>>    x=[1; 2; 3; 4];
>>    u=househ(x);
>>    y=apphouse(u,x)


y = -5.4772
           0
           0
           0  ■
```

As plane rotations can be embedded in unit matrices, in order to apply the transformation in a structured way, we similarly can embed Householder transformations. Assume, for instance that we have transformed the first column in a matrix to a unit vector and that we then want to zero all the elements in the second column below the main diagonal. Thus, in an example with a 5×4 matrix, we want to compute the transformation

$$P_2 A^{(1)} = P_2 \begin{pmatrix} \times & \times & \times & \times \\ 0 & \times & \times & \times \\ 0 & \times & \times & \times \\ 0 & \times & \times & \times \\ 0 & \times & \times & \times \end{pmatrix} = \begin{pmatrix} \times & \times & \times & \times \\ 0 & \times & \times & \times \\ 0 & 0 & \times & \times \\ 0 & 0 & \times & \times \\ 0 & 0 & \times & \times \end{pmatrix} =: A^{(2)}. \qquad (4.2)$$

Partition the second column of $A^{(1)}$ as follows:

$$\begin{pmatrix} a_{12}^{(1)} \\ a_{.2}^{(1)} \end{pmatrix},$$

where $a_{12}^{(1)}$ is a scalar. We know how to transform $a_{.2}^{(1)}$ to a unit vector; let $\hat{P}_2$ be a Householder transformation that does this. Then the transformation (4.2) can be implemented by embedding $\hat{P}_2$ in a unit matrix:

$$P_2 = \begin{pmatrix} 1 & 0 \\ 0 & \hat{P}_2 \end{pmatrix}. \qquad (4.3)$$

It is obvious that P_2 leaves the first row of $A^{(1)}$ unchanged and computes the transformation (4.2). Also, it is easy to see that the newly created zeros in the first column are not destroyed.

Similar to the case of plane rotations, one should not explicitly embed a Householder transformation in an identity matrix of larger dimension. Instead one should apply it to the rows (in the case of multiplication from the left) that are affected in the transformation.

Example 4.14. The transformation in (4.2) is done by the following statements.

```
u=househ(A(2:m,2)); A(2:m,2:n)=apphouse(u,A(2:m,2:n));
```

```
>> A = -0.8992    -0.6708    -0.7788    -0.9400
       -0.0000     0.3299     0.7400     0.3891
       -0.0000     0.0000    -0.1422    -0.6159
       -0.0000    -0.0000     0.7576     0.1632
       -0.0000    -0.0000     0.3053     0.4680   ∎
```

4.3   Number of Floating Point Operations

We shall compare the number of flops to transform the first column of an $m \times n$ matrix A to a multiple of a unit vector κe_1 using plane and Householder transformations. Consider first plane rotations. Obviously, the computation of

$$\begin{pmatrix} c & s \\ -s & c \end{pmatrix} \begin{pmatrix} x \\ y \end{pmatrix} = \begin{pmatrix} cx + sy \\ -sx + cy \end{pmatrix}$$

requires four multiplications and two additions, i.e., six flops. Applying such a transformation to an $m \times n$ matrix requires $6n$ flops. In order to zero all elements but one in the first column of the matrix, we apply $m - 1$ rotations. Thus the overall flop count is $6(m - 1)n \approx 6mn$.

If the corresponding operation is performed by a Householder transformation as in (4.1), then only $4mn$ flops are needed. (Note that multiplication by 2 is not a flop, as it is implemented by the compiler as a shift, which is much faster than a flop; alternatively one can scale the vector u by $\sqrt{2}$.)

4.4   Orthogonal Transformations in Floating Point Arithmetic

Orthogonal transformations are very stable in floating point arithmetic. For instance, it can be shown [50, p. 367] that a computed Householder transformation in floating point $\hat{P}$ that approximates an exact P satisfies

$$\| P - \hat{P} \|_2 = O(\mu),$$

where μ is the unit round-off of the floating point system. We also have the backward error result

$$fl(\hat{P}A) = P(A + E), \qquad \| E \|_2 = O(\mu \| A \|_2).$$

Thus the floating point result is equal to the product of the exact orthogonal matrix and a data matrix that has been perturbed by a very small amount. Analogous results hold for plane rotations.

Chapter 5

QR Decomposition

One of the main themes of this book is decomposition of matrices to compact (e.g., triangular or diagonal) form by orthogonal transformations. We will now introduce the first such decomposition, the *QR decomposition*, which is a factorization of a matrix A in a product of an orthogonal matrix and a triangular matrix. This is more ambitious than computing the LU decomposition, where the two factors are both required only to be triangular.

5.1 Orthogonal Transformation to Triangular Form

By a sequence of Householder transformations[7] we can transform any matrix $A \in \mathbb{R}^{m \times n}$, $m \geq n$,

$$A \longrightarrow Q^T A = \begin{pmatrix} R \\ 0 \end{pmatrix}, \qquad R \in \mathbb{R}^{n \times n},$$

where R is upper triangular and $Q \in \mathbb{R}^{m \times m}$ is orthogonal. The procedure can be conveniently illustrated using a matrix of small dimension. Let $A \in \mathbb{R}^{5 \times 4}$. In the first step we zero the elements below the main diagonal in the first column,

$$H_1 A = H_1 \begin{pmatrix} \times & \times & \times & \times \\ \times & \times & \times & \times \\ \times & \times & \times & \times \\ \times & \times & \times & \times \\ \times & \times & \times & \times \end{pmatrix} = \begin{pmatrix} + & + & + & + \\ 0 & + & + & + \\ 0 & + & + & + \\ 0 & + & + & + \\ 0 & + & + & + \end{pmatrix},$$

where +'s denote elements that have changed in the transformation. The orthogonal matrix H_1 can be taken equal to a Householder transformation. In the second step we use an embedded Householder transformation as in (4.3) to zero the elements

---

[7]In this chapter we use Householder transformations, but analogous algorithms can be formulated in terms of plane rotations.

below the main diagonal in the second column:

$$H_2 \begin{pmatrix} \times & \times & \times & \times \\ 0 & \times & \times & \times \\ 0 & \times & \times & \times \\ 0 & \times & \times & \times \\ 0 & \times & \times & \times \end{pmatrix} = \begin{pmatrix} \times & \times & \times & \times \\ 0 & + & + & + \\ 0 & 0 & + & + \\ 0 & 0 & + & + \\ 0 & 0 & + & + \end{pmatrix}.$$

Again, on the right-hand side, +'s denote elements that have been changed in the transformation, and ×'s denote elements that are unchanged in the present transformation.

In the third step we annihilate elements below the diagonal in the third column:

$$H_3 \begin{pmatrix} \times & \times & \times & \times \\ 0 & \times & \times & \times \\ 0 & 0 & \times & \times \\ 0 & 0 & \times & \times \\ 0 & 0 & \times & \times \end{pmatrix} = \begin{pmatrix} \times & \times & \times & \times \\ 0 & \times & \times & \times \\ 0 & 0 & + & + \\ 0 & 0 & 0 & + \\ 0 & 0 & 0 & + \end{pmatrix}.$$

After the fourth step we have computed the upper triangular matrix R. The sequence of transformations is summarized

$$Q^T A = \begin{pmatrix} R \\ 0 \end{pmatrix}, \qquad Q^T = H_4 H_3 H_2 H_1.$$

Note that the matrices H_i have the following structure (here we assume that $A \in \mathbb{R}^{m \times n}$):

$$H_1 = I - 2u_1 u_1^T, \quad u_1 \in \mathbb{R}^m,$$

$$H_2 = \begin{pmatrix} 1 & 0 \\ 0 & P_2 \end{pmatrix}, \quad P_2 = I - 2u_2 u_2^T, \quad u_2 \in \mathbb{R}^{m-1}, \tag{5.1}$$

$$H_3 = \begin{pmatrix} 1 & 0 & 0 \\ 0 & 1 & 0 \\ 0 & 0 & P_3 \end{pmatrix}, \quad P_3 = I - 2u_3 u_3^T, \quad u_3 \in \mathbb{R}^{m-2},$$

etc. Thus we embed the Householder transformations of successively smaller dimension in identity matrices, and the vectors u_i become shorter in each step. It is easy to see that the matrices H_i are also Householder transformations. For instance,

$$H_3 = I - 2u^{(3)} u^{(3)^T}, \quad u^{(3)} = \begin{pmatrix} 0 \\ 0 \\ u_3 \end{pmatrix}.$$

The transformation to triangular form is equivalent to a decomposition of the matrix A.

Theorem 5.1 (QR decomposition). *Any matrix $A \in \mathbb{R}^{m \times n}$, $m \geq n$, can be transformed to upper triangular form by an orthogonal matrix. The transformation is equivalent to a decomposition*

$$A = Q \begin{pmatrix} R \\ 0 \end{pmatrix},$$

where $Q \in \mathbb{R}^{m \times m}$ is orthogonal and $R \in \mathbb{R}^{n \times n}$ is upper triangular. If the columns of A are linearly independent, then R is nonsingular.

Proof. The constructive procedure outlined in the preceding example can easily be adapted to the general case, under the provision that if the vector to be transformed to a unit vector is a zero vector, then the orthogonal transformation is chosen equal to the identity.

The linear independence of the columns of

$$\begin{pmatrix} R \\ 0 \end{pmatrix}$$

follows from Proposition 2.4. Since R is upper triangular, the linear independence implies that its diagonal elements are nonzero. (If one column had a zero on the diagonal, then it would be a linear combination of those to the left of it.) Thus, the determinant of R is nonzero, which means that R is nonsingular.   ☐

We illustrate the QR decomposition symbolically in Figure 5.1.

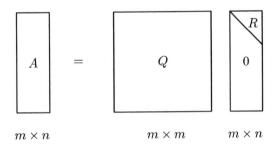

$m \times n$ $m \times m$ $m \times n$

Figure 5.1. *Symbolic illustration of the QR decomposition.*

Quite often it is convenient to write the decomposition in an alternative way, where the only part of Q that is kept corresponds to an orthogonalization of the columns of A; see Figure 5.2.

This *thin QR decomposition* can be derived by partitioning $Q = (Q_1 \ Q_2)$, where $Q_1 \in \mathbb{R}^{m \times n}$, and noting that in the multiplication the block Q_2 is multiplied by zero:

$$A = (Q_1 \ Q_2) \begin{pmatrix} R \\ 0 \end{pmatrix} = Q_1 R. \tag{5.2}$$

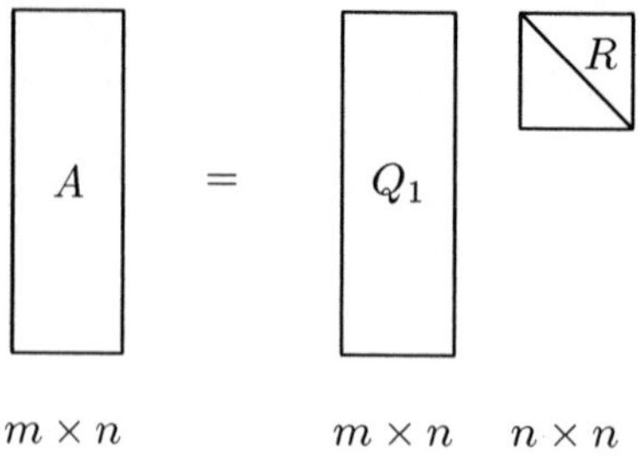

Figure 5.2. *Thin QR decomposition $A = Q_1 R$.*

It is seen from this equation that $\mathcal{R}(A) = \mathcal{R}(Q_1)$; thus we have now computed an *orthogonal basis* of the range space $\mathcal{R}(A)$. Furthermore, if we write out column j in (5.2),

$$a_j = Q_1 r_j = \sum_{i=1}^{j} r_{ij} q_i,$$

we see that *column j in R holds the coordinates of a_j in the orthogonal basis.*

Example 5.2. We give a simple numerical illustration of the computation of a QR decomposition in MATLAB:

```
A =   1       1       1
      1       2       4
      1       3       9
      1       4      16
>> [Q,R]=qr(A)


Q =-0.5000     0.6708      0.5000      0.2236
   -0.5000     0.2236     -0.5000     -0.6708
   -0.5000    -0.2236     -0.5000      0.6708
   -0.5000    -0.6708      0.5000     -0.2236


R =-2.0000     -5.0000   -15.0000
        0      -2.2361   -11.1803
        0           0      2.0000
        0           0           0
```

The thin QR decomposition is obtained by the command `qr(A,0)`:

```
>> [Q,R]=qr(A,0)


Q =-0.5000     0.6708      0.5000
   -0.5000     0.2236     -0.5000
   -0.5000    -0.2236     -0.5000
   -0.5000    -0.6708      0.5000
```

```
R =-2.0000    -5.0000  -15.0000
        0     -2.2361  -11.1803
        0           0    2.0000  ∎
```

5.2 Solving the Least Squares Problem

Using the QR decomposition, we can solve the least squares problem

$$\min_x \| b - Ax \|_2,\qquad(5.3)$$

where $A \in \mathbb{R}^{m \times n}$, $m \geq n$, without forming the normal equations. To do this we use the fact that the Euclidean vector norm is invariant under orthogonal transformations (Proposition 4.8):

$$\|Qy\|_2 = \|y\|_2.$$

Introducing the QR decomposition of A in the residual vector, we get

$$\|r\|_2^2 = \|b - Ax\|_2^2 = \left\| b - Q \begin{pmatrix} R \\ 0 \end{pmatrix} x \right\|_2^2$$
$$= \left\| Q(Q^T b - \begin{pmatrix} R \\ 0 \end{pmatrix} x) \right\|_2^2 = \left\| Q^T b - \begin{pmatrix} R \\ 0 \end{pmatrix} x \right\|_2^2.$$

Then we partition $Q = (Q_1\ Q_2)$, where $Q_1 \in \mathbb{R}^{m \times n}$, and denote

$$Q^T b = \begin{pmatrix} b_1 \\ b_2 \end{pmatrix} := \begin{pmatrix} Q_1^T b \\ Q_2^T b \end{pmatrix}.$$

Now we can write

$$\|r\|_2^2 = \left\| \begin{pmatrix} b_1 \\ b_2 \end{pmatrix} - \begin{pmatrix} Rx \\ 0 \end{pmatrix} \right\|_2^2 = \|b_1 - Rx\|_2^2 + \|b_2\|_2^2. \qquad(5.4)$$

Under the assumption that the columns of A are linearly independent, we can solve

$$Rx = b_1$$

and minimize $\|r\|_2$ by making the first term in (5.4) equal to zero. We now have proved the following theorem.

Theorem 5.3 (least squares solution by QR decomposition). *Let the matrix $A \in \mathbb{R}^{m \times n}$ have full column rank and thin QR decomposition $A = Q_1 R$. Then the least squares problem $\min_x \| Ax - b \|_2$ has the unique solution*

$$x = R^{-1} Q_1^T b.$$

Example 5.4. As an example we solve the least squares problem from the beginning of Section 3.6. The matrix and right-hand side are

```
A =  1    1              b = 7.9700
     1    2                 10.2000
     1    3                 14.2000
     1    4                 16.0000
     1    5                 21.2000
```

with thin QR decomposition and least squares solution

```
>> [Q1,R]=qr(A,0)        % thin QR

Q1 = -0.4472    -0.6325
     -0.4472    -0.3162
     -0.4472     0.0000
     -0.4472     0.3162
     -0.4472     0.6325

R = -2.2361    -6.7082
          0     3.1623

>> x=R\(Q1'*b)

x = 4.2360
    3.2260
```

Note that the MATLAB statement x=A\b gives the same result, using exactly the same algorithm. ∎

5.3 Computing or Not Computing Q

The orthogonal matrix Q can be computed at the same time as R by applying the transformations to the identity matrix. Similarly, Q_1 in the thin QR decomposition can be computed by applying the transformations to the partial identity matrix

$$\begin{pmatrix} I_n \\ 0 \end{pmatrix}.$$

However, in many situations we do not need Q explicitly. Instead, it may be sufficient to apply the same sequence of Householder transformations. Due to the structure of the embedded Householder matrices exhibited in (5.1), the vectors that are used to construct the Householder transformations for reducing the matrix A to upper triangular form can be stored below the main diagonal in A, in the positions that were made equal to zero. An extra vector is then needed to store the elements on the diagonal of R.

In the solution of the least squares problem (5.3) there is no need to compute Q at all. By adjoining the right-hand side to the matrix, we compute

$$\begin{pmatrix} A & b \end{pmatrix} \quad \rightarrow \quad Q^T \begin{pmatrix} A & b \end{pmatrix} = \begin{pmatrix} Q_1^T \\ Q_2^T \end{pmatrix} \begin{pmatrix} A & b \end{pmatrix} = \begin{pmatrix} R & Q_1^T b \\ 0 & Q_2^T b \end{pmatrix},$$

and the least squares solution is obtained by solving $Rx = Q_1^T b$. We also see that

$$\min_x \| Ax - b \|_2 = \min_x \left\| \begin{pmatrix} Rx - Q_1^T b \\ Q_2^T b \end{pmatrix} \right\|_2 = \| Q_2^T b \|_2.$$

Thus the norm of the optimal residual is obtained as a by-product of the triangularization procedure.

5.4 Flop Count for QR Factorization

As shown in Section 4.3, applying a Householder transformation to an $m \times n$ matrix to zero the elements of the first column below the diagonal requires approximately $4mn$ flops. In the following transformation, only rows 2 to m and columns 2 to n are changed (see (5.1)), and the dimension of the submatrix that is affected by the transformation is reduced by one in each step. Therefore the number of flops for computing R is approximately

$$4 \sum_{k=0}^{n-1} (m - k)(n - k) \approx 2mn^2 - \frac{2n^3}{3}.$$

Then the matrix Q is available in factored form, as a product of Householder transformations. If we compute explicitly the full matrix Q, then in step $k + 1$ we need $4(m - k)m$ flops, which leads to a total of

$$4 \sum_{k=0}^{n-1} (m - k)m \approx 4mn \left(m - \frac{n}{2} \right).$$

It is possible to take advantage of structure in the accumulation of Q to reduce the flop count somewhat [42, Section 5.1.6].

5.5 Error in the Solution of the Least Squares Problem

As we stated in Section 4.4, Householder transformations and plane rotations have excellent properties with respect to floating point rounding errors. Here we give a theorem, the proof of which can be found in [50, Theorem 19.3].

Theorem 5.5. *Assume that $A \in \mathbb{R}^{m \times n}$, $m \geq n$, has full column rank and that the least squares problem $\min_x \| Ax - b \|_2$ is solved using QR factorization by Householder transformations. Then the computed solution $\hat{x}$ is the exact least squares solution of*

$$\min_x \| (A + \Delta A)\hat{x} - (b + \delta b) \|_2,$$

where

$$\| \Delta A \|_F \leq c_1 mn\mu \| A \|_F + O(\mu^2), \quad \| \delta b \|_2 \leq c_2 mn\mu \| b \| + O(\mu^2),$$

and c_1 and c_2 are small integers.

It is seen that, in the sense of backward errors, the solution is as good as can be hoped for (i.e., the method is *backward stable*). Using the perturbation theory in Section 6.6 one can estimate the forward error in the computed solution. In Section 3.6 we suggested that the normal equations method for solving the least squares problem has less satisfactory properties in floating point arithmetic. It can be shown that that method is not backward stable, unless the matrix A is well-conditioned. The pros and cons of the two methods are nicely summarized in [50, p. 399]. Here we give an example that, although somewhat extreme, demonstrates that for certain least squares problems the solution given by the method of normal equations can be much less accurate than that produced using a QR decomposition; cf. Example 3.12.

Example 5.6. Let $\epsilon = 10^{-7}$, and consider the matrix

$$A = \begin{pmatrix} 1 & 1 \\ \epsilon & 0 \\ 0 & \epsilon \end{pmatrix}.$$

The condition number of A is of the order 10^7. The following MATLAB script

```
x=[1;1]; b=A*x;
xq=A\b;                % QR decomposition
xn=(A'*A)\(A'*b);      % Normal equations
[xq xn]
```

gave the result

```
1.00000000000000    1.01123595505618
1.00000000000000    0.98876404494382
```

which shows that the normal equations method is suffering from the fact that the condition number of the matrix $A^T A$ is the square of that of A. ∎

5.6 Updating the Solution of a Least Squares Problem

In some applications the rows of A and the corresponding elements of b are measured in real time. Let us call one row and the element of b an *observation*. Every time an observation arrives, a new least squares solution is to be computed. If we were to recompute the solution from scratch, it would cost $O(mn^2)$ flops for each new observation. This is too costly in most situations and is an unnecessarily heavy computation, since the least squares solution can be computed by *updating* the QR decomposition in $O(n^2)$ flops every time a new observation is available. Furthermore, the updating algorithm does not require that we save the orthogonal matrix Q!

Assume that we have reduced the matrix and the right-hand side

$$\begin{pmatrix} A & b \end{pmatrix} \quad \rightarrow \quad Q^T \begin{pmatrix} A & b \end{pmatrix} = \begin{pmatrix} R & Q_1^T b \\ 0 & Q_2^T b \end{pmatrix}, \tag{5.5}$$

from which the least squares solution is readily available. Assume that we have not saved Q. Then let a new observation be denoted $(a^T \; \beta)$, where $a \in \mathbb{R}^n$ and β is a scalar. We then want to find the solution of the augmented least squares problem

$$\min_x \left\| \begin{pmatrix} A \\ a^T \end{pmatrix} x - \begin{pmatrix} b \\ \beta \end{pmatrix} \right\|. \qquad (5.6)$$

In terms of the new matrix, we can write the reduction (5.5) in the form

$$\begin{pmatrix} A & b \\ a^T & \beta \end{pmatrix} \quad \rightarrow \quad \begin{pmatrix} Q^T & 0 \\ 0 & 1 \end{pmatrix} \begin{pmatrix} A & b \\ a^T & \beta \end{pmatrix} = \begin{pmatrix} R & Q_1^T b \\ 0 & Q_2^T b \\ a^T & \beta \end{pmatrix}.$$

Therefore, we can find the solution of the augmented least squares problem (5.6) if we reduce

$$\begin{pmatrix} R & Q_1^T b \\ 0 & Q_2^T b \\ a^T & \beta \end{pmatrix}$$

to triangular form by a sequence of orthogonal transformations. The vector $Q_2^T b$ will play no part in this reduction, and therefore we exclude it from the derivation.

We will now show how to perform the reduction to triangular form using a sequence of plane rotations. The ideas of the algorithm will be illustrated using a small example with $n = 4$. We start with

$$\begin{pmatrix} R & b_1 \\ a^T & \beta \end{pmatrix} = \begin{pmatrix} \times & \times & \times & \times & \times \\ & \times & \times & \times & \times \\ & & \times & \times & \times \\ & & & \times & \times \\ & & & & \times \\ \times & \times & \times & \times & \times \end{pmatrix}.$$

By a rotation in the $(1, n + 1)$ plane, we zero the first element of the bottom row vector. The result is

$$\begin{pmatrix} + & + & + & + & + \\ & \times & \times & \times & \times \\ & & \times & \times & \times \\ & & & \times & \times \\ & & & & \times \\ 0 & + & + & + & + \end{pmatrix},$$

where $+$'s denote elements that have been changed in the present transformation. Then the second element of the bottom vector is zeroed by a rotation in $(2, n + 1)$:

$$\begin{pmatrix} \times & \times & \times & \times & \times \\ & + & + & + & + \\ & & \times & \times & \times \\ & & & \times & \times \\ & & & & \times \\ & 0 & + & + & + \end{pmatrix}.$$

Note that the zero that was introduced in the previous step is not destroyed. After three more analogous steps, the final result is achieved:

$$\begin{pmatrix} \tilde{R} & \tilde{b}_1 \\ 0 & \tilde{\beta} \end{pmatrix} = \begin{pmatrix} \times & \times & \times & \times & \times \\ & \times & \times & \times & \times \\ & & \times & \times & \times \\ & & & \times & \times \\ & & & & \times \end{pmatrix}.$$

A total of n rotations are needed to compute the reduction. The least squares solution of (5.6) is now obtained by solving $\tilde{R}x = \tilde{b}_1$.

Chapter 6

Singular Value Decomposition

Even if the QR decomposition is very useful for solving least squares problems and has excellent stability properties, it has the drawback that it treats the rows and columns of the matrix differently: it gives a basis only for the *column space*. The singular value decomposition (SVD) deals with the rows and columns in a symmetric fashion, and therefore it supplies more information about the matrix. It also "orders" the information contained in the matrix so that, loosely speaking, the "dominating part" becomes visible. This is the property that makes the SVD so useful in data mining and many other areas.

6.1   The Decomposition

Theorem 6.1 (SVD). *Any $m \times n$ matrix A, with $m \geq n$, can be factorized*

$$A = U \begin{pmatrix} \Sigma \\ 0 \end{pmatrix} V^T, \tag{6.1}$$

where $U \in \mathbb{R}^{m \times m}$ and $V \in \mathbb{R}^{n \times n}$ are orthogonal, and $\Sigma \in \mathbb{R}^{n \times n}$ is diagonal,

$$\Sigma = \mathrm{diag}(\sigma_1, \sigma_2, \ldots, \sigma_n),$$

$$\sigma_1 \geq \sigma_2 \geq \cdots \geq \sigma_n \geq 0.$$

Proof. The assumption $m \geq n$ is no restriction: in the other case, just apply the theorem to A^T. We give a proof along the lines of that in [42]. Consider the maximization problem

$$\sup_{\|x\|_2 = 1} \|Ax\|_2.$$

Since we are seeking the supremum of a continuous function over a closed set, the supremum is attained for some vector x. Put $Ax = \sigma_1 y$, where $\|y\|_2 = 1$ and

57

$\sigma_1 = \|A\|_2$ (by definition). Using Proposition 4.7 we can construct orthogonal matrices

$$Z_1 = (y \, \bar{Z}_2) \in \mathbb{R}^{m \times m}, \quad W_1 = (x \, \bar{W}_2) \in \mathbb{R}^{n \times n}.$$

Then

$$Z_1^T A W_1 = \begin{pmatrix} \sigma_1 & y^T A \bar{W}_2 \\ 0 & \bar{Z}_2^T A \bar{W}_2 \end{pmatrix},$$

since $y^T A x = \sigma_1$, and $Z_2^T A x = \sigma_1 \bar{Z}_2^T y = 0$. Put

$$A_1 = Z_1^T A W_1 = \begin{pmatrix} \sigma_1 & w^T \\ 0 & B \end{pmatrix}.$$

Then

$$\frac{1}{\sigma_1^2 + w^T w} \left\| A_1 \begin{pmatrix} \sigma_1 \\ w \end{pmatrix} \right\|_2^2 = \frac{1}{\sigma_1^2 + w^T w} \left\| \begin{pmatrix} \sigma_1^2 + w^T w \\ Bw \end{pmatrix} \right\|_2^2 \geq \sigma_1^2 + w^T w.$$

But $\|A_1\|_2^2 = \|Z_1^T A W_1\|_2^2 = \sigma_1^2$; therefore $w = 0$ must hold. Thus we have taken one step toward a diagonalization of A. The proof is now completed by induction. Assume that

$$B = Z_2 \begin{pmatrix} \Sigma_2 \\ 0 \end{pmatrix} W_2, \quad \Sigma_2 = \text{diag}(\sigma_2, \ldots, \sigma_n).$$

Then we have

$$A = Z_1 \begin{pmatrix} \sigma_1 & 0 \\ 0 & B \end{pmatrix} W_1^T = Z_1 \begin{pmatrix} 1 & 0 \\ 0 & Z_2 \end{pmatrix} \begin{pmatrix} \sigma_1 & 0 \\ 0 & \Sigma_2 \\ 0 & 0 \end{pmatrix} \begin{pmatrix} 1 & 0 \\ 0 & W_2^T \end{pmatrix} W_1^T.$$

Thus, by defining

$$U = Z_1 \begin{pmatrix} 1 & 0 \\ 0 & Z_2 \end{pmatrix}, \quad \Sigma = \begin{pmatrix} \sigma_1 & 0 \\ 0 & \Sigma_2 \end{pmatrix}, \quad V = W_1 \begin{pmatrix} 1 & 0 \\ 0 & W_2 \end{pmatrix},$$

the theorem is proved. □

The columns of U and V are called *singular vectors* and the diagonal elements σ_i *singular values*.

We emphasize at this point that not only is this an important theoretical result, but also there are very efficient and accurate algorithms for computing the SVD; see Section 6.8.

The SVD appears in other scientific areas under different names. In statistics and data analysis, the singular vectors are closely related to *principal components* (see Section 6.4), and in image processing the SVD goes by the name *Karhunen–Loewe expansion*.

We illustrate the SVD symbolically:

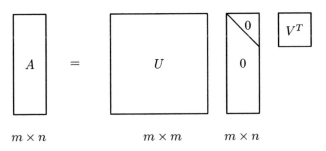

$$m \times n \qquad m \times m \qquad m \times n$$

With the partitioning $U = (U_1 \, U_2)$, where $U_1 \in \mathbb{R}^{m \times n}$, we get the *thin SVD*,

$$A = U_1 \Sigma V^T,$$

illustrated symbolically,

$$m \times n \qquad m \times n \qquad n \times n$$

If we write out the matrix equations

$$AV = U_1 \Sigma, \qquad A^T U_1 = V \Sigma$$

column by column, we get the equivalent equations

$$A v_i = \sigma_i u_i, \qquad A^T u_i = \sigma_i v_i, \qquad i = 1, 2, \ldots, n.$$

The SVD can also be written as an expansion of the matrix:

$$A = \sum_{i=1}^{n} \sigma_i u_i v_i^T. \tag{6.2}$$

This is usually called the *outer product form*, and it is derived by starting from the thin version:

$$A = U_1 \Sigma V^T = \begin{pmatrix} u_1 & u_2 & \cdots & u_n \end{pmatrix} \begin{pmatrix} \sigma_1 & & & \\ & \sigma_2 & & \\ & & \ddots & \\ & & & \sigma_n^T \end{pmatrix} \begin{pmatrix} v_1^T \\ v_2^T \\ \vdots \\ v_n^T \end{pmatrix}$$

$$= \begin{pmatrix} u_1 & u_2 & \cdots & u_n \end{pmatrix} \begin{pmatrix} \sigma_1 v_1^T \\ \sigma_2 v_2^T \\ \vdots \\ \sigma_n v_n^T \end{pmatrix} = \sum_{i=1}^{n} \sigma_i u_i v_i^T.$$

The outer product form of the SVD is illustrated as

$$A = \sum_{i=1}^{n} \sigma_i u_i v_i^T = \quad\begin{vmatrix} \end{vmatrix}\rule[3ex]{3em}{0.4pt} \quad + \quad \begin{vmatrix} \end{vmatrix}\rule[3ex]{3em}{0.4pt} \quad + \quad \cdots .$$

Example 6.2. We compute the SVD of a matrix with full column rank:

```
A =   1      1
      1      2
      1      3
      1      4
>> [U,S,V]=svd(A)

U =  0.2195    -0.8073     0.0236     0.5472
     0.3833    -0.3912    -0.4393    -0.7120
     0.5472     0.0249     0.8079    -0.2176
     0.7110     0.4410    -0.3921     0.3824

S =  5.7794          0
          0     0.7738
          0          0
          0          0

V =  0.3220    -0.9467
     0.9467     0.3220
```

The thin version of the SVD is

```
>> [U,S,V]=svd(A,0)

U =  0.2195    -0.8073
     0.3833    -0.3912
     0.5472     0.0249
     0.7110     0.4410

S =  5.7794          0
          0     0.7738

V =  0.3220    -0.9467
     0.9467     0.3220       ∎
```

The matrix 2-norm was defined in Section 2.4. From the proof of Theorem 6.1 we know already that $\| A \|_2 = \sigma_1$. This is such an important fact that it is worth a separate proposition.

Proposition 6.3. *The 2-norm of a matrix is given by*

$$\|A\|_2 = \sigma_1.$$

Proof. The following is an alternative proof. Without loss of generality, assume that $A \in \mathbb{R}^{m \times n}$ with $m \geq n$, and let the SVD of A be $A = U\Sigma V^T$. The norm is invariant under orthogonal transformations, and therefore

$$\|A\|_2 = \|\Sigma\|_2.$$

The result now follows, since the 2-norm of a diagonal matrix is equal to the absolute value of the largest diagonal element:

$$\|\Sigma\|_2^2 = \sup_{\|y\|_2 = 1} \|\Sigma y\|_2^2 = \sup_{\|y\|_2 = 1} \sum_{i=1}^n \sigma_i^2 y_i^2 \leq \sigma_1^2 \sum_{i=1}^n y_i^2 = \sigma_1^2$$

with equality for $y = e_1$. □

6.2 Fundamental Subspaces

The SVD gives orthogonal bases of the four fundamental subspaces of a matrix. The *range of the matrix A* is the linear subspace

$$\mathcal{R}(A) = \{y \mid y = Ax, \text{ for arbitrary } x\}.$$

Assume that A has rank r:

$$\sigma_1 \geq \cdots \geq \sigma_r > \sigma_{r+1} = \cdots = \sigma_n = 0.$$

Then, using the outer product form, we have

$$y = Ax = \sum_{i=1}^r \sigma_i u_i v_i^T x = \sum_{i=1}^r (\sigma_i v_i^T x) u_i = \sum_{i=1}^r \alpha_i u_i.$$

The *null-space of the matrix A* is the linear subspace

$$\mathcal{N}(A) = \{x \mid Ax = 0\}.$$

Since $Ax = \sum_{i=1}^r \sigma_i u_i v_i^T x$, we see that any vector $z = \sum_{i=r+1}^n \beta_i v_i$ is in the null-space:

$$Az = \left(\sum_{i=1}^r \sigma_i u_i v_i^T\right)\left(\sum_{i=r+1}^n \beta_i v_i\right) = 0.$$

After a similar demonstration for A^T we have the following theorem.

Theorem 6.4 (fundamental subspaces).

1. *The singular vectors $u_1, u_2, \ldots, u_r$ are an orthonormal basis in $\mathcal{R}(A)$ and*

$$\text{rank}(A) = \dim(\mathcal{R}(A)) = r.$$

2. *The singular vectors $v_{r+1}, v_{r+2}, \ldots, v_n$ are an orthonormal basis in $\mathcal{N}(A)$ and*

$$\dim(\mathcal{N}(A)) = n - r.$$

3. *The singular vectors $v_1, v_2, \ldots, v_r$ are an orthonormal basis in $\mathcal{R}(A^T)$.*

4. *The singular vectors $u_{r+1}, u_{r+2}, \ldots, u_m$ are an orthonormal basis in $\mathcal{N}(A^T)$.*

Example 6.5. We create a rank deficient matrix by constructing a third column in the previous example as a linear combination of columns 1 and 2:

```
>> A(:,3)=A(:,1)+0.5*A(:,2)


A = 1.0000     1.0000      1.5000
    1.0000     2.0000      2.0000
    1.0000     3.0000      2.5000
    1.0000     4.0000      3.0000

>> [U,S,V]=svd(A,0)

U = 0.2612    -0.7948     -0.5000
    0.4032    -0.3708      0.8333
    0.5451     0.0533     -0.1667
    0.6871     0.4774     -0.1667

S = 7.3944          0           0
          0     0.9072           0
          0          0           0

V = 0.2565    -0.6998      0.6667
    0.7372     0.5877      0.3333
    0.6251    -0.4060     -0.6667
```

The third singular value is equal to zero and the matrix is rank deficient. Obviously, the third column of V is a basis vector in $\mathcal{N}(A)$:

```
>> A*V(:,3)

ans =
    1.0e-15 *
          0
    -0.2220
    -0.2220
          0
```
■

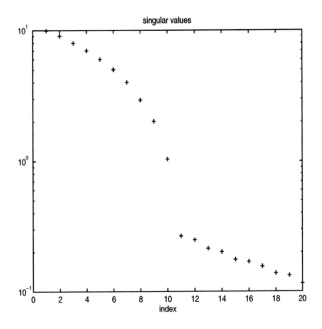

Figure 6.1. *Singular values of a matrix of rank* 10 *plus noise.*

6.3   Matrix Approximation

Assume that A is a low-rank matrix plus noise: $A = A_0 + N$, where the noise N is small compared with A_0. Then typically the singular values of A have the behavior illustrated in Figure 6.1. In such a situation, if the noise is sufficiently small in magnitude, the number of large singular values is often referred to as the *numerical rank* of the matrix. If we know the correct rank of A_0, or can estimate it, e.g., by inspecting the singular values, then we can "remove the noise" by approximating A by a matrix of the correct rank. The obvious way to do this is simply to truncate the singular value expansion (6.2). Assume that the numerical rank is equal to k. Then we approximate

$$A = \sum_{i=1}^{n} \sigma_i u_i v_i^T \approx \sum_{i=1}^{k} \sigma_i u_i v_i^T =: A_k.$$

The truncated SVD is very important, not only for removing noise but also for compressing data (see Chapter 11) and for stabilizing the solution of problems that are extremely ill-conditioned.

It turns out that the truncated SVD is the solution of approximation problems where one wants to approximate a given matrix by one of lower rank. We will consider low-rank approximation of a matrix A in two norms. First we give the theorem for the matrix 2-norm.

Theorem 6.6. *Assume that the matrix $A \in \mathbb{R}^{m \times n}$ has rank $r > k$. The matrix* *approximation problem*

$$\min_{\text{rank}(Z)=k} \|A - Z\|_2$$

has the solution

$$Z = A_k := U_k \Sigma_k V_k^T,$$

where $U_k = (u_1, \ldots, u_k)$, $V_k = (v_1, \ldots, v_k)$, *and* $\Sigma_k = \text{diag}(\sigma_1, \ldots, \sigma_k)$. *The minimum is*

$$\|A - A_k\|_2 = \sigma_{k+1}.$$

A proof of this theorem can be found, e.g., in [42, Section 2.5.5]. Next recall the definition of the *Frobenius matrix norm* (2.7)

$$\|A\|_F = \sqrt{\sum_{i,j} a_{ij}^2}.$$

It turns out that the approximation result is the same for this case.

Theorem 6.7. *Assume that the matrix* $A \in \mathbb{R}^{m \times n}$ *has rank* $r > k$. *The Frobenius norm matrix approximation problem*

$$\min_{\text{rank}(Z)=k} \|A - Z\|_F$$

has the solution

$$Z = A_k = U_k \Sigma_k V_k^T,$$

where $U_k = (u_1, \ldots, u_k)$, $V_k = (v_1, \ldots, v_k)$, *and* $\Sigma_k = \text{diag}(\sigma_1, \ldots, \sigma_k)$. *The minimum is*

$$\|A - A_k\|_F = \left(\sum_{i=k+1}^{p} \sigma_i^2 \right)^{1/2},$$

where $p = \min(m, n)$.

For the proof of this theorem we need a lemma.

Lemma 6.8. *Consider the* mn-*dimensional vector space* $\mathbb{R}^{m \times n}$ *with inner product*

$$\langle A, B \rangle = \text{tr}(A^T B) = \sum_{i=1}^{m} \sum_{j=1}^{n} a_{ij} b_{ij} \qquad (6.3)$$

and norm

$$\|A\|_F = \langle A, A \rangle^{1/2}.$$

Let $A \in \mathbb{R}^{m \times n}$ with SVD $A = U\Sigma V^T$. Then the matrices

$$u_i v_j^T, \qquad i = 1, 2, \ldots, m, \qquad j = 1, 2, \ldots, n, \tag{6.4}$$

are an orthonormal basis in $\mathbb{R}^{m \times n}$.

Proof. Using the identities $\langle A, B \rangle = \mathrm{tr}(A^T B) = \mathrm{tr}(BA^T)$ we get

$$\langle u_i v_j^T, u_k v_l^T \rangle = \mathrm{tr}(v_j u_i^T u_k v_l^T) = \mathrm{tr}(v_l^T v_j\, u_i^T u_k) = (v_l^T v_j)\,(u_i^T u_k),$$

which shows that the matrices are orthonormal. Since there are mn such matrices, they constitute a basis in $\mathbb{R}^{m \times n}$. ☐

Proof (Theorem 6.7). This proof is based on that in [41]. Write the matrix $Z \in \mathbb{R}^{m \times n}$ in terms of the basis (6.4),

$$Z = \sum_{i,j} \zeta_{ij} u_i v_j^T,$$

where the coefficients are to be chosen. For the purpose of this proof we denote the elements of Σ by σ_{ij}. Due to the orthonormality of the basis, we have

$$\|A - Z\|_F^2 = \sum_{i,j} (\sigma_{ij} - \zeta_{ij})^2 = \sum_i (\sigma_{ii} - \zeta_{ii})^2 + \sum_{i \neq j} \zeta_{ij}^2.$$

Obviously, we can choose the second term as equal to zero. We then have the following expression for Z:

$$Z = \sum_i \zeta_{ii} u_i v_i^T.$$

Since the rank of Z is equal to the number of terms in this sum, we see that the constraint $\mathrm{rank}(Z) = k$ implies that we should have exactly k nonzero terms in the sum. To minimize the objective function, we then choose

$$\zeta_{ii} = \sigma_{ii}, \quad i = 1, 2, \ldots, k,$$

which gives the desired result. ☐

The low-rank approximation of a matrix is illustrated as

6.4   Principal Component Analysis

The approximation properties of the SVD can be used to elucidate the equivalence between the SVD and *principal component analysis (PCA)*. Assume that $X \in \mathbb{R}^{m \times n}$ is a data matrix, where each column is an observation of a real-valued random vector with mean zero. The matrix is assumed to be centered, i.e., the mean of each column is equal to zero. Let the SVD of X be $X = U \Sigma V^T$. The right singular vectors v_i are called *principal components directions* of X [47, p. 62]. The vector

$$z_1 = X v_1 = \sigma_1 u_1$$

has the largest sample variance among all normalized linear combinations of the columns of X:

$$\text{Var}(z_1) = \text{Var}(X v_1) = \frac{\sigma_1^2}{m}.$$

Finding the vector of maximal variance is equivalent, using linear algebra terminology, to maximizing the Rayleigh quotient:

$$\sigma_1^2 = \max_{v \neq 0} \frac{v^T X^T X v}{v^T v}, \qquad v_1 = \arg\max_{v \neq 0} \frac{v^T X^T X v}{v^T v}.$$

The normalized variable $u_1 = (1/\sigma_1) X v_1$ is called the *normalized first principal component* of X.

Having determined the vector of largest sample variance, we usually want to go on and find the vector of second largest sample variance *that is orthogonal to the first*. This is done by computing the vector of largest sample variance of the *deflated data matrix* $X - \sigma_1 u_1 v_1^T$. Continuing this process we can determine all the principal components in order, i.e., we compute the singular vectors. In the general step of the procedure, the subsequent principal component is defined as the vector of maximal variance subject to the constraint that it is orthogonal to the previous ones.

Example 6.9. PCA is illustrated in Figure 6.2. Five hundred data points from a correlated normal distribution were generated and collected in a data matrix $X \in \mathbb{R}^{3 \times 500}$. The data points and the principal components are illustrated in the top plot of the figure. We then deflated the data matrix, $X_1 := X - \sigma_1 u_1 v_1^T$; the data points corresponding to X_1 are given in the bottom plot. ∎

6.5   Solving Least Squares Problems

The least squares problem can be solved using the SVD. Assume that we have an overdetermined system $Ax \sim b$, where the matrix A has full column rank. Write the SVD

$$A = (U_1 \, U_2) \begin{pmatrix} \Sigma \\ 0 \end{pmatrix} V^T,$$

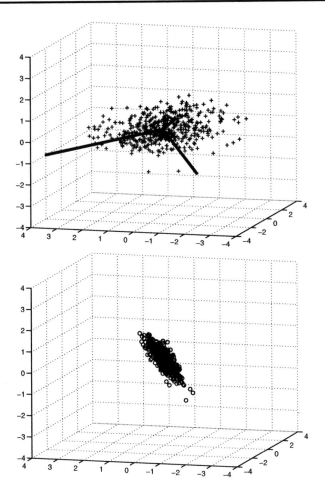

Figure 6.2. *Top: Cluster of points in* $\mathbb{R}^3$ *with (scaled) principal components. Bottom: same data with the contributions along the first principal component deflated.*

where $U_1 \in \mathbb{R}^{m \times n}$. Using the SVD and the fact that the norm is invariant under orthogonal transformations, we have

$$\|r\|^2 = \|b - Ax\|^2 = \left\| b - U \begin{pmatrix} \Sigma \\ 0 \end{pmatrix} V^T x \right\|^2 = \left\| \begin{pmatrix} b_1 \\ b_2 \end{pmatrix} - \begin{pmatrix} \Sigma \\ 0 \end{pmatrix} y \right\|^2,$$

where $b_i = U_i^T b$ and $y = V^T x$. Thus

$$\|r\|^2 = \|b_1 - \Sigma y\|^2 + \|b_2\|^2.$$

We can now minimize $\|r\|^2$ by putting $y = \Sigma^{-1}b_1$. The least squares solution is given by

$$x = Vy = V\Sigma^{-1}b_1 = V\Sigma^{-1}U_1^T b. \tag{6.5}$$

Recall that Σ is diagonal,

$$\Sigma^{-1} = \text{diag}\left(\frac{1}{\sigma_1}, \frac{1}{\sigma_2}, \ldots, \frac{1}{\sigma_n}\right),$$

so the solution can also be written

$$x = \sum_{i=1}^{n} \frac{u_i^T b}{\sigma_i}\, v_i.$$

The assumption that A has full column rank implies that all the singular values are nonzero: $\sigma_i > 0$, $i = 1, 2, \ldots, n$. We also see that in this case, the solution is unique.

Theorem 6.10 (least squares solution by SVD). *Let the matrix $A \in \mathbb{R}^{m \times n}$ have full column rank and thin SVD $A = U_1 \Sigma V^T$. Then the least squares problem $\min_x \| Ax - b \|_2$ has the unique solution*

$$x = V\Sigma^{-1}U_1^T b = \sum_{i=1}^{n} \frac{u_i^T b}{\sigma_i}\, v_i.$$

Example 6.11. As an example, we solve the least squares problem given at the beginning of Chapter 3.6. The matrix and right-hand side are

```
A =  1     1              b = 7.9700
     1     2                 10.2000
     1     3                 14.2000
     1     4                 16.0000
     1     5                 21.2000

>> [U1,S,V]=svd(A,0)

U1 =0.1600    -0.7579
    0.2853    -0.4675
    0.4106    -0.1772
    0.5359     0.1131
    0.6612     0.4035

S = 7.6912          0
        0      0.9194

V = 0.2669    -0.9637
    0.9637     0.2669
```

The two column vectors in A are linearly independent since the singular values are both nonzero. The least squares problem is solved using (6.5):

```
>> x=V*(S\(U1'*b))
```

```
x = 4.2360
    3.2260
```
 ∎

6.6 Condition Number and Perturbation Theory for the Least Squares Problem

The condition number of a rectangular matrix is defined in terms of the SVD. Let A have rank r, i.e., its singular values satisfy

$$\sigma_1 \geq \cdots \geq \sigma_r > \sigma_{r+1} = \cdots = \sigma_p = 0,$$

where $p = \min(m, n)$. Then the condition number is defined

$$\kappa(A) = \frac{\sigma_1}{\sigma_r}.$$

Note that in the case of a square, nonsingular matrix, this reduces to the definition (3.3).

The following perturbation theorem was proved by Wedin [106].

Theorem 6.12. *Assume that the matrix $A \in \mathbb{R}^{m \times n}$, where $m \geq n$ has full column rank, and let x be the solution of the least squares problem $\min_x \| Ax - b \|_2$. Let δA and δb be perturbations such that*

$$\eta = \frac{\| \delta A \|_2}{\sigma_n} = \kappa \epsilon_A < 1, \qquad \epsilon_A = \frac{\| \delta A \|_2}{\| A \|_2}.$$

Then the perturbed matrix $A + \delta A$ has full rank, and the perturbation of the solution δx satisfies

$$\| \delta x \|_2 \leq \frac{\kappa}{1 - \eta} \left(\epsilon_A \| x \|_2 + \frac{\| \delta b \|_2}{\| A \|_2} + \epsilon_A \kappa \frac{\| r \|_2}{\| A \|_2} \right),$$

where r is the residual $r = b - Ax$.

There are at least two important observations to make here:

1. The number κ determines the condition of the least squares problem, and if $m = n$, then the residual r is equal to zero and the inequality becomes a perturbation result for a linear system of equations; cf. Theorem 3.5.

2. In the overdetermined case the residual is usually not equal to zero. Then the conditioning depends on κ^2. This dependence may be significant if the norm of the residual is large.

6.7   Rank-Deficient and Underdetermined Systems

Assume that A is rank-deficient, i.e., $\text{rank}(A) = r < \min(m, n)$. The least squares problem can still be solved, but the solution is no longer unique. In this case we write the SVD

$$A = \begin{pmatrix} U_1 & U_2 \end{pmatrix} \begin{pmatrix} \Sigma_1 & 0 \\ 0 & 0 \end{pmatrix} \begin{pmatrix} V_1^T \\ V_2^T \end{pmatrix}, \tag{6.6}$$

where

$$U_1 \in \mathbb{R}^{m \times r}, \qquad \Sigma_1 \in \mathbb{R}^{r \times r}, \qquad V_1 \in \mathbb{R}^{n \times r}, \tag{6.7}$$

and the diagonal elements of Σ_1 are all nonzero. The norm of the residual can now be written

$$\| r \|_2^2 = \| Ax - b \|_2^2 = \left\| \begin{pmatrix} U_1 & U_2 \end{pmatrix} \begin{pmatrix} \Sigma_1 & 0 \\ 0 & 0 \end{pmatrix} \begin{pmatrix} V_1^T \\ V_2^T \end{pmatrix} x - b \right\|_2^2.$$

Putting

$$y = V^T x = \begin{pmatrix} V_1^T x \\ V_2^T x \end{pmatrix} = \begin{pmatrix} y_1 \\ y_2 \end{pmatrix}, \qquad \begin{pmatrix} b_1 \\ b_2 \end{pmatrix} = \begin{pmatrix} U_1^T b \\ U_2^T b \end{pmatrix}$$

and using the invariance of the norm under orthogonal transformations, the residual becomes

$$\| r \|_2^2 = \left\| \begin{pmatrix} \Sigma_1 & 0 \\ 0 & 0 \end{pmatrix} \begin{pmatrix} y_1 \\ y_2 \end{pmatrix} - \begin{pmatrix} b_1 \\ b_2 \end{pmatrix} \right\|_2^2 = \| \Sigma_1 y_1 - b_1 \|_2^2 + \| b_2 \|_2^2.$$

Thus, we can minimize the residual by choosing $y_1 = \Sigma_1^{-1} b_1$. In fact,

$$y = \begin{pmatrix} \Sigma_1^{-1} b_1 \\ y_2 \end{pmatrix},$$

where y_2 is arbitrary, solves the least squares problem. Therefore, *the solution of the least squares problem is not unique*, and, since the columns of V_2 span the null-space of A, it is in this null-space, where the indeterminacy is. We can write

$$\| x \|_2^2 = \| y \|_2^2 = \| y_1 \|_2^2 + \| y_2 \|_2^2,$$

and therefore we obtain the solution of *minimum norm* by choosing $y_2 = 0$.

We summarize the derivation in a theorem.

Theorem 6.13 (minimum norm solution). *Assume that the matrix A is rank deficient with SVD (6.6), (6.7). Then the least squares problem $\min_x \| Ax - b \|_2$ does not have a unique solution. However, the problem*

$$\min_{x \in \mathcal{L}} \| x \|_2, \qquad \mathcal{L} = \{ x \mid \| Ax - b \|_2 = \min \},$$

has the unique solution

$$x = V \begin{pmatrix} \Sigma_1^{-1} & 0 \\ 0 & 0 \end{pmatrix} U^T b = V_1 \Sigma_1^{-1} U_1^T b.$$

The matrix

$$A^\dagger = V \begin{pmatrix} \Sigma_1^{-1} & 0 \\ 0 & 0 \end{pmatrix} U^T$$

is called the *pseudoinverse* of A. It is defined for any nonzero matrix of arbitrary dimensions.

The SVD can also be used to solve *underdetermined linear systems*, i.e., systems with more unknowns than equations. Let $A \in \mathbb{R}^{m \times n}$, with $m < n$, be given. The SVD of A is

$$A = U \begin{pmatrix} \Sigma & 0 \end{pmatrix} \begin{pmatrix} V_1^T \\ V_2^T \end{pmatrix}, \qquad V_1 \in \mathbb{R}^{m \times m}. \tag{6.8}$$

Obviously A has full row rank if and only Σ is nonsingular.

We state a theorem concerning the solution of a linear system

$$Ax = b \tag{6.9}$$

for the case when A has full row rank.

Theorem 6.14 (solution of an underdetermined linear system). *Let $A \in \mathbb{R}^{m \times n}$ have full row rank with SVD (6.8). Then the linear system (6.9) always has a solution, which, however, is nonunique. The problem*

$$\min_{x \in \mathcal{K}} \| x \|_2, \qquad \mathcal{K} = \{x \mid Ax = b\}, \tag{6.10}$$

has the unique solution

$$x = V_1 \Sigma^{-1} U^T b. \tag{6.11}$$

Proof. Using the SVD (6.8) we can write

$$Ax = U \begin{pmatrix} \Sigma & 0 \end{pmatrix} \begin{pmatrix} V_1^T x \\ V_2^T x \end{pmatrix} =: U \begin{pmatrix} \Sigma & 0 \end{pmatrix} \begin{pmatrix} y_1 \\ y_2 \end{pmatrix} = U \Sigma y_1.$$

Since Σ is nonsingular, we see that for any right-hand side, (6.11) is a solution of the linear system. However, we can add an arbitrary solution component in the null-space of A, $y_2 = V_2^T x$, and we still have a solution. The minimum norm solution, i.e., the solution of (6.10), is given by (6.11). $\square$

The rank-deficient case may or may not have a solution depending on the right-hand side, and that case can be easily treated as in Theorem 6.13.

6.8   Computing the SVD

The SVD is computed in MATLAB by the statement [U,S,V]=svd(A). This statement is an implementation of algorithms from LAPACK [1]. (The double precision
high-level driver algorithm for SVD is called DGESVD.) In the algorithm the matrix
is first reduced to bidiagonal form by a series of Householder transformations from
the left and right. Then the bidiagonal matrix is iteratively reduced to diagonal
form using a variant of the QR algorithm; see Chapter 15.

The SVD of a dense (full) matrix can be computed in $\mathcal{O}(mn^2)$ flops. Depending on how much is computed, the constant is of the order 5–25.

The computation of a partial SVD of a large, sparse matrix is done in MAT-
LAB by the statement [U,S,V]=svds(A,k). This statement is based on Lanczos
methods from ARPACK. We give a brief description of Lanczos algorithms in
Chapter 15. For a more comprehensive treatment, see [4].

6.9   Complete Orthogonal Decomposition

In the case when the matrix is rank deficient, computing the SVD is the most
reliable method for determining the rank. However, it has the drawbacks that it is
comparatively expensive to compute, and it is expensive to update (when new rows
and/or columns are added). Both these issues may be critical, e.g., in a real-time
application. Therefore, methods have been developed that approximate the SVD,
so-called *complete orthogonal decompositions*, which in the noise-free case and in
exact arithmetic can be written

$$A = Q \begin{pmatrix} T & 0 \\ 0 & 0 \end{pmatrix} Z^T$$

for orthogonal Q and Z and triangular $T \in \mathbb{R}^{r \times r}$ when A has rank r. Obviously,
the SVD is a special case of a complete orthogonal decomposition.

In this section we will assume that the matrix $A \in \mathbb{R}^{m \times n}$, $m \geq n$, has exact
or numerical rank r. (Recall the definition of numerical rank on p. 63.)

6.9.1   QR with Column Pivoting

The first step toward obtaining a complete orthogonal decomposition is to perform
column pivoting in the computation of a QR decomposition [22]. Consider the
matrix before the algorithm has started: compute the 2-norm of each column, and
move the column with largest norm to the leftmost position. This is equivalent to
multiplying the matrix by a permutation matrix P_1 from the right. In the first step
of the reduction to triangular form, a Householder transformation is applied that
annihilates elements in the first column:

$$A \longrightarrow AP_1 \longrightarrow Q_1^T AP_1 = \begin{pmatrix} r_{11} & r_1^T \\ 0 & B \end{pmatrix}.$$

Then in the next step, find the column with largest norm in B, permute the columns
so that the column with largest norm is moved to position 2 in A (this involves only

columns 2 to n, of course), and reduce the first column of B:

$$Q_1^T A P_1 \longrightarrow Q_2^T Q_1^T A P_1 P_2 = \begin{pmatrix} r_{11} & r_{12} & \bar{r}_1^T \\ 0 & r_{22} & \bar{r}_2^T \\ 0 & 0 & C \end{pmatrix}.$$

It is seen that $|r_{11}| \geq |r_{22}|$.

After n steps we have computed

$$AP = Q \begin{pmatrix} R \\ 0 \end{pmatrix}, \qquad Q = Q_1 Q_2 \cdots Q_n, \qquad P = P_1 P_2 \cdots P_{n-1}.$$

The product of permutation matrices is itself a permutation matrix.

Proposition 6.15. *Assume that A has rank r. Then, in exact arithmetic, the QR decomposition with column pivoting is given by*

$$AP = Q \begin{pmatrix} R_{11} & R_{12} \\ 0 & 0 \end{pmatrix}, \qquad R_{11} \in \mathbb{R}^{r \times r},$$

and the diagonal elements of R_{11} are nonzero (R_{11} is nonsingular).

Proof. Obviously the diagonal elements occurring in the process are nonincreasing:

$$|r_{11}| \geq |r_{22}| \geq \cdots.$$

Assume that $r_{r+1,r+1} > 0$. That would imply that the rank of R in the QR decomposition is larger than r, which is a contradiction, since R and A must have the same rank.   □

Example 6.16. The following MATLAB script performs QR decomposition with column pivoting on a matrix that is constructed to be rank deficient:

```
[U,ru]=qr(randn(3)); [V,rv]=qr(randn(3));
D=diag([1 0.5 0]); A=U*D*V';
[Q,R,P]=qr(A);  % QR with column pivoting

R = -0.8540     0.4311     -0.0642
         0      0.4961     -0.2910
         0          0       0.0000

>> R(3,3) = 2.7756e-17
```

In many cases QR decomposition with pivoting gives reasonably accurate information about the numerical rank of a matrix. We modify the matrix in the previous script by adding noise:

```
[U,ru]=qr(randn(3)); [V,rv]=qr(randn(3));
D=diag([1 0.5 0]);   A=U*D*V'+1e-4*randn(3);
[Q,R,P]=qr(A);
```

```
>> R =  0.8172    -0.4698    -0.1018
             0    -0.5758     0.1400
             0          0     0.0001
```

The smallest diagonal element is of the same order of magnitude as the smallest singular value:

```
>> svd(A) = 1.0000
            0.4999
            0.0001   ■
```

It turns out, however, that one cannot rely completely on this procedure to give correct information about possible rank deficiency. We give an example due to Kahan; see [50, Section 8.3].

Example 6.17. Let $c^2 + s^2 = 1$. For n large enough, the triangular matrix

$$T_n(c) = \mathrm{diag}(1, s, s^2, \dots, s^{n-1}) \begin{pmatrix} 1 & -c & -c & \cdots & -c \\ & 1 & -c & \cdots & -c \\ & & \ddots & & \vdots \\ & & & 1 & -c \\ & & & & 1 \end{pmatrix}$$

is very ill-conditioned. For $n = 200$ and $c = 0.2$, we have

$$\kappa_2(T_n(c)) = \frac{\sigma_1}{\sigma_n} \approx \frac{12.7}{5.7 \cdot 10^{-18}}.$$

Thus, in IEEE double precision, the matrix is singular. The columns of the triangular matrix all have length 1. Therefore, because the elements in each row to the right of the diagonal are equal, QR decomposition with column pivoting will not introduce any column interchanges, and the upper triangular matrix R is equal to $T_n(c)$. However, the bottom diagonal element is equal to $s^{199} \approx 0.0172$, so for this matrix QR with column pivoting does not give any information whatsoever about the ill-conditioning.   ■

Chapter 7

Reduced-Rank Least Squares Models

Consider a linear model

$$b = Ax + \eta, \qquad A \in \mathbb{R}^{m \times n},$$

where η is random noise and A and b are given. If one chooses to determine x by minimizing the Euclidean norm of the residual $b - Ax$, then one has a linear least squares problem

$$\min_x \|Ax - b\|_2. \tag{7.1}$$

In some situations the actual solution x itself is not the primary object of interest, but rather it is an auxiliary, intermediate variable. This is the case, e.g., in certain classification methods, when the norm of the residual is the interesting quantity; see Chapter 10.

Least squares prediction is another area in which the solution x is an intermediate quantity and is not interesting in itself (except that it should be robust and reliable in a numerical sense). The columns of A consist of observations of *explanatory variables*, which are used to explain the variation of a *dependent variable b*. In this context it is essential that the variation of b is well explained by an approximate solution $\hat{x}$, in the sense that the *relative residual* $\|A\hat{x} - b\|_2/\|b\|_2$ should be rather small. Given $\hat{x}$ and a new row vector a_{new}^T of observations of the explanatory variables, one can predict the corresponding value of the dependent variable:

$$b_{\text{predicted}} = a_{\text{new}}^T \hat{x}. \tag{7.2}$$

Often in this context it is not necessary, or even desirable, to find the solution that actually minimizes the residual in (7.1). For instance, in prediction it is common that several of the explanatory variables are (almost) linearly dependent. Therefore the matrix A is often very ill-conditioned, and the least squares solution is highly influenced by measurement errors and floating point roundoff errors.

Example 7.1. The MATLAB script

```
A=[1 0
   1 1
   1 1];
B=[A A*[1;0.5]+1e-7*randn(3,1)];
b=B*[1;1;1]+1e-4*randn(3,1);
x=B\b
```

creates a matrix B, whose third column is almost a linear combination of the other two. The matrix is quite ill-conditioned: the condition number is $\kappa_2(B) \approx 5.969 \cdot 10^7$. The script gives the least squares solution

```
x = -805.95
    -402.47
     807.95
```

This approximate solution explains the variation of the dependent variable very well, as the residual is small:

```
resn = norm(B*x-b)/norm(b) = 1.9725e-14
```

However, because the components of the solution are large, there will be considerable cancellation (see Section 1.5) in the evaluation of (7.2), which leads to numerical errors. Furthermore, in an application it may be very difficult to interpret such a solution.

The large deviation of the least squares solution from the vector that was used to construct the right-hand side is due to the fact that the *numerical rank* of the matrix is two. (The singular values are 3.1705, 0.6691, and $8.4425 \cdot 10^{-8}$.) In view of this, it is reasonable to accept the approximate solution

```
xt = 0.7776
     0.8891
     1.2222
```

obtained using a truncated SVD

$$x_{\text{tsvd}} = \sum_{i=1}^{2} \frac{u_i^T b}{\sigma_i} v_i$$

(cf. Section 7.1). This solution candidate has residual norm $1.2 \cdot 10^{-5}$, which is of the same order of magnitude as the perturbation of the right-hand side. Such a solution vector may be much better for prediction, as the cancellation in the evaluation of (7.2) is much smaller or is eliminated completely (depending on the vector a_{new}). ∎

To reduce the ill-conditioning of the problem, and thus make the solution less sensitive to perturbations of the data, one sometimes introduces an approximate orthogonal basis of low dimension in $\mathbb{R}^n$, where the solution x lives. Let the basis vectors be $\begin{pmatrix} z_1 & z_2 & \ldots & z_k \end{pmatrix} =: Z_k$, for some (small) value of k. Then to determine the coordinates of the solution in terms of the approximate basis, we make the *ansatz* $x = Z_k y$ in the least squares problem and solve

$$\min_y \| A Z_k y - b \|_2. \tag{7.3}$$

This is a least squares problem corresponding to a *reduced-rank model*. In the following two sections we describe two methods for determining such a matrix of basis vectors. The first is based on the SVD of the data matrix A. The second method is a *Krylov subspace method*, in which the right-hand side influences the choice of basis.

7.1 Truncated SVD: Principal Component Regression

Assume that the data matrix has the SVD

$$A = U\Sigma V^T = \sum_{i=1}^r \sigma_i u_i v_i^T,$$

where r is the rank of A (note that we allow $m \geq n$ or $m \leq n$). The minimum norm solution (see Section 6.7) of the least squares problem (7.1) is

$$x = \sum_{i=1}^r \frac{u_i^T b}{\sigma_i} v_i. \tag{7.4}$$

As the SVD "orders the variation" of the data matrix A starting with the dominating direction, we see that the terms in the sum (7.4) are also organized in this way: the first term is the solution component along the dominating direction of the data matrix, the second term is the component along the second most dominating direction, and so forth.[8]

Thus, if we prefer to use the ordering induced by the SVD, then we should choose the matrix Z_k in (7.3) equal to the first k right singular vectors of A (we assume that $k \leq r$):

$$Z_k = V_k = \begin{pmatrix} v_1 & v_2 & \ldots & v_k \end{pmatrix}.$$

Using the fact that

$$V^T V_k = \begin{pmatrix} I_k \\ 0 \end{pmatrix},$$

---

[8]However, this does not mean that the terms in the sum are ordered by magnitude.

where $I_k \in \mathbb{R}^{k \times k}$, we get

$$\|AV_k y - b\|_2^2 = \|U\Sigma V^T V_k y - b\|_2^2 = \left\| U \left(\Sigma \begin{pmatrix} I_k \\ 0 \end{pmatrix} y - U^T b \right) \right\|_2^2$$

$$= \left\| \begin{pmatrix} \sigma_1 & & \\ & \ddots & \\ & & \sigma_k \end{pmatrix} \begin{pmatrix} y_1 \\ \vdots \\ y_k \end{pmatrix} - \begin{pmatrix} u_1^T b \\ \vdots \\ u_k^T b \end{pmatrix} \right\|_2^2 + \sum_{i=k+1}^{r} (u_i^T b)^2.$$

We see that the least squares problem $\min_y \|AV_k y - b\|_2$ has the solution

$$y = \begin{pmatrix} u_1^T b / \sigma_1 \\ \vdots \\ u_k^T b / \sigma_k \end{pmatrix},$$

which is equivalent to taking

$$x_k := \sum_{i=1}^{k} \frac{u_i^T b}{\sigma_i} v_i$$

as an approximate solution of (7.1). This is often referred to as the *truncated SVD solution*.

Often one wants to find as low a value of k such that the reduction of the residual is substantial enough. The procedure can be formulated as an algorithm, which is sometimes referred to as *principal component regression*.

Principal component regression (truncated SVD)

1. Find the smallest value of k such that $\sum_{i=k+1}^{r} (u_i^T b)^2 < \text{tol} \|b\|_2^2$.

2. Put

$$x_k := \sum_{i=1}^{k} \frac{u_i^T b}{\sigma_i} v_i.$$

The parameter tol is a predefined tolerance.

Example 7.2. We use the matrix from Example 1.1. Let

$$A = \begin{pmatrix} 0 & 0 & 0 & 1 & 0 \\ 0 & 0 & 0 & 0 & 1 \\ 0 & 0 & 0 & 0 & 1 \\ 1 & 0 & 1 & 0 & 0 \\ 1 & 0 & 0 & 0 & 0 \\ 0 & 1 & 0 & 0 & 0 \\ 1 & 0 & 1 & 1 & 0 \\ 0 & 1 & 1 & 0 & 0 \\ 0 & 0 & 1 & 1 & 1 \\ 0 & 1 & 1 & 0 & 0 \end{pmatrix}.$$

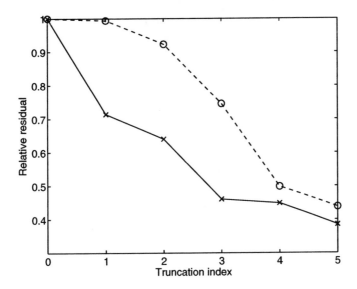

Figure 7.1. *The relative norm of the residuals for the query vectors q_1 (solid line) and q_2 (dashed) as functions of the truncation index k.*

Recall that each column corresponds to a document (here a sentence). We want to see how well two query vectors q_1 and q_2 can be represented in terms of the first few terms of the singular value expansion (7.4) of the solution, i.e., we will solve the least squares problems

$$\min_y \|AV_k y - q_i\|_2, \qquad i = 1, 2,$$

for different values of k. The two vectors are

$$q_1 = \begin{pmatrix} 0 \\ 0 \\ 0 \\ 0 \\ 0 \\ 0 \\ 0 \\ 1 \\ 1 \\ 1 \end{pmatrix}, \qquad q_2 = \begin{pmatrix} 0 \\ 1 \\ 1 \\ 0 \\ 0 \\ 0 \\ 0 \\ 0 \\ 0 \\ 0 \end{pmatrix},$$

corresponding to the words *rank, page, Web* and *England, FIFA*, respectively. In Figure 7.1 we plot the relative norm of residuals, $\|Ax_k - b\|_2/\|b\|_2$, for the two vectors as functions of k. From Example 1.1 we see that the main contents of the documents are related to the ranking of Web pages using the Google matrix, and this is reflected in the dominant singular vectors.[9] Since q_1 "contains Google

---

[9]See also Example 11.8 in Chapter 11.

terms," it can be well represented in terms of the first few singular vectors. On the other hand, the q_2 terms are related only to the "football document." Therefore, it is to be expected that the residual for q_1 decays faster than that of q_2 as a function of k.

The coordinates of q_1 and q_2 in terms of the first five left singular vectors are

```
U'*[q1 q2] =  1.2132      0.1574
             -0.5474      0.5215
              0.7698      0.7698
             -0.1817      0.7839
              0.3981     -0.3352
```

The vector q_1 has a substantial component in the first left singular vector u_1, and therefore the residual is reduced substantially for $k = 1$. Since q_2 has a small component in terms of u_1, there is only a marginal reduction of the residual in the first step.

If we want to reduce the relative residual to under 0.7 in this example, then we should choose $k = 2$ for q_1 and $k = 4$ for q_2. ■

7.2   A Krylov Subspace Method

When we use the truncated SVD (principal component regression) for a reduced-rank model, the right-hand side does not influence the choice of basis vectors z_i at all. The effect of this is apparent in Example 7.2, where the rate of decay of the residual is considerably slower for the vector q_2 than for q_1.

In many situations one would like to have a fast decay of the residual as a function of the number of basis vectors for any right-hand side. Then it is necessary to let the right-hand side influence the choice of basis vectors. This is done in an algorithm called *Lanczos–Golub–Kahan (LGK) bidiagonalization*, in the field of numerical linear algebra.[10] A closely related method is known in chemometrics and other areas as *partial least squares* or *projection to latent structures* (PLS). It is an algorithm out of a large class of *Krylov subspace methods*, often used for the solution of sparse linear systems; see, e.g., [42, Chapters 9–10], [80] or, for eigenvalue–singular value computations, see Section 15.8.

Krylov subspace methods are recursive, but in our derivation we will start with the reduction of a matrix to bidiagonal form using Householder transformations. The presentation in this section is largely influenced by [15].

7.2.1   Bidiagonalization Using Householder Transformations

The first step in the algorithm for computing the SVD of a dense matrix[11] $C \in \mathbb{R}^{m \times (n+1)}$ is to reduce it to upper bidiagonal form by Householder transformations

---

[10]The algorithm is often called Lanczos bidiagonalization, but it was first described by Golub and Kahan in [41].

[11]We choose these particular dimensions here because later in this chapter we will have $C = (b \ A)$.

from the left and right. We assume that $m > n$. The result is

$$C = P \begin{pmatrix} \hat{B} \\ 0 \end{pmatrix} W^T, \tag{7.5}$$

where P and W are orthogonal and $\hat{B}$ is upper bidiagonal. The decomposition in itself is useful also for other purposes. For instance, it is often used for the approximate solution of least squares problems, both dense and sparse.

We illustrate the Householder bidiagonalization procedure with a small example, where $C \in \mathbb{R}^{6 \times 5}$. First, all subdiagonal elements in the first column are zeroed by a transformation P_1^T from the left (the elements that are changed in the transformation are denoted by $*$):

$$P_1^T C = P_1^T \begin{pmatrix} \times & \times & \times & \times & \times \\ \times & \times & \times & \times & \times \\ \times & \times & \times & \times & \times \\ \times & \times & \times & \times & \times \\ \times & \times & \times & \times & \times \\ \times & \times & \times & \times & \times \end{pmatrix} = \begin{pmatrix} * & * & * & * & * \\ 0 & * & * & * & * \\ 0 & * & * & * & * \\ 0 & * & * & * & * \\ 0 & * & * & * & * \\ 0 & * & * & * & * \end{pmatrix}.$$

Then, by a different Householder transformation W_1 from the right, we zero elements in the first row, from position 3 to n. To achieve this we choose

$$\mathbb{R}^{5 \times 5} \ni W_1 = \begin{pmatrix} 1 & 0 \\ 0 & Z_1 \end{pmatrix},$$

where Z_1 is a Householder transformation. Since this transformation does not change the elements in the first column, the zeros that we just introduced in the first column remain. The result of the first step is

$$P_1^T C W_1 = \begin{pmatrix} \times & \times & \times & \times & \times \\ 0 & \times & \times & \times & \times \\ 0 & \times & \times & \times & \times \\ 0 & \times & \times & \times & \times \\ 0 & \times & \times & \times & \times \\ 0 & \times & \times & \times & \times \end{pmatrix} W_1 = \begin{pmatrix} \times & * & 0 & 0 & 0 \\ 0 & * & * & * & * \\ 0 & * & * & * & * \\ 0 & * & * & * & * \\ 0 & * & * & * & * \\ 0 & * & * & * & * \end{pmatrix} =: C_1.$$

We now continue in an analogous way and zero all elements below the diagonal in the second column by a transformation from the left. The matrix P_2 is constructed so that it does not change the elements in the first row of C_1, i.e., P_2 has the structure

$$\mathbb{R}^{6 \times 6} \ni P_2 = \begin{pmatrix} 1 & 0 \\ 0 & \tilde{P}_2 \end{pmatrix},$$

where $\tilde{P}_2 \in \mathbb{R}^{5 \times 5}$ is a Householder transformation. We get

$$
P_2^T C_1 = \begin{pmatrix}
\times & \times & 0 & 0 & 0 \\
0 & * & * & * & * \\
0 & 0 & * & * & * \\
0 & 0 & * & * & * \\
0 & 0 & * & * & * \\
0 & 0 & * & * & *
\end{pmatrix}.
$$

Then, by a transformation from the right,

$$
W_2 = \begin{pmatrix} I_2 & 0 \\ 0 & Z_2 \end{pmatrix}, \qquad I_2 = \begin{pmatrix} 1 & 0 \\ 0 & 1 \end{pmatrix},
$$

we annihilate elements in the second row without destroying the newly introduced zeros:

$$
P_1^T C_1 W_2 = \begin{pmatrix}
\times & \times & 0 & 0 & 0 \\
0 & \times & * & 0 & 0 \\
0 & 0 & * & * & * \\
0 & 0 & * & * & * \\
0 & 0 & * & * & * \\
0 & 0 & * & * & *
\end{pmatrix} =: C_2.
$$

We continue in an analogous manner and finally obtain

$$
P^T C W = \begin{pmatrix}
\times & \times & & & \\
 & \times & \times & & \\
 & & \times & \times & \\
 & & & \times & \times \\
 & & & & \times \\
 & & & &
\end{pmatrix} = \begin{pmatrix} \hat{B} \\ 0 \end{pmatrix}. \tag{7.6}
$$

In the general case,

$$
P = P_1 P_2 \cdots P_n \in \mathbb{R}^{m \times m}, \qquad W = W_1 W_2 \cdots W_{n-2} \in \mathbb{R}^{(n+1) \times (n+1)}
$$

are products of Householder transformations, and

$$
\hat{B} = \begin{pmatrix}
\beta_1 & \alpha_1 & & & \\
 & \beta_2 & \alpha_2 & & \\
 & & \ddots & \ddots & \\
 & & & \beta_n & \alpha_n \\
 & & & & \beta_{n+1}
\end{pmatrix} \in \mathbb{R}^{(n+1) \times (n+1)}
$$

is upper bidiagonal.

Due to the way the orthogonal matrices were constructed, they have a particular structure that will be used in the rest of this chapter.

Proposition 7.3. *Denote the columns of P in the bidiagonal decomposition (7.6) by p_i, $i = 1, 2, \ldots, m$. Then*

$$p_1 = \beta_1 c_1, \qquad W = \begin{pmatrix} 1 & 0 \\ 0 & Z \end{pmatrix},$$

where c_1 is the first column of C and $Z \in \mathbb{R}^{n \times n}$ is orthogonal.

Proof. The first relation follows immediately from $P^T c_1 = \beta_1 e_1$. The second follows from the fact that all W_i have the structure

$$W_i = \begin{pmatrix} I_i & 0 \\ 0 & Z_i \end{pmatrix},$$

where $I_i \in \mathbb{R}^{i \times i}$ are identity matrices and Z_i are orthogonal. □

The reduction to bidiagonal form by Householder transformation requires $4mn^2 - 4n^3/3$ flops. If $m \gg n$, then it is more efficient to first reduce A to upper triangular form and then bidiagonalize the R factor.

Assume now that we want to solve the least squares problem $\min_x \|b - Ax\|_2$, where $A \in \mathbb{R}^{m \times n}$. If we choose $C = (b \quad A)$ in the bidiagonalization procedure, then we get an equivalent bidiagonal least squares problem. Using (7.6) and Proposition 7.3 we obtain

$$P^T C W = P^T (b \quad A) \begin{pmatrix} 1 & 0 \\ 0 & Z \end{pmatrix} = (P^T b \quad P^T A Z) = \begin{pmatrix} \beta_1 e_1 & B \\ 0 & 0 \end{pmatrix}, \tag{7.7}$$

where

$$B = \begin{pmatrix} \alpha_1 & & & \\ \beta_2 & \alpha_2 & & \\ & \ddots & \ddots & \\ & & \beta_n & \alpha_n \\ & & & \beta_{n+1} \end{pmatrix} \in \mathbb{R}^{(n+1) \times n}.$$

Then, defining $y = Z^T x$ we can write the norm of the residual,

$$\|b - Ax\|_2 = \left\| (b \quad A) \begin{pmatrix} 1 \\ -x \end{pmatrix} \right\|_2 = \left\| P^T (b \quad A) \begin{pmatrix} 1 & 0 \\ 0 & Z \end{pmatrix} \begin{pmatrix} 1 \\ -y \end{pmatrix} \right\|_2$$

$$= \left\| (P^T b \quad P^T A Z) \begin{pmatrix} 1 \\ -y \end{pmatrix} \right\|_2 = \|\beta_1 e_1 - By\|_2. \tag{7.8}$$

The bidiagonal least squares problem $\min_y \|\beta_1 e_1 - By\|_2$ can be solved in $O(n)$ flops, if we reduce B to upper bidiagonal form using a sequence of plane rotations (see below).

7.2.2   LGK Bidiagonalization

We will now give an alternative description of the bidiagonalization procedure of the preceding section that allows us to compute the decomposition (7.7) in a recursive manner. This is the LGK bidiagonalization. Part of the last equation of (7.7) can be written

$$P^T A = \begin{pmatrix} BZ^T \\ 0 \end{pmatrix}, \qquad BZ^T \in \mathbb{R}^{(n+1)\times n},$$

which implies

$$A^T \begin{pmatrix} p_1 & p_2 & \cdots & p_{n+1} \end{pmatrix}$$

$$= ZB^T = \begin{pmatrix} z_1 & z_2 & \cdots & z_n \end{pmatrix} \begin{pmatrix} \alpha_1 & \beta_2 & & & & & \\ & \alpha_2 & \beta_3 & & & & \\ & & \ddots & \ddots & & & \\ & & & & \beta_i & & \\ & & & & \alpha_i & & \\ & & & & & \ddots & \ddots \\ & & & & & & \alpha_n & \beta_{n+1} \end{pmatrix}.$$

Equating column i $(i \geq 2)$ on both sides, we get

$$A^T p_i = \beta_i z_{i-1} + \alpha_i z_i,$$

which can be written

$$\alpha_i z_i = A^T p_i - \beta_i z_{i-1}. \tag{7.9}$$

Similarly, by equating column i in

$$AZ = A \begin{pmatrix} z_1 & z_2 & \cdots & z_n \end{pmatrix}$$

$$= PB = \begin{pmatrix} p_1 & p_2 & \cdots & p_{n+1} \end{pmatrix} \begin{pmatrix} \alpha_1 & & & & & & \\ \beta_2 & \alpha_2 & & & & & \\ & \ddots & \ddots & & & & \\ & & & \alpha_i & & & \\ & & & \beta_{i+1} & & & \\ & & & & \ddots & \ddots & \\ & & & & & \beta_n & \alpha_n \\ & & & & & & \beta_{n+1} \end{pmatrix},$$

we get

$$Az_i = \alpha_i p_i + \beta_{i+1} p_{i+1},$$

which can be written

$$\beta_{i+1} p_{i+1} = Az_i - \alpha_i p_i. \tag{7.10}$$

Now, by compiling the starting equation $\beta_1 p_1 = b$ from Proposition 7.3, equations (7.9) and (7.10), we have derived a recursion:

LGK Bidiagonalization

---

1. $\beta_1 p_1 = b$, $z_0 = 0$

2. **for** $i = 1 : n$

$$\alpha_i z_i = A^T p_i - \beta_i z_{i-1},$$
$$\beta_{i+1} p_{i+1} = A z_i - \alpha_i p_i$$

3. **end**

The coefficients α_{i-1} and β_i are determined so that $\|p_i\| = \|z_i\| = 1$.

The recursion breaks down if any α_i or β_i becomes equal to zero. It can be shown (see, e.g., [15, Section 7.2]) that in the solution of least squares problems, these occurrences are harmless in the sense that they correspond to well-defined special cases.

The recursive bidiagonalization procedure gives, *in exact arithmetic*, the same result as the Householder bidiagonalization of $\begin{pmatrix} b & A \end{pmatrix}$, and thus the generated vectors $(p_i)_{i=1}^n$ and $(z_i)_{i=1}^n$ satisfy $p_i^T p_j = 0$ and $z_i^T z_j = 0$ if $i \neq j$. However, in floating point arithmetic, the vectors lose orthogonality as the recursion proceeds; see Section 7.2.7.

7.2.3 Approximate Solution of a Least Squares Problem

Define the matrices $P_k = \begin{pmatrix} p_1 & p_2 & \dots & p_k \end{pmatrix}$, $Z_k = \begin{pmatrix} z_1 & z_2 & \dots & z_k \end{pmatrix}$, and

$$B_k = \begin{pmatrix} \alpha_1 & & & \\ \beta_2 & \alpha_2 & & \\ & \ddots & \ddots & \\ & & \beta_{k-1} & \alpha_{k-1} \\ & & & \beta_k \end{pmatrix} \in \mathbb{R}^{k \times (k-1)}.$$

In the same way we could write the relations $AZ = PB$ and $A^T P = ZB^T$ as a recursion, we can now write the *first k steps of the recursion* as a matrix equation

$$AZ_k = P_{k+1} B_{k+1}. \tag{7.11}$$

Consider the least squares problem $\min_x \|Ax - b\|_2$. Note that the column vectors z_i are orthogonal vectors in $\mathbb{R}^n$, where the solution x lives. Assume that we want to *find the best approximate solution in the subspace spanned by the vectors $z_1, z_2, \dots, z_k$.* That is equivalent to solving the least squares problem

$$\min_y \|AZ_k y - b\|_2,$$

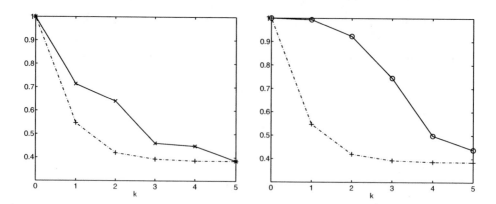

Figure 7.2. *The relative norm of the residuals for the query vectors q_1 (left) and q_2 (right) as a function of subspace dimension k. The residual curves for the truncated SVD solutions are solid and for the bidiagonalization solutions are dash-dotted.*

where $y \in \mathbb{R}^k$. From (7.11) we see that this is the same as solving

$$\min_y \| P_{k+1} B_{k+1} y - b \|_2,$$

which, using the orthogonality of $P = \begin{pmatrix} P_{k+1} & P_\perp \end{pmatrix}$, we can rewrite

$$\| P_{k+1} B_{k+1} y - b \|_2 = \| P^T (P_{k+1} B_{k+1} y - b) \|_2$$
$$= \left\| \begin{pmatrix} P_{k+1}^T \\ P_\perp^T \end{pmatrix} (P_{k+1} B_{k+1} y - b) \right\|_2 = \left\| \begin{pmatrix} B_{k+1} y \\ 0 \end{pmatrix} - \begin{pmatrix} \beta_1 e_1 \\ 0 \end{pmatrix} \right\|_2,$$

since $b = \beta_1 p_1$. It follows that

$$\min_y \| A Z_k y - b \|_2 = \min_y \| B_{k+1} y - \beta_1 e_1 \|_2, \tag{7.12}$$

which, due to the bidiagonal structure, we can solve in $O(n)$ flops; see below.

Example 7.4. Using bidiagonalization, we compute approximate solutions to the same least squares problems as in Example 7.2. The relative norm of the residual, $\| A Z_k y - b \|_2 / \| b \|_2$, is plotted as a function of k in Figure 7.2 for the truncated SVD solution and the bidiagonalization procedure. It is seen that in both cases, the bidiagonalization-based method give a faster decay of the residual than the truncated SVD solutions. Thus in this example, the fact that we let the basis vectors z_i be influenced by the right-hand sides q_1 and q_2 leads to reduced rank models of smaller dimensions. If we want to reduce the relative residual to below 0.7, then in both cases we can choose $k = 1$ with the bidiagonalization method.   ∎

The least squares problem (7.12) with bidiagonal structure can be solved using a sequence of plane rotations. Consider the reduction of

$$\begin{pmatrix} B_{k+1} & \beta e_1 \end{pmatrix} = \begin{pmatrix} \alpha_1 & & & & & \beta_1 \\ \beta_2 & \alpha_2 & & & & 0 \\ & \beta_3 & \alpha_3 & & & 0 \\ & & \ddots & \ddots & & \vdots \\ & & & \beta_k & \alpha_k & 0 \\ & & & & \beta_{k+1} & 0 \end{pmatrix}$$

to upper triangular form. We will now demonstrate that the norm of the residual can be easily computed. In the first step we zero β_2 by a rotation in the $(1,2)$ plane, with cosine and sine c_1 and s_1. The result is

$$\begin{pmatrix} \hat{\alpha}_1 & + & & & & \beta_1 \\ 0 & \hat{\alpha}_2 & & & & -\beta_1 s_1 \\ & \beta_3 & \alpha_3 & & & 0 \\ & & \ddots & \ddots & & \vdots \\ & & & \beta_k & \alpha_k & 0 \\ & & & & \beta_{k+1} & 0 \end{pmatrix},$$

where matrix elements that have changed are marked with a hat, and the new nonzero element is marked with a +. In the next step, we zero β_3 by a rotation with cosine and sine c_2 and s_2:

$$\begin{pmatrix} \hat{\alpha}_1 & + & & & & \beta_1 \\ 0 & \hat{\alpha}_2 & + & & & -\beta_1 s_1 \\ & 0 & \hat{\alpha}_3 & & & \beta_1 s_1 s_2 \\ & & \ddots & \ddots & & \vdots \\ & & & \beta_k & \alpha_k & 0 \\ & & & & \beta_{k+1} & 0 \end{pmatrix}.$$

The final result after k steps is

$$\begin{pmatrix} \hat{\alpha}_1 & + & & & \gamma_0 \\ & \hat{\alpha}_2 & + & & \gamma_1 \\ & & \hat{\alpha}_3 & + & \gamma_2 \\ & & & \ddots & \vdots \\ & & & \hat{\alpha}_k & \gamma_{k-1} \\ & & & & \gamma_k \end{pmatrix} =: \begin{pmatrix} \widehat{B}_k & \gamma \\ 0 & \gamma_k \end{pmatrix},$$

where $\gamma_i = (-1)^i \beta_1 s_1 s_2 \cdots s_i$ and $\gamma^{(k)} = \begin{pmatrix} \gamma_0 & \gamma_1 & \cdots & \gamma_{k-1} \end{pmatrix}^T$. If we define the product of plane rotations to be the orthogonal matrix $Q_{k+1} \in \mathbb{R}^{(k+1)\times(k+1)}$, we have the QR decomposition

$$B_{k+1} = Q_{k+1} \begin{pmatrix} \widehat{B}_k \\ 0 \end{pmatrix} \tag{7.13}$$

and

$$\begin{pmatrix} \gamma^{(k)} \\ \gamma_k \end{pmatrix} = \begin{pmatrix} \gamma_0 \\ \gamma_1 \\ \vdots \\ \gamma_k \end{pmatrix} = Q_{k+1}^T \begin{pmatrix} \beta_1 \\ 0 \\ \vdots \\ 0 \end{pmatrix}. \tag{7.14}$$

Using the QR decomposition we can write

$$\|B_{k+1}y - \beta_1 e_1\|_2^2 = \|\widehat{B}_k y - \gamma\|_2^2 + |\gamma_k|^2,$$

and the norm of the residual in the least squares problem is equal to $|\gamma_k| = |\beta_1 s_1 \cdots s_k|$. It follows that the norm of the residual can be computed recursively as we generate the scalar coefficients α_i and β_i, and thus it is possible to monitor the decay of the residual.

7.2.4   Matrix Approximation

The bidiagonalization procedure also gives a low-rank approximation of the matrix A. Here it is slightly more convenient to consider the matrix A^T for the derivation. Assume that we want to use the columns of Z_k as approximate basis vectors in $\mathbb{R}^n$. Then we can determine the coordinates of the columns of A^T in terms of this basis by solving the least squares problem

$$\min_{S_k \in \mathbb{R}^{m \times k}} \|A^T - Z_k S_k^T\|_F. \tag{7.15}$$

Lemma 7.5. *Given the matrix* $A \in \mathbb{R}^{m \times n}$ *and the matrix* $Z_k \in \mathbb{R}^{n \times k}$ *with orthonormal columns, the least squares problem* (7.15) *has the solution*

$$S_k = P_{k+1} B_{k+1}.$$

Proof. Since the columns of Z_k are orthonormal, the least squares problem has the solution

$$S_k^T = Z_k^T A^T,$$

which by (7.11) is the same as $S_k = P_{k+1} B_{k+1}$.   □

From the lemma we see that we have a least squares approximation $A^T \approx Z_k (P_{k+1} B_{k+1})^T$ or, equivalently,

$$A \approx P_{k+1} B_{k+1} Z_k^T.$$

However, this is not a "proper" rank-k approximation, since $P_{k+1} \in \mathbb{R}^{m \times (k+1)}$ and $B_{k+1} \in \mathbb{R}^{(k+1) \times k}$. Now, with the QR decomposition (7.13) of B_{k+1} we have

$$P_{k+1} B_{k+1} = (P_{k+1} Q_{k+1})(Q_{k+1}^T B_{k+1}) = (P_{k+1} Q_{k+1}) \begin{pmatrix} \widehat{B}_k \\ 0 \end{pmatrix} = W_k \widehat{B}_k,$$

where W_k is defined to be the first k columns of $P_{k+1}Q_{k+1}$. With $Y_k^T = \widehat{B}_k Z_k^T$ we now have a proper rank-k approximation of A:

$$A \approx P_{k+1}B_{k+1}Z_k^T = W_kY_k^T, \qquad W_k \in \mathbb{R}^{m \times k}, \qquad Y_k \in \mathbb{R}^{n \times k}. \tag{7.16}$$

The low-rank approximation of A is illustrated as

$$A \quad \approx \qquad\qquad = \quad W_kY_k^T.$$

As before, we can interpret the low-rank approximation as follows. *The columns of W_k are a basis in a subspace of R^m. The coordinates of column j of A in this basis are given in column j of Y_k^T.*

7.2.5 Krylov Subspaces

In the LGK bidiagonalization, we create two sets of basis vectors—the p_i and the z_i. It remains to demonstrate what subspaces they span. From the recursion we see that z_1 is a multiple of $A^T b$ and that p_2 is a linear combination of b and $AA^T b$. By an easy induction proof one can show that

$$p_k \in \text{span}\{b, AA^Tb, (AA^T)^2b, \ldots, (AA^T)^{k-1}b\},$$
$$z_k \in \text{span}\{A^Tb, (A^TA)A^Tb, \ldots, (A^TA)^{k-1}A^Tb\}$$

for $k = 1, 2, \ldots$. Denote

$$\mathcal{K}_k(C, b) = \text{span}\{b, Cb, C^2, \ldots, C^{k-1}b\}.$$

This a called a *Krylov subspace*. We have the following result.

Proposition 7.6. *The columns of P_k are an orthonormal basis of $\mathcal{K}_k(AA^T, b)$, and the columns of Z_k are an orthonormal basis of $\mathcal{K}_k(A^TA, A^Tb)$.*

7.2.6 Partial Least Squares

Partial least squares (PLS) [109, 111] is a recursive algorithm for computing approximate least squares solutions and is often used in chemometrics. Different variants of the algorithm exist, of which perhaps the most common is the so-called NIPALS formulation.

The NIPALS PLS algorithm

---

1. $A_0 = A$

2. **for i=1,2,...,k**

   (a) $w_i = \frac{1}{\|A_{i-1}^T b\|} A_{i-1}^T b$

   (b) $\tilde{u}_i = \frac{1}{\|A_{i-1} w_i\|} A_{i-1} w_i$

   (c) $\tilde{v}_i = A_{i-1}^T \tilde{u}_i$

   (d) $A_i = A_{i-1} - \tilde{u}_i \tilde{v}_i^T$

This algorithm differs from LGK bidiagonalization in a few significant ways, the most important being that the data matrix is deflated as soon as a new pair of vectors $(\tilde{u}_i, \tilde{v}_i)$ has been computed. However, it turns out [32, 110] that the PLS algorithm is mathematically equivalent to a variant of LGK bidiagonalization that is started by choosing not p_1 but instead $\alpha_1 z_1 = A^T b$. This implies that the vectors $(w_i)_{i=1}^k$ form an orthonormal basis in $\mathcal{K}_k(A^T A, A^T b)$, and $(\tilde{u}_i)_{i=1}^k$ form an orthonormal basis in $\mathcal{K}_k(AA^T, AA^T b)$.

7.2.7   Computing the Bidiagonalization

The recursive versions of the bidiagonalization suffers from the weakness that the generated vectors lose orthogonality. This can be remedied by *reorthogonalizing* the vectors, using a Gram–Schmidt process. Householder bidiagonalization, on the other hand, generates vectors that are as orthogonal as can be expected in floating point arithmetic; cf. Section 4.4. Therefore, for dense matrices A of moderate dimensions, one should use this variant.[12]

For large and sparse or otherwise structured matrices, it is usually necessary to use the recursive variant. This is because the Householder algorithm modifies the matrix by orthogonal transformations and thus destroys the structure. Note that for such problems, the PLS algorithm has the same disadvantage because it deflates the matrix (step (d) in the algorithm above).

A version of LGK bidiagonalization that avoids storing all the vectors p_i and z_i has been developed [75].

---

[12]However, if there are missing entries in the matrix, which is often the case in certain applications, then the PLS algorithm can be modified to estimate those; see, e.g., [111].

Chapter 8

Tensor Decomposition

8.1 Introduction

So far in this book we have considered linear algebra, where the main objects are vectors and matrices. These can be thought of as one-dimensional and two-dimensional arrays of data, respectively. For instance, in a term-document matrix, each element is associated with one term and one document. In many applications, data commonly are organized according to more than two categories. The corresponding mathematical objects are usually referred to as *tensors*, and the area of mathematics dealing with tensors is *multilinear algebra*. Here, for simplicity, we restrict ourselves to tensors $\mathcal{A} = (a_{ijk}) \in \mathbb{R}^{l \times m \times n}$ that are arrays of data with three subscripts; such a tensor can be illustrated symbolically as

$$\mathcal{A} = \quad \text{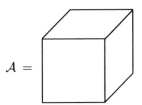}$$

Example 8.1. In the classification of handwritten digits, the *training set* is a collection of images, manually classified into 10 classes. Each such class is a set of digits of one kind, which can be considered as a tensor; see Figure 8.1. If each digit is represented as a 16×16 matrix of numbers representing gray scale, then a set of n digits can be organized as a tensor $\mathcal{A} \in \mathbb{R}^{16 \times 16 \times n}$. ∎

We will use the terminology of [60] and refer to a tensor $\mathcal{A} \in \mathbb{R}^{l \times m \times n}$ as a 3-mode array,[13] i.e., the different "dimensions" of the array are called *modes*. The *dimensions* of a tensor $\mathcal{A} \in \mathbb{R}^{l \times m \times n}$ are l, m, and n. In this terminology, a matrix is a 2-mode array.

---

[13]In some literature, the terminology 3-way and, in the general case, n-way, is used.

91

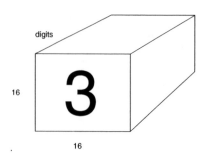

Figure 8.1. *The image of one digit is a 16×16 matrix, and a collection of digits is a tensor.*

In this chapter we present a generalization of the matrix SVD to 3-mode tensors, and then, in Chapter 14, we describe how it can be used for face recognition. The further generalization to n-mode tensors is easy and can be found, e.g., in [60]. In fact, the face recognition application requires 5-mode arrays.

The use of tensors in data analysis applications was pioneered by researchers in psychometrics and chemometrics in the 1960s; see, e.g., [91].

8.2   Basic Tensor Concepts

First define the *inner product* of two tensors:

$$\langle A, B \rangle = \sum_{i,j,k} a_{ijk} b_{ijk}. \tag{8.1}$$

The corresponding norm is

$$\| A \|_F = \langle A, A \rangle^{1/2} = \left(\sum_{i,j,k} a_{ijk}^2 \right)^{1/2}. \tag{8.2}$$

If we specialize the definition to matrices (2-mode tensors), we see that this is equivalent to the matrix Frobenius norm; see Section 2.4.

Next we define *i-mode multiplication* of a tensor by a matrix. The 1-mode product of a tensor $A \in \mathbb{R}^{l \times m \times n}$ by a matrix $U \in \mathbb{R}^{l_0 \times l}$, denoted by $A \times_1 U$, is an $l_0 \times m \times n$ tensor in which the entries are given by

$$(A \times_1 U)(j, i_2, i_3) = \sum_{k=1}^{l} u_{j,k} \, a_{k, i_2, i_3}. \tag{8.3}$$

For comparison, consider the matrix multiplication

$$A \times_1 U = UA, \quad (UA)(i,j) = \sum_{k=1}^{l} u_{i,k}\, a_{k,j}. \tag{8.4}$$

We recall from Section 2.2 that matrix multiplication is equivalent to multiplying each column in A by the matrix U. Comparing (8.3) and (8.4) we see that the corresponding property is true for tensor-matrix multiplication: in the 1-mode product, all column vectors in the 3-mode array are multiplied by the matrix U.

Similarly, 2-mode multiplication of a tensor by a matrix V

$$(\mathcal{A} \times_2 V)(i_1, j, i_3) = \sum_{k=1}^{l} v_{j,k}\, a_{i_1,k,i_3}$$

means that all row vectors of the tensor are multiplied by V. Note that 2-mode multiplication of a matrix by V is equivalent to matrix multiplication by V^T from the right,

$$A \times_2 V = AV^T;$$

3-mode multiplication is analogous.

It is sometimes convenient to *unfold* a tensor into a matrix. The unfolding of a tensor $\mathcal{A}$ along the three modes is defined (using (semi-)MATLAB notation; for a general definition,[14] see [60]) as

$$\mathbb{R}^{l \times mn} \ni \mathrm{unfold}_1(\mathcal{A}) := A_{(1)} := \big(\mathcal{A}(:,1,:) \quad \mathcal{A}(:,2,:) \quad \ldots \quad \mathcal{A}(:,m,:) \big),$$

$$\mathbb{R}^{m \times ln} \ni \mathrm{unfold}_2(\mathcal{A}) := A_{(2)} := \big(\mathcal{A}(:,:,1)^T \quad \mathcal{A}(:,:,2)^T \quad \ldots \quad \mathcal{A}(:,:,n)^T \big),$$

$$\mathbb{R}^{n \times lm} \ni \mathrm{unfold}_3(\mathcal{A}) := A_{(3)} := \big(\mathcal{A}(1,:,:)^T \quad \mathcal{A}(2,:,:)^T \quad \ldots \quad \mathcal{A}(l,:,:)^T \big).$$

It is seen that the unfolding along mode i makes that mode the first mode of the matrix $A_{(i)}$, and the other modes are handled cyclically. For instance, row i of $A_{(j)}$ contains all the elements of $\mathcal{A}$, which have the jth index equal to i. The following is another way of putting it.

1. The column vectors of $\mathcal{A}$ are column vectors of $A_{(1)}$.

2. The row vectors of $\mathcal{A}$ are column vectors of $A_{(2)}$.

3. The 3-mode vectors of $\mathcal{A}$ are column vectors of $A_{(3)}$.

The 1-unfolding of $\mathcal{A}$ is equivalent to dividing the tensor into *slices* $\mathcal{A}(:,i,:)$ (which are matrices) and arranging the slices in a long matrix $A_{(1)}$.

---

[14]For the matrix case, $\mathrm{unfold}_1(A) = A$, and $\mathrm{unfold}_2(A) = A^T$.

Example 8.2. Let $\mathcal{B} \in \mathbb{R}^{3 \times 3 \times 3}$ be a tensor, defined in MATLAB as

```
B(:,:,1) =            B(:,:,2) =            B(:,:,3) =
    1    2    3           11   12   13           21   22   23
    4    5    6           14   15   16           24   25   26
    7    8    9           17   18   19           27   28   29
```

Then unfolding along the third mode gives

```
>> B3 = unfold(B,3)

b3 =    1    2    3    4    5    6    7    8    9
       11   12   13   14   15   16   17   18   19
       21   22   23   24   25   26   27   28   29   ∎
```

The inverse of the unfolding operation is written

$$\mathrm{fold}_i(\mathrm{unfold}_i(\mathcal{A})) = \mathcal{A}.$$

For the folding operation to be well defined, information about the target tensor must be supplied. In our somewhat informal presentation we suppress this.

Using the unfolding-folding operations, we can now formulate a matrix multiplication equivalent of i-mode tensor multiplication:

$$\mathcal{A} \times_i U = \mathrm{fold}_i(U \ \mathrm{unfold}_i(\mathcal{A})) = \mathrm{fold}_i(U A_{(i)}). \tag{8.5}$$

It follows immediately from the definition that i-mode and j-mode multiplication commute if $i \neq j$:

$$(\mathcal{A} \times_i F) \times_j G = (\mathcal{A} \times_j G) \times_i F = \mathcal{A} \times_i F \times_j G.$$

Two i-mode multiplications satisfy the identity

$$(\mathcal{A} \times_i F) \times_i G = \mathcal{A} \times_i (GF).$$

This is easily proved using (8.5):

$$
\begin{aligned}
(\mathcal{A} \times_i F) \times_i G &= (\mathrm{fold}_i(F(\mathrm{unfold}_i(\mathcal{A})))) \times_i G \\
&= \mathrm{fold}_i(G(\mathrm{unfold}_i(\mathrm{fold}_i(F(\mathrm{unfold}_i(\mathcal{A})))))) \\
&= \mathrm{fold}_i(GF \, \mathrm{unfold}_i(\mathcal{A})) = \mathcal{A} \times_i (GF).
\end{aligned}
$$

8.3   A Tensor SVD

The matrix SVD can be generalized to tensors in different ways. We present one such generalization that is analogous to an *approximate principal component analysis*. It is often referred to as the higher order SVD (HOSVD)[15] [60].

---

[15]HOSVD is related to the Tucker model in psychometrics and chemometrics [98, 99].

Theorem 8.3 (HOSVD). *The tensor* $\mathcal{A} \in \mathbb{R}^{l \times m \times n}$ *can be written as*

$$\mathcal{A} = \mathcal{S} \times_1 U^{(1)} \times_2 U^{(2)} \times_3 U^{(3)}, \tag{8.6}$$

where $U^{(1)} \in \mathbb{R}^{l \times l}$, $U^{(2)} \in \mathbb{R}^{m \times m}$, *and* $U^{(3)} \in \mathbb{R}^{n \times n}$ *are orthogonal matrices.* $\mathcal{S}$ *is a tensor of the same dimensions as* $\mathcal{A}$; *it has the property of* all-orthogonality: *any two slices of* $\mathcal{S}$ *are orthogonal in the sense of the scalar product* (8.1):

$$\langle \mathcal{S}(i,:,:), \mathcal{S}(j,:,:) \rangle = \langle \mathcal{S}(:,i,:), \mathcal{S}(:,j,:) \rangle = \langle \mathcal{S}(:,:,i), \mathcal{S}(:,:,j) \rangle = 0$$

for $i \neq j$. *The* 1-*mode singular values are defined by*

$$\sigma_j^{(1)} = \|\mathcal{S}(i,:,:)\|_F, \qquad j = 1, \dots, l,$$

and they are ordered

$$\sigma_1^{(1)} \geq \sigma_2^{(1)} \geq \cdots \geq \sigma_l^{(1)}. \tag{8.7}$$

The singular values in other modes and their ordering are analogous.

Proof. We give only the recipe for computing the orthogonal factors and the tensor $\mathcal{S}$; for a full proof, see [60]. Compute the SVDs,

$$A_{(i)} = U^{(i)} \Sigma^{(i)} (V^{(i)})^T, \quad i = 1, 2, 3, \tag{8.8}$$

and put

$$\mathcal{S} = \mathcal{A} \times_1 (U^{(1)})^T \times_2 (U^{(2)})^T \times_3 (U^{(3)})^T.$$

It remains to show that the slices of $\mathcal{S}$ are orthogonal and that the i-mode singular values are decreasingly ordered. $\square$

The all-orthogonal tensor $\mathcal{S}$ is usually referred to as the *core tensor*.
The HOSVD is visualized in Figure 8.2.

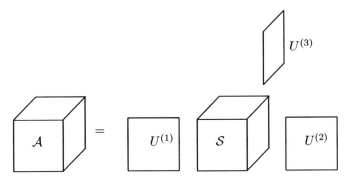

Figure 8.2. *Visualization of the HOSVD.*

Equation (8.6) can also be written

$$\mathcal{A}_{ijk} = \sum_{p=1}^{l} \sum_{q=1}^{m} \sum_{s=1}^{n} u_{ip}^{(1)} u_{jq}^{(2)} u_{ks}^{(3)} \mathcal{S}_{pqs},$$

which has the following interpretation: the element $\mathcal{S}_{pqs}$ reflects the variation by the combination of the singular vectors $u_p^{(1)}$, $u_q^{(2)}$, and $u_s^{(3)}$.

The computation of the HOSVD is straightforward and is implemented by the following MATLAB code, although somewhat inefficiently:[16]

```
function [U1,U2,U3,S,s1,s2,s3]=svd3(A);
% Compute the HOSVD of a 3-way tensor A

[U1,s1,v]=svd(unfold(A,1));
[U2,s2,v]=svd(unfold(A,2));
[U3,s3,v]=svd(unfold(A,3));

S=tmul(tmul(tmul(A,U1',1),U2',2),U3',3);
```

The function $\texttt{tmul(A,X,i)}$ is assumed to multiply the tensor $\texttt{A}$ by the matrix $\texttt{X}$ in mode i, $\mathcal{A} \times_i X$.

Let V be orthogonal of the same dimension as U_i; then from the identities [60]

$$\mathcal{S} \times_i U^{(i)} = \mathcal{S} \times_i (U^{(i)} V V^T) = (\mathcal{S} \times_i V^T) \times_i U^{(i)} V),$$

it may appear that the HOSVD is not unique. However, the property that the i-mode singular values are ordered is destroyed by such transformations. Thus, the HOSVD is essentially unique; the exception is when there are equal singular values along any mode. (This is the same type of nonuniqueness that occurs with the matrix SVD.)

In some applications it happens that the dimension of one mode is larger than the product of the dimensions of the other modes. Assume, for instance, that $\mathcal{A} \in \mathbb{R}^{l \times m \times n}$ with $l > mn$. Then it can be shown that the core tensor $\mathcal{S}$ satisfies

$$\mathcal{S}(i, :, :) = 0, \qquad i > mn,$$

and we can omit the zero part of the core and rewrite (8.6) as a *thin HOSVD*,

$$\mathcal{A} = \widehat{\mathcal{S}} \times_1 \widehat{U}^{(1)} \times_2 U^{(2)} \times_3 U^{(3)}, \tag{8.9}$$

where $\widehat{\mathcal{S}} \in \mathbb{R}^{mn \times m \times n}$ and $\widehat{U}^{(1)} \in \mathbb{R}^{l \times mn}$.

8.4 Approximating a Tensor by HOSVD

A matrix can be written in terms of the SVD as a sum of rank-1 terms; see (6.2). An analogous expansion of a tensor can be derived using the definition of tensor-matrix

---

[16]Exercise: In what sense is the computation inefficient?

multiplication: a tensor $\mathcal{A} \in \mathbb{R}^{l \times m \times n}$ can be expressed as a sum of matrices times singular vectors:

$$\mathcal{A} = \sum_{i=1}^{n} A_i \times_3 u_i^{(3)}, \qquad A_i = \mathcal{S}(:, :, i) \times_1 U^{(1)} \times_2 U^{(2)}, \tag{8.10}$$

where $u_i^{(3)}$ are column vectors in $U^{(3)}$. The A_i are to be identified as both matrices in $\mathbb{R}^{m \times n}$ and tensors in $\mathbb{R}^{m \times n \times 1}$. The expansion (8.10) is illustrated as

This expansion is analogous along the other modes.

It is easy to show that the A_i matrices are orthogonal in the sense of the scalar product (8.1):

$$\langle A_i, A_j \rangle = \text{tr}[U^{(2)} \mathcal{S}(:, :, i)^T (U^{(1)})^T U^{(1)} \mathcal{S}(:, :, j)(U^{(2)})^T]$$
$$= \text{tr}[\mathcal{S}(:, :, i)^T \mathcal{S}(:, :, j)] = 0.$$

(Here we have identified the slices $\mathcal{S}(:, :, i)$ with matrices and used the identity $\text{tr}(AB) = \text{tr}(BA)$.)

It is now seen that the expansion (8.10) can be interpreted as follows. Each slice along the third mode of the tensor $\mathcal{A}$ can be written (exactly) in terms of the orthogonal basis $(A_i)_{i=1}^{r_3}$, where r_3 is the number of positive 3-mode singular values of $\mathcal{A}$:

$$\mathcal{A}(:, :, j) = \sum_{i=1}^{r_3} z_i^{(j)} A_i, \tag{8.11}$$

where $z_i^{(j)}$ is the jth component of $u_i^{(3)}$. In addition, we have a simultaneous orthogonal factorization of the A_i,

$$A_i = \mathcal{S}(:, :, i) \times_1 U^{(1)} \times_2 U^{(2)},$$

which, due to the ordering (8.7) of all the j-mode singular values for different j, has the property that the "mass" of each $\mathcal{S}(:, :, i)$ is concentrated at the upper left corner.

We illustrate the HOSVD in the following example.

Example 8.4. Given 131 handwritten digits,[17] where each digit is a 16×16 matrix, we computed the HOSVD of the $16 \times 16 \times 131$ tensor. In Figure 8.3 we plot the

---

[17]From a U.S. Postal Service database, downloaded from the Web page of [47].

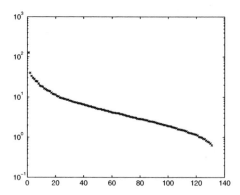

Figure 8.3. *The singular values in the digit (third) mode.*

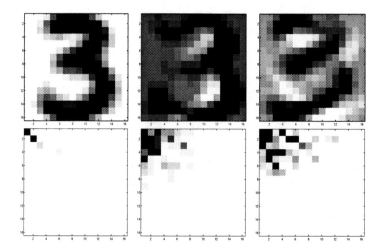

Figure 8.4. *The top row shows the three matrices A_1, A_2, and A_3, and the bottom row shows the three slices of the core tensor, $\mathcal{S}(:,:,1)$, $\mathcal{S}(:,:,2)$, and $\mathcal{S}(:,:,3)$ (absolute values of the components).*

singular values along the third mode (different digits); it is seen that quite a large percentage of the variation of the digits is accounted for by the first 20 singular values (note the logarithmic scale). In fact,

$$\frac{\sum_{i=1}^{20}(\sigma_i^{(3)})^2}{\sum_{i=1}^{131}(\sigma_i^{(3)})^2} \approx 0.91.$$

The first three matrices A_1, A_2, and A_3 are illustrated in Figure 8.4. It is seen that the first matrix looks like a mean value of different 3's; that is the dominating "direction" of the 131 digits, when considered as points in $\mathbb{R}^{256}$. The next two images represent the dominating directions of variation from the "mean value" among the different digits.

In the bottom row of Figure 8.4, we plot the absolute values of the three slices of the core tensor, $\mathcal{S}(:,:,1)$, $\mathcal{S}(:,:,2)$, and $\mathcal{S}(:,:,3)$. It is seen that the mass of these matrices is concentrated at the upper left corner. ∎

If we truncate the expansion (8.10),

$$\mathcal{A} = \sum_{i=1}^{k} A_i \times_3 u_i^{(3)}, \qquad A_i = \mathcal{S}(:,:,i) \times_1 U^{(1)} \times_2 U^{(2)},$$

for some k, then we have an approximation of the tensor (here in the third mode) in terms of an orthogonal basis. We saw in (8.11) that each 3-mode slice $\mathcal{A}(:,:,j)$ of $\mathcal{A}$ can be written as a linear combination of the orthogonal basis matrices A_j. In the classification of handwritten digits (cf. Chapter 10), one may want to compute the coordinates of an unknown digit in terms of the orthogonal basis. This is easily done due to the orthogonality of the basis.

Example 8.5. Let Z denote an unknown digit. For classification purposes we want to compute the coordinates of Z in terms of the basis of 3's from the previous example. This is done by solving the least squares problem

$$\min_z \left\| Z - \sum_j z_j A_j \right\|_F,$$

where the norm is the matrix Frobenius norm. Put

$$G(z) = \frac{1}{2} \left\| Z - \sum_j z_j A_j \right\|_F^2 = \frac{1}{2} \left\langle Z - \sum_j z_j A_j, Z - \sum_j z_j A_j \right\rangle.$$

Since the basis is orthogonal with respect to the scalar product,

$$\langle A_i, A_j \rangle = 0 \quad \text{for} \quad i \neq j,$$

we can rewrite

$$G(z) = \frac{1}{2} \langle Z, Z \rangle - \sum_j z_j \langle Z, A_j \rangle + \frac{1}{2} \sum_j z_j^2 \langle A_j, A_j \rangle.$$

To find the minimum, we compute the partial derivatives with respect to the z_j and put them equal to zero,

$$\frac{\partial G}{\partial z_j} = -\langle Z, A_j \rangle + z_j \langle A_j, A_j \rangle = 0,$$

which gives the solution of the least squares problem as

$$z_j = \frac{\langle Z, A_j \rangle}{\langle A_j, A_j \rangle}, \quad j = 1, 2, \ldots. \quad \blacksquare$$

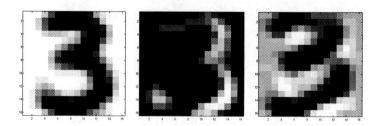

Figure 8.5. *Compressed basis matrices of handwritten 3's.*

Because the mass of the core tensor is concentrated for small values of the three indices, it is possible to perform a simultaneous data compression in all three modes by the HOSVD. Here we assume that we compress to k_i columns in mode i. Let $U_{k_i}^{(i)} = U^{(i)}(:, 1 : k_i)$ and $\hat{\mathcal{S}} = \mathcal{S}(1 : k_1, 1 : k_2, 1 : k_3)$. Then consider the approximation

$$\mathcal{A} \approx \hat{\mathcal{A}} = \hat{\mathcal{S}} \times_1 U_{k_1}^{(i)} \times_2 U_{k_2}^{(2)} \times_3 U_{k_3}^{(3)}.$$

We illustrate this as follows:

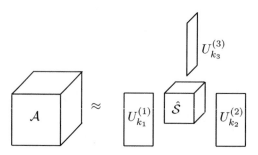

Example 8.6. We compressed the basis matrices A_j of 3's from Example 8.4. In Figure 8.5 we illustrate the compressed basis matrices

$$\hat{A}_j = \mathcal{S}(1 : 8, 1 : 8, j) \times_1 U_8^{(1)} \times_2 U_8^{(2)}.$$

See the corresponding full-basis matrices in Figure 8.4. Note that the new basis matrices $\hat{A}_j$ are no longer orthogonal. ■

Chapter 9

Clustering and Nonnegative Matrix Factorization

An important method for data compression and classification is to organize data points in *clusters*. A cluster is a subset of the set of data points that are close together in some distance measure. One can compute the mean value of each cluster separately and use the means as representatives of the clusters. Equivalently, the means can be used as basis vectors, and all the data points represented by their coordinates with respect to this basis.

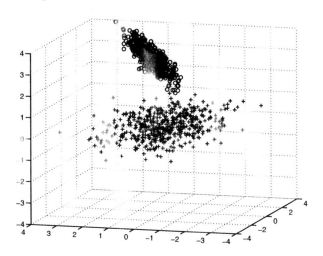

Figure 9.1. *Two clusters in* $\mathbb{R}^3$.

Example 9.1. In Figure 9.1 we illustrate a set of data points in $\mathbb{R}^3$, generated from two correlated normal distributions. Assuming that we know that we have two clusters, we can easily determine visually which points belong to which class. A clustering algorithm takes the complete set of points and classifies them using some distance measure. ∎

101

There are several methods for computing a clustering. One of the most important is the k-*means algorithm*. We describe it in Section 9.1.

In data mining applications, the matrix is often nonnegative. If we compute a low-rank approximation of the matrix using the SVD, then, due to the orthogonality of the singular vectors, we are very likely to obtain factors with negative elements. It may seem somewhat unnatural to approximate a nonnegative matrix by a low-rank approximation with negative elements. Instead one often wants to compute a low-rank approximation with nonnegative factors:

$$A \approx WH, \qquad W, H \geq 0. \tag{9.1}$$

In many applications, a nonnegative factorization facilitates the interpretation of the low-rank approximation in terms of the concepts of the application.

In Chapter 11 we will apply a clustering algorithm to a nonnegative matrix and use the cluster centers as basis vectors, i.e., as columns in the matrix W in (9.1). However, this does not guarantee that H also is nonnegative. Recently several algorithms for computing such *nonnegative matrix factorizations* have been proposed, and they have been used successfully in different applications. We describe such algorithms in Section 9.2.

9.1   The k-Means Algorithm

We assume that we have n data points $(a_j)_{j=1}^n \in \mathbb{R}^m$, which we organize as columns in a matrix $A \in \mathbb{R}^{m \times n}$. Let $\Pi = (\pi_i)_{i=1}^k$ denote a partitioning of the vectors $a_1, a_1, \ldots, a_n$ into k clusters:

$$\pi_j = \{\nu \mid a_\nu \text{ belongs to cluster } j\}.$$

Let the mean, or the *centroid*, of the cluster be

$$m_j = \frac{1}{n_j} \sum_{\nu \in \pi_j} a_\nu,$$

where n_j is the number of elements in π_j. We will describe a k-*means algorithm*, based on the Euclidean distance measure.

The tightness or *coherence* of cluster π_j can be measured as the sum

$$q_j = \sum_{\nu \in \pi_j} \|a_\nu - m_j\|_2^2.$$

The closer the vectors are to the centroid, the smaller the value of q_j. The quality of a clustering can be measured as the overall coherence:

$$Q(\Pi) = \sum_{j=1}^k q_j = \sum_{j=1}^k \sum_{\nu \in \pi_j} \|a_\nu - m_j\|_2^2.$$

In the k-means algorithm we seek a partitioning that has optimal coherence, in the sense that it is the solution of the minimization problem

$$\min_{\Pi} Q(\Pi).$$

The basic idea of the algorithm is straightforward: given a provisional partitioning, one computes the centroids. Then for each data point in a particular cluster, one checks whether there is another centroid that is closer than the present cluster centroid. If that is the case, then a redistribution is made.

The k-means algorithm

---

1. Start with an initial partitioning $\Pi^{(0)}$ and compute the corresponding centroid vectors, $(m_j^{(0)})_{j=1}^k$. Compute $Q(\Pi^{(0)})$. Put $t = 1$.

2. For each vector a_i, find the closest centroid. If the closest vector is $m_p^{(t-1)}$, assign a_i to $\pi_p^{(t)}$.

3. Compute the centroids $(m_j^{(t)})_{j=1}^k$ of the new partitioning $\Pi^{(t)}$.

4. if $|Q(\Pi^{(t-1)}) - Q(\Pi^{(t)})| <$ tol, then stop; otherwise increment t by 1 and go to step 2.

The initial partitioning is often chosen randomly. The algorithm usually has rather fast convergence, but one cannot guarantee that the algorithm finds the global minimum.

Example 9.2. A standard example in clustering is taken from a breast cancer diagnosis study [66].[18] The matrix $A \in \mathbb{R}^{9 \times 683}$ contains data from breast cytology tests. Out of the 683 tests, 444 represent a diagnosis of benign and 239 a diagnosis of malignant. We iterated with $k = 2$ in the k-means algorithm until the relative difference in the function $Q(\Pi)$ was less than 10^{-10}. With a random initial partitioning the iteration converged in six steps (see Figure 9.2), where we give the values of the objective function. Note, however, that the convergence is not monotone: the objective function was smaller after step 3 than after step 6. It turns out that in many cases the algorithm gives only a local minimum.

As the test data have been manually classified, it is known which patients had the benign and which the malignant cancer, and we can check the clustering given by the algorithm. The results are given in Table 9.1. Of the 239 patients with malignant cancer, the k-means algorithm classified 222 correctly but 17 incorrectly. ∎

In Chapter 11 and in the following example, we use clustering for information retrieval or text mining. The centroid vectors are used as basis vectors, and the documents are represented by their coordinates in terms of the basis vectors.

---

[18]See http://www.radwin.org/michael/projects/learning/about-breast-cancer-wisconsin.html.

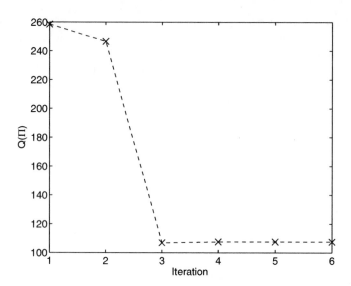

Figure 9.2. *The objective function in the k-means algorithm for the breast cancer data.*

Table 9.1. *Classification of cancer data with the k-means algorithm. B stands for benign and M for malignant cancer.*

	k-means	
	M	B
M	222	17
B	9	435

Example 9.3. Consider the term-document matrix in Example 1.1,

$$A = \begin{pmatrix} 0 & 0 & 0 & 1 & 0 \\ 0 & 0 & 0 & 0 & 1 \\ 0 & 0 & 0 & 0 & 1 \\ 1 & 0 & 1 & 0 & 0 \\ 1 & 0 & 0 & 0 & 0 \\ 0 & 1 & 0 & 0 & 0 \\ 1 & 0 & 1 & 1 & 0 \\ 0 & 1 & 1 & 0 & 0 \\ 0 & 0 & 1 & 1 & 1 \\ 0 & 1 & 1 & 0 & 0 \end{pmatrix},$$

and recall that the first four documents deal with Google and the ranking of Web pages, while the fifth is about football. With this knowledge, we can take the average of the first four column vectors as the centroid of that cluster and the fifth as the second centroid, i.e., we use the normalized basis vectors

$$C = \begin{pmatrix} 0.1443 & 0 \\ 0 & 0.5774 \\ 0 & 0.5774 \\ 0.2561 & 0 \\ 0.1443 & 0 \\ 0.1443 & 0 \\ 0.4005 & 0 \\ 0.2561 & 0 \\ 0.2561 & 0.5774 \\ 0.2561 & 0 \end{pmatrix}.$$

The coordinates of the columns of A in terms of this approximate basis are computed by solving

$$\min_D \|A - CH\|_F.$$

Given the thin QR decomposition $C = QR$, this least squares problem has the solution $H = R^{-1}Q^T A$ with

$$H = \begin{pmatrix} 1.7283 & 1.4168 & 2.8907 & 1.5440 & 0.0000 \\ -0.2556 & -0.2095 & 0.1499 & 0.3490 & 1.7321 \end{pmatrix}.$$

We see that the first two columns have negative coordinates in terms of the second basis vector. This is rather difficult to interpret in the term-document setting. For instance, it means that the first column a_1 is approximated by

$$a_1 \approx Ch_1 = \begin{pmatrix} 0.2495 \\ -0.1476 \\ -0.1476 \\ 0.4427 \\ 0.2495 \\ 0.2495 \\ 0.6921 \\ 0.4427 \\ 0.2951 \\ 0.4427 \end{pmatrix}.$$

It is unclear what it may signify that this "approximate document" has negative entries for the words *England* and *FIFA*.

Finally we note, for later reference, that the relative approximation error is rather high:

$$\frac{\|A - CH\|_F}{\|A\|_F} \approx 0.596. \quad \blacksquare \tag{9.2}$$

In the next section we will approximate the matrix in the preceding example, making sure that both the basis vectors and the coordinates are nonnegative.

9.2   Nonnegative Matrix Factorization

Given a data matrix $A \in \mathbb{R}^{m \times n}$, we want to compute a rank-k approximation that is constrained to have nonnegative factors. Thus, assuming that $W \in \mathbb{R}^{m \times k}$ and $H \in \mathbb{R}^{k \times n}$, we want to solve

$$\min_{W \geq 0,\, H \geq 0} \|A - WH\|_F. \tag{9.3}$$

Considered as an optimization problem for W and H at the same time, this problem is nonlinear. However, if one of the unknown matrices were known, W, say, then the problem of computing H would be a standard, nonnegatively constrained, least squares problem with a matrix right-hand side. Therefore the most common way of solving (9.3) is to use an *alternating least squares (ALS)* procedure [73]:

Alternating nonnegative least squares algorithm

---

1. Guess an initial value $W^{(1)}$.

2. for $k = 1, 2, \ldots$ until convergence

   (a) Solve $\min_{H \geq 0} \|A - W^{(k)}H\|_F$, giving $H^{(k)}$.

   (b) Solve $\min_{W \geq 0} \|A - WH^{(k)}\|_F$, giving $W^{(k+1)}$.

However, the factorization WH is not unique: we can introduce any diagonal matrix D with positive diagonal elements and its inverse between the factors,

$$WH = (WD)(D^{-1}H).$$

To avoid growth of one factor and decay of the other, we need to normalize one of them in every iteration. A common normalization is to scale the columns of W so that the largest element in each column becomes equal to 1.

Let a_j and h_j be the columns of A and H. Writing out the columns one by one, we see that the *matrix least squares problem* $\min_{H \geq 0} \|A - W^{(k)}H\|_F$ is equivalent to n independent *vector least squares problems*:

$$\min_{h_j \geq 0} \|a_j - W^{(k)}h_j\|_2, \qquad j = 1, 2, \ldots, n.$$

These can be solved by an active-set algorithm[19] from [61, Chapter 23]. By transposing the matrices, the least squares problem for determining W can be reformulated as m independent vector least squares problems. Thus the core of the ALS algorithm can be written in pseudo-MATLAB:

---

[19]The algorithm is implemented in MATLAB as a function `lsqnonneg`.

```
while (not converged)
    [W]=normalize(W);
    for i=1:n
        H(:,i)=lsqnonneg(W,A(:,i));
    end
    for i=1:m
        w=lsqnonneg(H',A(i,:)');
        W(i,:)=w';
    end
end
```

There are many variants of algorithms for nonnegative matrix factorization. The above algorithm has the drawback that the active set algorithm for nonnegative least squares is rather time-consuming. As a cheaper alternative, given the thin QR decomposition $W = QR$, one can take the unconstrained least squares solution,

$$H = R^{-1}Q^T A,$$

and then set all negative elements in H equal to zero, and similarly in the other step of the algorithm. Improvements that accentuate sparsity are described in [13].

A multiplicative algorithm was given in [63]:

```
while (not converged)
    W=W.*(W>=0);
    H=H.*(W'*V)./((W'*W)*H+epsilon);
    H=H.*(H>=0);
    W=W.*(V*H')./(W*(H*H')+epsilon);
    [W,H]=normalize(W,H);
end
```

(The variable epsilon should be given a small value and is used to avoid division by zero.) The matrix operations with the operators .* and ./ are equivalent to the componentwise statements

$$H_{ij} := H_{ij}\frac{(W^T A)_{ij}}{(W^T W H)_{ij} + \epsilon}, \qquad W_{ij} := W_{ij}\frac{(AH^T)_{ij}}{(WHH^T)_{ij} + \epsilon}.$$

The algorithm can be considered as a gradient descent method.

Since there are so many important applications of nonnegative matrix factorizations, algorithm development is an active research area. For instance, the problem of finding a termination criterion for the iterations does not seem to have found a good solution. A survey of different algorithms is given in [13].

A nonnegative factorization $A \approx WH$ can be used for clustering: the data vector a_j is assigned to cluster i if h_{ij} is the largest element in column j of H [20, 37].

Nonnegative matrix factorization is used in a large variety of applications: document clustering and email surveillance [85, 8], music transcription [90], bioinformatics [20, 37], and spectral analysis [78], to mention a few.

9.2.1   Initialization

A problem with several of the algorithms for nonnegative matrix factorization is that convergence to a global minimum is not guaranteed. It often happens that convergence is slow and that a suboptimal approximation is reached. An efficient procedure for computing a good initial approximation can be based on the SVD of A [18]. We know that the first k singular triplets $(\sigma_i, u_i, v_i)_{i=1}^k$ give the best rank-k approximation of A in the Frobenius norm. It is easy to see that if A is a nonnegative matrix, then u_1 and v_1 are nonnegative (cf. Section 6.4). Therefore, if $A = U\Sigma V^T$ is the SVD of A, we can take the first singular vector u_1 as the first column in $W^{(1)}$ (and v_1^T as the first row in an initial approximation $H^{(1)}$, if that is needed in the algorithm; we will treat only the approximation of $W^{(1)}$ in the following).

The next best vector, u_2, is very likely to have negative components, due to orthogonality. But if we compute the matrix $C^{(2)} = u_2 v_2^T$ and replace all negative elements with zero, giving the nonnegative matrix $C_+^{(2)}$, then we know that the first singular vector of this matrix is nonnegative. Furthermore, we can hope that it is a reasonably good approximation of u_2, so we can take it as the second column of $W^{(1)}$.

The procedure can be implemented by the following, somewhat simplified, MATLAB script:

```
[U,S,V]=svds(A,k);    % Compute only the k largest singular
                      %  values and the corresponding vectors
W(:,1)=U(:,1);
for j=2:k
    C=U(:,j)*V(:,j)';
    C=C.*(C>=0);
    [u,s,v]=svds(C,1);
    W(:,j)=u;
end
```

The MATLAB [U,S,V]=svds(A,k) computes only the k-largest singular values and the corresponding singular vectors using a Lanczos method; see Section 15.8.3. The standard SVD function svd(A) computes the full decomposition and is usually considerably slower, especially when the matrix is large and sparse.

Example 9.4. We computed a rank-2 nonnegative factorization of the matrix A in Example 9.3, using a random initialization and the SVD-based initialization. With the random initialization, convergence was slower (see Figure 9.3), and after 10 iterations it had not converged. The relative approximation error of the algorithm

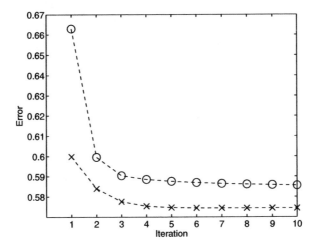

Figure 9.3. *Relative approximation error in the nonnegative matrix factorization as a function of the iteration number. The upper curve is with random initialization and the lower with the SVD-based initialization.*

with SVD initialization was 0.574 (cf. the error 0.596 with the k-means algorithm (9.2)). In some runs, the algorithm with the random initialization converged to a local, suboptimal minimum. The factorization with SVD initialization was

$$
WH = \begin{pmatrix}
0.3450 & 0 \\
0.1986 & 0 \\
0.1986 & 0 \\
0.6039 & 0.1838 \\
0.2928 & 0 \\
0 & 0.5854 \\
1.0000 & 0.0141 \\
0.0653 & 1.0000 \\
0.8919 & 0.0604 \\
0.0653 & 1.0000
\end{pmatrix}
\begin{pmatrix}
0.7740 & 0 & 0.9687 & 0.9120 & 0.5251 \\
0 & 1.0863 & 0.8214 & 0 & 0
\end{pmatrix}.
$$

It is now possible to interpret the decomposition. The first four documents are well represented by the basis vectors, which have large components for Google-related keywords. In contrast, the fifth document is represented by the first basis vector only, but its coordinates are smaller than those of the first four Google-oriented documents. In this way, the rank-2 approximation accentuates the Google-related contents, while the "football-document" is de-emphasized. In Chapter 11 we will see that other low-rank approximations, e.g., those based on SVD, have a similar effect.

On the other hand, if we compute a rank-3 approximation, then we get

$$
WH = \begin{pmatrix}
0.2516 & 0 & 0.1633 \\
0 & 0 & 0.7942 \\
0 & 0 & 0.7942 \\
0.6924 & 0.1298 & 0 \\
0.3786 & 0 & 0 \\
0 & 0.5806 & 0 \\
1.0000 & 0 & 0.0444 \\
0.0589 & 1.0000 & 0.0007 \\
0.4237 & 0.1809 & 1.0000 \\
0.0589 & 1.0000 & 0.0007
\end{pmatrix}
\begin{pmatrix}
1.1023 & 0 & 1.0244 & 0.8045 & 0 \\
0 & 1.0815 & 0.8314 & 0 & 0 \\
0 & 0 & 0.1600 & 0.3422 & 1.1271
\end{pmatrix}.
$$

We see that now the third vector in W is essentially a "football" basis vector, while the other two represent the Google-related documents.

Part II

Data Mining Applications

Chapter 10

Classification of Handwritten Digits

Classification by computer of handwritten digits is a standard problem in pattern recognition. The typical application is automatic reading of zip codes on envelopes. A comprehensive review of different algorithms is given in [62].

10.1 Handwritten Digits and a Simple Algorithm

In Figure 10.1 we illustrate handwritten digits that we will use in the examples in this chapter.

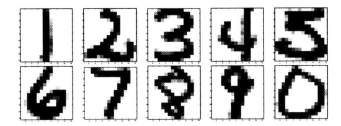

Figure 10.1. *Handwritten digits from the U.S. Postal Service database; see, e.g.,* [47].

We will treat the digits in three different but equivalent formats:

1. As 16×16 gray scale images, as in Figure 10.1;

2. As functions of two variables, $s = s(x, y)$, as in Figure 10.2; and

3. As vectors in $\mathbb{R}^{256}$.

In the classification of an unknown digit we need to compute the distance to known digits. Different distance measures can be used, and perhaps the most natural one to use is the Euclidean distance: stack the columns of the image in a

113

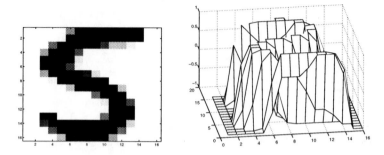

Figure 10.2. *A digit considered as a function of two variables.*

vector and identify each digit as a vector in $\mathbb{R}^{256}$. Then define the distance function

$$(x, y) = \| x - y \|_2.$$

An alternative distance function is the cosine between two vectors.

    In a real application of handwritten digit classification, e.g., zip code reading, there are hardware and real-time factors that must be taken into account. In this chapter we describe an idealized setting. The problem is as follows:

> *Given a set of manually classified digits (the training set), classify a set of unknown digits (the test set).*

In the U.S. Postal Service database, the training set contains 7291 handwritten digits. Here we will use a subset of 1707 digits, relatively equally distributed between 0 and 9. The test set has 2007 digits.

    If we consider the training set digits as vectors or points, then it is reasonable to assume that all digits of one kind form a cluster of points in a Euclidean 256-dimensional vector space. Ideally the clusters are well separated (otherwise the task of classifying unknown digits will be very difficult), and the separation between the clusters depends on how well written the training digits are.

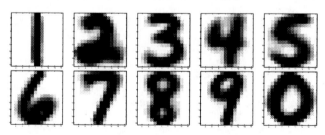

Figure 10.3. *The means (centroids) of all digits in the training set.*

    In Figure 10.3 we illustrate the means (centroids) of the digits in the training set. From the figure we get the impression that a majority of the digits are well written. (If there were many badly written digits, the means would be very diffuse.)

This indicates that the clusters are rather well separated. Therefore, it seems likely that a simple classification algorithm that computes the distance from each unknown digit to the means may be reasonably accurate.

A simple classification algorithm

Training: Given the manually classified training set, compute the means (centroids) m_i, $i = 0, \ldots, 9$, of all the 10 classes.

Classification: For each digit in the test set, classify it as k if m_k is the closest mean.

It turns out that for our test set, the success rate of this algorithm is around 75%, which is not good enough. The reason for this relatively bad performance is that the algorithm does not use any information about the variation within each class of digits.

10.2   Classification Using SVD Bases

We will now describe a classification algorithm that is based on the modeling of the variation within each digit class using orthogonal basis vectors computed using the SVD. This can be seen as a least squares algorithm based on a *reduced rank model*; cf. Chapter 7.

If we consider the images as 16×16 matrices, then the data are multidimensional; see Figure 10.4. Stacking all the columns of each image above each other gives a matrix. Let $A \in \mathbb{R}^{m \times n}$, with $m = 256$, be the matrix consisting of all the training digits of one kind, the 3's, say. The columns of A span a linear subspace of $\mathbb{R}^m$. However, this subspace cannot be expected to have a large dimension, because if it did, then the subspaces of the different kinds of digits would intersect (remember that we are considering subspaces of $\mathbb{R}^{256}$).

Now the idea is to "model" the variation within the set of training (and test) digits of one kind using an orthogonal basis of the subspace. An orthogonal basis can be computed using the SVD, and any matrix A is a sum of rank 1 matrices:

$$A = \sum_{i=1}^{m} \sigma_i u_i v_i^T = \quad \Bigg| \qquad\qquad + \quad \Bigg| \qquad\qquad + \quad \cdots . \qquad (10.1)$$

Each column in A represents an image of a digit 3, and therefore the left singular vectors u_i are an orthogonal basis in the "image space of 3's." We will refer to the left singular vectors as "singular images." From (10.1) the jth column of A is equal to

$$a_j = \sum_{i=1}^{m} (\sigma_i v_{ij}) u_i,$$

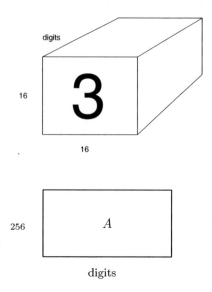

Figure 10.4. *The image of one digit is a matrix, and the set of images of one kind form a tensor. In the lower part of the figure, each digit (of one kind) is represented by a column in the matrix.*

and we see that the coordinates of image j in A in terms of this basis are $\sigma_i u_{ij}$. From the matrix approximation properties of the SVD (Theorems 6.6 and 6.7), we know that the first singular vector represents the "dominating" direction of the data matrix. Therefore, if we fold the vectors u_i back into images, we expect the first singular vector to look like a 3, and the following singular images should represent the dominating variations of the training set around the first singular image. In Figure 10.5 we illustrate the singular values and the first three singular images for the training set 3's. In the middle graph we plot the coordinates of each of the 131 digits in terms of the first three singular vectors. We see that all the digits have a large portion (between 0.05 and 0.1) of the first singular image, which, in fact, looks very much like the mean of 3's in Figure 10.3. We then see that there is a rather large variation in the coordinates in terms of the second and third singular images.

The SVD basis classification algorithm will be based on the following assumptions:

1. Each digit (in the training set and the test set) is well characterized by a few of the first singular images of its own kind. The more precise meaning of "few" should be investigated in experiments.

2. An expansion in terms of the first few singular images discriminates well between the different classes of digits.

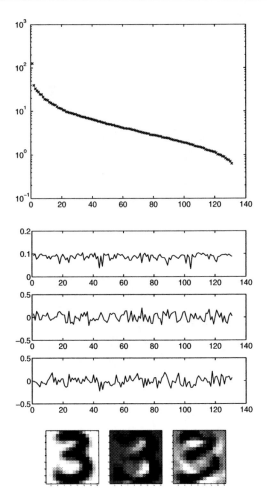

Figure 10.5. *Singular values (top), coordinates of the 131 test digits in terms of the first three right singular vectors v_i (middle), and the first three singular images (bottom).*

3. If an unknown digit can be better approximated in one particular basis of singular images, the basis of 3's say, than in the bases of the other classes, then it is likely that the unknown digit is a 3.

Thus we should compute how well an unknown digit can be represented in the 10 different bases. This can be done by computing the residual vector in *least squares problems* of the type

$$\min_{\alpha_i} \left\| z - \sum_{i=1}^{k} \alpha_i u_i \right\|,$$

where z represents an unknown digit and u_i represents the singular images. We can

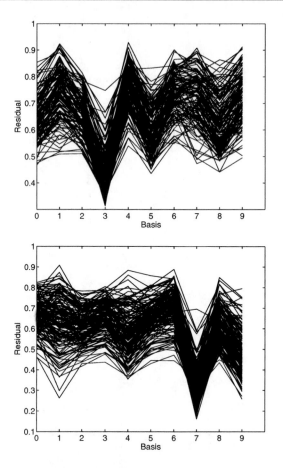

Figure 10.6. *Relative residuals of all test 3's (top) and 7's (bottom) in terms of all bases. Ten basis vectors were used for each class.*

write this problem in the form

$$\min_{\alpha} \| z - U_k \alpha \|_2,$$

where $U_k = \begin{pmatrix} u_1 & u_2 & \cdots & u_k \end{pmatrix}$. Since the columns of U_k are orthogonal, the solution of this problem is given by $\alpha = U_k^T z$, and the norm of the residual vector of the least squares problems is

$$\| (I - U_k U_k^T) z \|_2, \tag{10.2}$$

i.e., the norm of the projection of the unknown digit onto the subspace orthogonal to span(U_k).

To demonstrate that the assumptions above are reasonable, we illustrate in Figure 10.6 the relative residual norm for all test 3's and 7's in terms of all 10 bases.

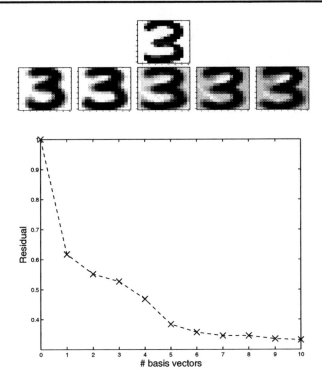

Figure 10.7. *Unknown digit (nice 3) and approximations using* 1, 3, 5, 7, *and* 9 *terms in the 3-basis (top). Relative residual* $\| (I - U_k U_k^T)z \|_2 / \| z \|_2$ *in least squares problem (bottom).*

In the two figures, there is one curve for each unknown digit, and naturally it is not possible to see the individual curves. However, one can see that most of the test 3's and 7's are best approximated in terms of their own basis. The graphs also give information about which classification errors are more likely than others. (For example, 3's and 5's are similar, whereas 3's and 4's are quite different; of course this only confirms what we already know.)

It is also interesting to see how the residual depends on the number of terms in the basis. In Figure 10.7 we illustrate the approximation of a nicely written 3 in terms of the 3-basis with different numbers of basis images. In Figures 10.8 and 10.9 we show the approximation of an ugly 3 in the 3-basis and a nice 3 in the 5-basis.

From Figures 10.7 and 10.9 we see that the relative residual is considerably smaller for the nice 3 in the 3-basis than in the 5-basis. We also see from Figure 10.8 that the ugly 3 is not well represented in terms of the 3-basis. Therefore, naturally, if the digits are very badly drawn, then we cannot expect to get a clear classification based on the SVD bases.

It is possible to devise several classification algorithms based on the model of expanding in terms of SVD bases. Below we give a simple variant.

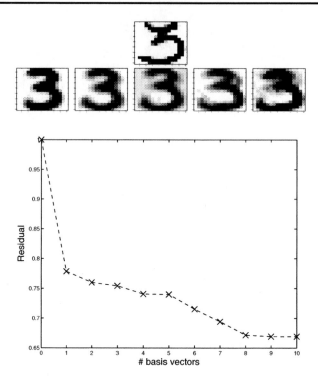

Figure 10.8. *Unknown digit (ugly 3) and approximations using 1, 3, 5, 7, and 9 terms in the 3-basis (top). Relative residual in least squares problem (bottom).*

An SVD basis classification algorithm

Training: For the training set of known digits, compute the SVD of each set of digits of one kind.

Classification: For a given test digit, compute its relative residual in all 10 bases. If one residual is significantly smaller than all the others, classify as that. Otherwise give up.

The work in this algorithm can be summarized as follows:

Training: Compute SVDs of 10 matrices of dimension $m^2 \times n_i$.
Each digit is an $m \times m$ digitized image.
n_i: the number of training digits i.

Test: Compute 10 least squares residuals (10.2).

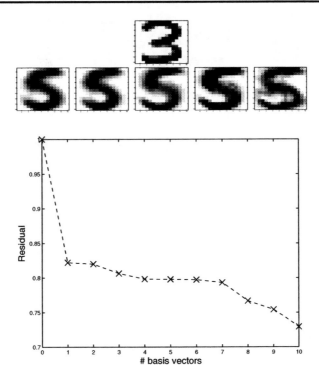

Figure 10.9. *Unknown digit (nice 3) and approximations using 1, 3, 5, 7, and 9 terms in the 5-basis (top). Relative residual in least squares problem (bottom).*

Table 10.1. *Correct classifications as a function of the number of basis images (for each class).*

# basis images	1	2	4	6	8	10
correct (%)	80	86	90	90.5	92	93

Thus the test phase is quite fast, and this algorithm should be suitable for real-time computations. The algorithm is related to the SIMCA method [89].

We next give some test results (from [82]) for the U.S. Postal Service database, here with 7291 training digits and 2007 test digits [47]. In Table 10.1 we give classification results as a function of the number of basis images for each class.

Even if there is a very significant improvement in performance compared to the method in which one used only the centroid images, the results are not good enough, as the best algorithms reach about 97% correct classifications. The training and test contain some digits that are very difficult to classify; we give a few examples in Figure 10.10. Such badly written digits are very difficult to handle automatically.

Figure 10.10. *Ugly digits in the U.S. Postal Service database.*

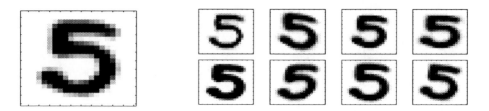

Figure 10.11. *A digit (left) and acceptable transformations (right). Columnwise from left to right the digit has been (1) written with a thinner and a thicker pen, (2) stretched diagonally, (3) compressed and elongated vertically, and (4) rotated.*

10.3 Tangent Distance

A good classification algorithm should be able to classify unknown digits that are rather well written but still deviate considerably in Euclidean distance from the ideal digit. There are some deviations that humans can easily handle and which are quite common and acceptable. We illustrate a few such variations[20] in Figure 10.11. Such transformations constitute no difficulties for a human reader, and ideally they should be very easy to deal with in automatic digit recognition. A distance measure, *tangent distance*, that is invariant under small such transformations is described in [86, 87].

16 × 16 images can be interpreted as points in $\mathbb{R}^{256}$. Let p be a fixed pattern in an image. We shall first consider the case of only one allowed transformation, translation of the pattern (digit) in the x-direction, say. This translation can be thought of as moving the pattern along a curve in $\mathbb{R}^{256}$. Let the curve be parameterized by a real parameter α so that the curve is given by $s(p, \alpha)$ and in such a way that $s(p, 0) = p$. In general, the curve is nonlinear and can be approximated by the first two terms in the Taylor expansion,

$$s(p, \alpha) = s(p, 0) + \frac{ds}{d\alpha}(p, 0)\, \alpha + O(\alpha^2) \approx p + t_p \alpha,$$

where $t_p = \frac{ds}{d\alpha}(p, 0)$ is a vector in $\mathbb{R}^{256}$. By varying α slightly around 0, we make a small movement of the pattern along the tangent at the point p on the curve. Assume that we have another pattern e that is approximated similarly:

$$s(e, \alpha) \approx e + t_e \alpha.$$

---

[20]Note that the transformed digits have been written not manually but by using the techniques described later in this section. The presentation in this section is based on the papers [86, 87, 82].

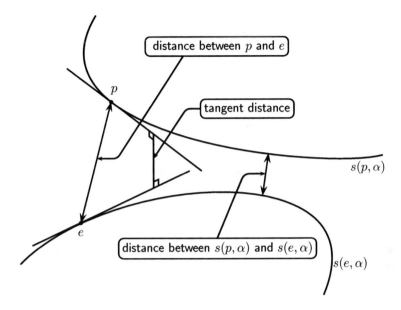

Figure 10.12. *The distance between the points p and e, and the tangent distance.*

Since we consider small movements along the curves as allowed, such small movements should not influence the distance function. Therefore, ideally we would like to define our measure of closeness between p and e as the closest distance between the two curves; see Figure 10.12 (cf. [87]).

However, since in general we cannot compute the distance between the curves, we can use the first order approximations and compute the closest distance between the two tangents in the points p and e. Thus we shall move the patterns independently along their respective tangents, until we find the smallest distance. If we measure this distance in the usual Euclidean norm, we solve the least squares problem,

$$\min_{\alpha_p,\alpha_e} \left\| p + t_p\alpha_p - e - t_e\alpha_e \right\|_2 = \min_{\alpha_p,\alpha_e} \left\| (p-e) - \begin{pmatrix} -t_p & t_e \end{pmatrix} \begin{pmatrix} \alpha_p \\ \alpha_e \end{pmatrix} \right\|_2.$$

Now consider the case when we are allowed to move the pattern p along l different curves in $\mathbb{R}^{256}$, parameterized by $\alpha = (\alpha_1 \cdots \alpha_l)^T$. This is equivalent to moving the pattern on an l-dimensional surface (manifold) in $\mathbb{R}^{256}$. Assume that we have two patterns, p and e, each of which is allowed to move on its surface of allowed transformations. Ideally we would like to find the closest distance between the surfaces, but instead, since that is impossible to compute, we now define a distance measure, where we compute the distance between the two *tangent planes* of the surface in the points p and e.

As before, the tangent plane is given by the first two terms in the Taylor expansion of the function $s(p, \alpha)$:

$$s(p, \alpha) = s(p, 0) + \sum_i^l \frac{ds}{d\alpha_i}(p, 0)\,\alpha_i + O(\|\,\alpha\,\|_2^2) \approx p + T_p\alpha,$$

where T_p is the matrix

$$T_p = \left(\frac{ds}{d\alpha_1} \quad \frac{ds}{d\alpha_2} \quad \cdots \quad \frac{ds}{d\alpha_l} \right),$$

and the derivatives are all evaluated in the point $(p, 0)$.

Thus the *tangent distance* between the points p and e is defined as the smallest possible residual in the least squares problem,

$$\min_{\alpha_p, \alpha_e} \| p + T_p\alpha_p - e - T_e\alpha_e \|_2 = \min_{\alpha_p, \alpha_e} \left\| (p - e) - \begin{pmatrix} -T_p & T_e \end{pmatrix} \begin{pmatrix} \alpha_p \\ \alpha_e \end{pmatrix} \right\|_2.$$

The least squares problem can be solved, e.g., using the SVD of $A = \begin{pmatrix} -T_p & T_e \end{pmatrix}$. Note that we are interested not in the solution itself but only in the norm of the residual. Write the least squares problem in the form

$$\min_\alpha \| b - A\alpha \|_2, \qquad b = p - e, \quad \alpha = \begin{pmatrix} \alpha_p \\ \alpha_e \end{pmatrix}.$$

If we use the QR decomposition[21]

$$A = Q \begin{pmatrix} R \\ 0 \end{pmatrix} = \begin{pmatrix} Q_1 & Q_2 \end{pmatrix} \begin{pmatrix} R \\ 0 \end{pmatrix} = Q_1 R,$$

the norm of the residual is given by

$$\min_\alpha \| b - A\alpha \|_2^2 = \min_\alpha \left\| \begin{pmatrix} Q_1^T b - R\alpha \\ Q_2^T b \end{pmatrix} \right\|^2$$

$$= \min_\alpha \left[\| (Q_1^T b - R\alpha) \|_2^2 + \| Q_2^T b \|_2^2 \right] = \| Q_2^T b \|_2^2.$$

The case when the matrix A should happen to not have full column rank is easily dealt with using the SVD; see Section 6.7. The probability is high that the columns of the tangent matrix are almost linearly dependent when the two patterns are close.

The most important property of this distance function is that it is *invariant under movements of the patterns on the tangent planes*. For instance, if we make a small translation in the x-direction of a pattern, then with this measure, the distance it has been moved is equal to zero.

10.3.1   Transformations

Here we consider the image pattern as a function of two variables, $p = p(x, y)$, and we demonstrate that the derivative of each transformation can be expressed as a differentiation operator that is a linear combination of the derivatives $p_x = \frac{dp}{dx}$ and $p_y = \frac{dp}{dy}$.

---

[21] A has dimension $256 \times 2l$; since the number of transformations is usually less than 10, the linear system is overdetermined.

Figure 10.13. *A pattern, its x-derivative, and x-translations of the pattern.*

Translation.   The simplest transformation is the one where the pattern is translated by α_x in the x-direction, i.e.,

$$s(p, \alpha_x)(x, y) = p(x + \alpha_x, y).$$

Obviously, using the chain rule,

$$\frac{d}{d\alpha_x}\left(s(p, \alpha_x)(x, y)\right)|_{\alpha_x=0} = \frac{d}{d\alpha_x}p(x + \alpha_x, y)|_{\alpha_x=0} = p_x(x, y).$$

In Figure 10.13 we give a pattern and its x-derivative. Then we demonstrate that by adding a small multiple of the derivative, the pattern can be translated to the left and to the right.

Analogously, for y-translation we get

$$\frac{d}{d\alpha_y}\left(s(p, \alpha_y)(x, y)\right)|_{\alpha_y=0} = p_y(x, y).$$

Rotation.   A rotation of the pattern by an angle α_r is made by replacing the value of p in the point (x, y) with the value in the point

$$\begin{pmatrix} \cos\alpha_r & \sin\alpha_r \\ -\sin\alpha_r & \cos\alpha_r \end{pmatrix}\begin{pmatrix} x \\ y \end{pmatrix}.$$

Thus we define the function

$$s(p, \alpha_r)(x, y) = p(x\cos\alpha_r + y\sin\alpha_r, -x\sin\alpha_r + y\cos\alpha_r),$$

and we get the derivative

$$\frac{d}{d\alpha_r}\left(s(p, \alpha_r)(x, y)\right) = (-x\sin\alpha_r + y\cos\alpha_r)p_x + (-x\cos\alpha_r - y\sin\alpha_r)p_y.$$

Setting $\alpha_r = 0$, we have

$$\frac{d}{d\alpha_r}\left(s(p, \alpha_r)(x, y)\right)|_{\alpha_r=0} = yp_x - xp_y,$$

where the derivatives are evaluated at (x, y).

An example of a rotation transformation is given in Figure 10.14.

Figure 10.14. *A pattern, its rotational derivative, and a rotation of the pattern.*

Figure 10.15. *A pattern, its scaling derivative, an* *an "up-scaling" of the pattern.*

Scaling. A scaling of the pattern is achieved by defining

$$s(p, \alpha_s)(x, y) = p((1 + \alpha_s)x, (1 + \alpha_s)y),$$

and we get the derivative

$$\frac{d}{d\alpha_s}(s(p, \alpha_s)(x, y))|_{\alpha_s=0} = xp_x + yp_y.$$

The scaling transformation is illustrated in Figure 10.15.

Parallel Hyperbolic Transformation. By defining

$$s(p, \alpha_p)(x, y) = p((1 + \alpha_p)x, (1 - \alpha_p)y),$$

we can stretch the pattern parallel to the axis. The derivative is

$$\frac{d}{d\alpha_p}(s(p, \alpha_p)(x, y))|_{\alpha_p=0} = xp_x - yp_y.$$

In Figure 10.16 we illustrate the parallel hyperbolic transformation.

Diagonal Hyperbolic Transformation. By defining

$$s(p, \alpha_h)(x, y) = p(x + \alpha_h y, y + \alpha_h x),$$

we can stretch the pattern along diagonals. The derivative is

$$\frac{d}{d\alpha_h}(s(p, \alpha_h)(x, y))|_{\alpha_h=0} = yp_x + xp_y.$$

In Figure 10.17 we illustrate the diagonal hyperbolic transformation.

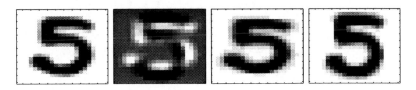

Figure 10.16. *A pattern, its parallel hyperbolic derivative, and two stretched patterns.*

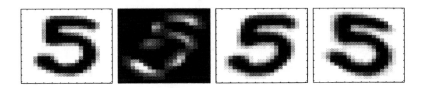

Figure 10.17. *A pattern, its diagonal hyperbolic derivative, and two stretched patterns.*

Figure 10.18. *A pattern, its thickening derivative, a thinner pattern, and a thicker pattern.*

Thickening. The pattern can be made thinner or thicker using similar techniques; for details, see [87]. The "thickening" derivative is

$$(p_x)^2 + (p_y)^2.$$

Thickening and thinning are illustrated in Figure 10.18.

A tangent distance classification algorithm

Training: For each digit in the training set, compute its tangent matrix T_p.

Classification: For each test digit,

- compute its tangent matrix;
- compute the tangent distance to all training digits and classify the test digit as the closest training digit.

Although this algorithm is quite good in terms of classification performance (96.9% correct classification for the U.S. Postal Service database [82]), it is very expensive, since each test digit is compared to all the training digits. To be competitive, it must be combined with some other algorithm that reduces the number of tangent distance comparisons.

We end this chapter by remarking that it is necessary to preprocess the digits in different ways in order to enhance the classification; see [62]. For instance, performance is improved if the images are smoothed (convolved with a Gaussian kernel) [87]. In [82] the derivatives p_x and p_y are computed numerically by finite differences.

Chapter 11

Text Mining

By *text mining* we mean methods for extracting useful information from large and often unstructured collections of texts. Another, closely related term is *information retrieval*. A typical application is searching databases of abstracts of scientific papers. For instance, in a medical application one may want to find all the abstracts in the database that deal with a particular syndrome. So one puts together a search phrase, a *query*, with keywords that are relevant to the syndrome. Then the retrieval system is used to match the query to the documents in the database and presents to the user the documents that are relevant, ranked according to relevance.

Example 11.1. The following is a typical query for search in a collection of medical abstracts:

> 9. *the use of induced hypothermia in heart surgery, neurosurgery, head injuries, and infectious diseases.*

The query is taken from a test collection for information retrieval, called Medline.[22] We will refer to this query as Q9. ∎

Library catalogues are another example of text mining applications.

Example 11.2. To illustrate one issue in information retrieval, we performed a search in the Linköping University library journal catalogue:

Search phrases	Results
computer science engineering	Nothing found
computing science engineering	IEEE: Computing in Science and Engineering

Naturally we would like the system to be insensitive to small errors on the part of the user. Anyone can see that the IEEE journal is close to the query. From

---

[22]See, e.g., http://www.dcs.gla.ac.uk/idom/ir_resources/test_collections/.

this example we conclude that in many cases straightforward word matching is not good enough. ∎

A very well known area of text mining is Web search engines, where the search phrase is usually very short, and often there are so many relevant documents that it is out of the question to present them all to the user. In that application the ranking of the search result is critical for the efficiency of the search engine. We will come back to this problem in Chapter 12.

For an overview of information retrieval, see, e.g., [43]. In this chapter we will describe briefly one of the most common methods for text mining, namely, the *vector space model* [81]. Here we give a brief overview of the vector space model and some variants: latent semantic indexing (LSI), which uses the SVD of the term-document matrix, a clustering-based method, nonnegative matrix factorization, and LGK bidiagonalization. For a more detailed account of the different techniques used in connection with the vector space model, see [12].

11.1   Preprocessing the Documents and Queries

In this section we discuss the preprocessing that is done to the texts before the vector space model of a particular collection of documents is set up.

In information retrieval, keywords that carry information about the contents of a document are called *terms*. A basic step in information retrieval is to create a list of all the terms in a document collection, a so-called index. For each term, a list is stored of all the documents that contain that particular term. This is called an inverted index.

But before the index is made, two preprocessing steps must be done: elimination of all stop words and stemming.

Stop words are words that one can find in virtually any document. Therefore, the occurrence of such a word in a document does not distinguish this document from other documents. The following is the beginning of one particular stop list:[23]

a, a's, able, about, above, according, accordingly, across, actually, after, afterwards, again, against, ain't, all, allow, allows, almost, alone, along, already, also, although, always, am, among, amongst, an, and, another, any, anybody, anyhow, anyone, anything, anyway, anyways, anywhere, apart, appear, appreciate, appropriate, are, aren't, around, as, aside, ask, ...

Stemming is the process of reducing each word that is conjugated or has a suffix to its stem. Clearly, from the point of view of information retrieval, no information is lost in the following reduction:

---

[23]ftp://ftp.cs.cornell.edu/pub/smart/english.stop.

$$
\left.\begin{array}{l}
\textbf{comput}\text{able} \\
\textbf{comput}\text{ation} \\
\textbf{comput}\text{ing} \\
\textbf{comput}\text{ed} \\
\textbf{comput}\text{ational}
\end{array}\right\} \quad \longrightarrow \quad \textbf{comput}
$$

Public domain stemming algorithms are available on the Internet.[24]

Table 11.1. *The beginning of the index for the Medline collection. The Porter stemmer and the GTP parser [38] were used.*

without stemming	with stemming
action	action
actions	
activation	activ
active	
actively	
activities	
activity	
acts	
actual	actual
actually	
acuity	acuiti
acute	acut
ad	ad
adaptation	adapt
adaptations	
adaptive	
add	add
added	
addition	addit
additional	

Example 11.3. We parsed the 1063 documents (actually 30 queries and 1033 documents) in the Medline collection, with and without stemming, in both cases removing stop words. For consistency it is necessary to perform the same stemming to the stop list. In the first case, the number of terms was 5839 and in the second was 4281. We show partial lists of terms in Table 11.1. ∎

11.2   The Vector Space Model

The main idea in the vector space model is to create a *term-document matrix*, where each document is represented by a column vector. The column has nonzero

---

[24]http://www.comp.lancs.ac.uk/computing/research/stemming/ and http://www.tartarus.org/~martin/PorterStemmer/.

entries in the positions that correspond to terms that can be found in the document. Consequently, each row represents a term and has nonzero entries in those positions that correspond to the documents where the term can be found; cf. the inverted index in Section 11.1.

A simplified example of a term-document matrix is given in Chapter 1. There we manually counted the frequency of the terms. For realistic problems one uses a *text parser* to create the term-document matrix. Two public-domain parsers are described in [38, 113]. Unless otherwise stated, we have used the one from [113] for the larger examples in this chapter. Text parsers for information retrieval usually include both a stemmer and an option to remove stop words. In addition there are filters, e.g., for removing formatting code in the documents, e.g., HTML or XML.

It is common not only to count the occurrence of terms in documents but also to apply a *term weighting scheme*, where the elements of A are weighted depending on the characteristics of the document collection. Similarly, document weighting is usually done. A number of schemes are described in [12, Section 3.2.1]. For example, one can define the elements in A by

$$a_{ij} = f_{ij} \log(n/n_i), \tag{11.1}$$

where f_{ij} is term frequency, the number of times term i appears in document j, and n_i is the number of documents that contain term i (inverse document frequency). If a term occurs frequently in only a few documents, then both factors are large. In this case the term discriminates well between different groups of documents, and the log-factor in (11.1) gives it a large weight in the documents where it appears.

Normally, the term-document matrix is *sparse*: most of the matrix elements are equal to zero. Then, of course, one avoids storing all the zeros and uses instead a sparse matrix storage scheme; see Section 15.7.

Example 11.4. For the stemmed Medline collection, parsed using GTP [38], the matrix (including 30 query columns) is 4163×1063 with 48263 nonzero elements, i.e., approximately 1%. The first 500 rows and columns of the matrix are illustrated in Figure 11.1.   ∎

11.2.1   Query Matching and Performance Modeling

Query matching is the process of finding the documents that are relevant to a particular query q. This is often done using the cosine distance measure: a document a_j is deemed relevant if the angle between the query q and a_j is small enough. Equivalently, a_j is retrieved if

$$\cos(\theta(q, a_j)) = \frac{q^T a_j}{\| q \|_2 \| a_j \|_2} > \text{tol},$$

where tol is a predefined tolerance. If the tolerance is lowered, then more documents are returned, and it is likely that many of those are relevant to the query. But at

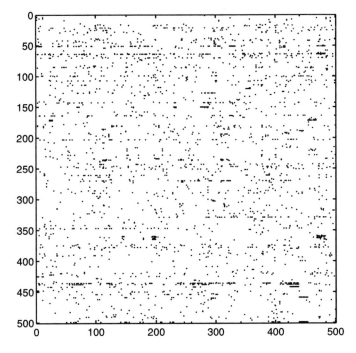

Figure 11.1. *The first 500 rows and columns of the Medline matrix. Each dot represents a nonzero element.*

the same time there is a risk that when the tolerance is lowered, more and more documents that are not relevant are also returned.

Example 11.5. We did query matching for query Q9 in the stemmed Medline collection. With tol $= 0.19$ for the cosine measure, only document 409 was considered relevant. When the tolerance was lowered to 0.17, documents 415 and 467 also were retrieved. ∎

We illustrate the different categories of documents in a query matching for two values of the tolerance in Figure 11.2. The query matching produces a good result when the intersection between the two sets of returned and relevant documents is as large as possible and the number of returned irrelevant documents is small. For a high value of the tolerance, the retrieved documents are likely to be relevant (the small circle in Figure 11.2). When the cosine tolerance is lowered, the intersection is increased, but at the same time, more irrelevant documents are returned.

In performance modeling for information retrieval we define the following measures:

$$Precision: \quad P = \frac{D_r}{D_t}, \tag{11.2}$$

where D_r is the number of relevant documents retrieved and D_t the total number

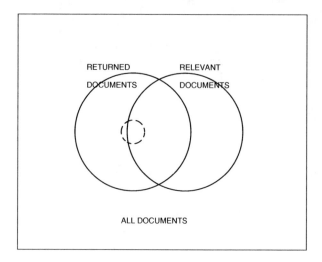

Figure 11.2. *Retrieved and relevant documents for two values of the tolerance. The dashed circle represents the retrieved documents for a high value of the cosine tolerance.*

of documents retrieved, and

$$Recall: \qquad R = \frac{D_r}{N_r}, \tag{11.3}$$

where N_r is the total number of relevant documents in the database. With a large value of tol for the cosine measure, we expect to have high precision but low recall. For a small value of tol, we will have high recall but low precision.

In the evaluation of different methods and models for information retrieval, usually a number of queries are used. For testing purposes, all documents have been read by a human, and those that are relevant for a certain query are marked. This makes it possible to draw diagrams of recall versus precision that illustrate the performance of a certain method for information retrieval.

Example 11.6. We did query matching for query Q9 in the Medline collection (stemmed) using the cosine measure. For a specific value of the tolerance, we computed the corresponding recall and precision from (11.2) and (11.3). By varying the tolerance from close to 1 down to zero, we obtained vectors of recall and precision that gave information about the quality of the retrieval method for this query. In the comparison of different methods it is illustrative to draw the recall versus precision diagram as in Figure 11.3. Ideally a method has high recall at the same time as the precision is high. Thus, the closer the curve is to the upper right corner, the higher the retrieval quality.

In this example and the following examples, the matrix elements were computed using term frequency and inverse document frequency weighting (11.1). ■

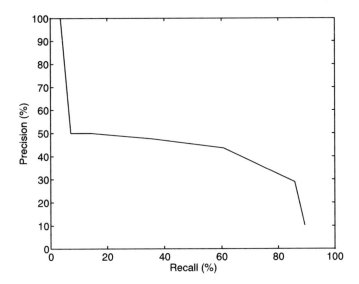

Figure 11.3. *Query matching for $Q9$ using the vector space method. Recall versus precision.*

11.3 Latent Semantic Indexing

Latent semantic indexing[25] (LSI) [28, 9] "is based on the assumption that there is some underlying latent semantic structure in the data ... that is corrupted by the wide variety of words used" [76] and that this semantic structure can be discovered and enhanced by projecting the data (the term-document matrix and the queries) onto a lower-dimensional space using the SVD.

Let $A = U\Sigma V^T$ be the SVD of the term-document matrix and approximate it by a matrix of rank k:

$$A \quad \approx \qquad\qquad = U_k \Sigma_k V_k^T =: U_k H_k.$$

The columns of U_k live in the document space and are an orthogonal basis that we use to approximate the documents. Write H_k in terms of its column vectors, $H_k = (h_1, h_2, \ldots, h_n)$. From $A \approx U_k H_k$ we have $a_j \approx U_k h_j$, which means that column j of H_k holds the coordinates of document j in terms of the orthogonal

---

[25]Sometimes also called latent semantic analysis (LSA) [52].

basis. With this rank-k approximation the term-document matrix is represented by $A_k = U_k H_k$ and in query matching we compute $q^T A_k = q^T U_k H_k = (U_k^T q)^T H_k$. Thus, we compute the coordinates of the query in terms of the new document basis and compute the cosines from

$$\cos\theta_j = \frac{q_k^T h_j}{\|q_k\|_2 \|h_j\|_2}, \qquad q_k = U_k^T q. \qquad (11.4)$$

This means that the query matching is performed in a k-dimensional space.

Example 11.7. We did query matching for Q9 in the Medline collection, approximating the matrix using the truncated SVD of rank 100.

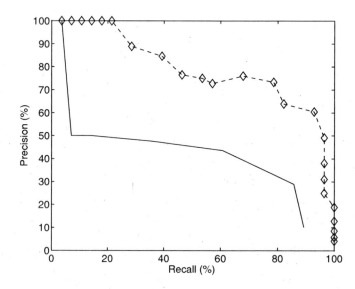

Figure 11.4. *Query matching for Q9. Recall versus precision for the full vector space model (solid line) and the rank 100 approximation (dashed line and diamonds).*

The recall precision curve is given in Figure 11.4. It is seen that for this query, LSI improves the retrieval performance. In Figure 11.5 we also demonstrate a fact that is common to many term-document matrices: it is rather well-conditioned and there is no gap in the sequence of singular values. Therefore, we cannot find a suitable rank of the LSI approximation by inspecting the singular values; it must be determined by retrieval experiments.

Another remarkable fact is that with $k = 100$ the approximation error in the matrix approximation,

$$\frac{\|A - A_k\|_F}{\|A\|_F} \approx 0.8,$$

is large, and we still get *improved retrieval performance*. In view of the large approximation error in the truncated SVD approximation of the term-document matrix,

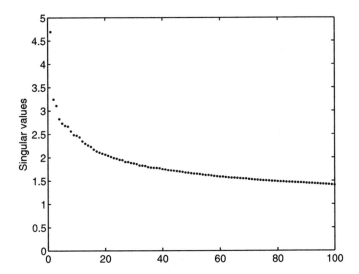

Figure 11.5. *First* 100 *singular values of the Medline (stemmed) matrix. The matrix columns are scaled to unit Euclidean length.*

one may question whether the "optimal" singular vectors constitute the best basis for representing the term-document matrix. On the other hand, since we get such good results, perhaps a more natural conclusion may be that the Frobenius norm is not a good measure of the information contents in the term-document matrix.

It is also interesting to see what are the most important "directions" in the data. From Theorem 6.6 we know that the first few left singular vectors are the dominant directions in the document space, and their largest components should indicate what these directions are. The MATLAB statement `find(abs(U(:,k))>0.13)`, combined with look-up in the index of terms, gave the following results for `k=1,2`:

U(:,1)	U(:,2)
cell	case
growth	cell
hormone	children
patient	defect
	dna
	growth
	patient
	ventricular

In Chapter 13 we will come back to the problem of extracting the keywords from texts. ∎

It should be said that LSI does not give significantly better results for all queries in the Medline collection: there are some in which it gives results comparable to the full vector model and some in which it gives worse performance. However, it is often the average performance that matters.

A systematic study of different aspects of LSI was done in [52]. It was shown that LSI improves retrieval performance for surprisingly small values of the reduced rank k. At the same time, the relative matrix approximation errors are large. It is probably not possible to prove any general results that explain in what way and for which data LSI can improve retrieval performance. Instead we give an artificial example (constructed using similar ideas as a corresponding example in [12]) that gives a partial explanation.

Example 11.8. Consider the term-document matrix from Example 1.1 and the query "**ranking** of **Web pages**." Obviously, Documents 1–4 are relevant with respect to the query, while Document 5 is totally irrelevant. However, we obtain cosines for the query and the original data as

$$\begin{pmatrix} 0 & 0.6667 & 0.7746 & 0.3333 & 0.3333 \end{pmatrix},$$

which indicates that Document 5 (the football document) is as relevant to the query as Document 4. Further, since none of the words of the query occurs in Document 1, this document is orthogonal to the query.

We then compute the SVD of the term-document matrix and use a rank-2 approximation. After projection to the two-dimensional subspace, the cosines, computed according to (11.4), are

$$\begin{pmatrix} 0.7857 & 0.8332 & 0.9670 & 0.4873 & 0.1819 \end{pmatrix}.$$

It turns out that Document 1, which was deemed totally irrelevant for the query in the original representation, is now highly relevant. In addition, the cosines for the relevant Documents 2–4 have been reinforced. At the same time, the cosine for Document 5 has been significantly reduced. Thus, in this artificial example, the dimension reduction enhanced the retrieval performance.

In Figure 11.6 we plot the five documents and the query in the coordinate system of the first two left singular vectors. Obviously, in this representation, the first document is closer to the query than Document 5. The first two left singular vectors are

$$u_1 = \begin{pmatrix} 0.1425 \\ 0.0787 \\ 0.0787 \\ 0.3924 \\ 0.1297 \\ 0.1020 \\ 0.5348 \\ 0.3647 \\ 0.4838 \\ 0.3647 \end{pmatrix}, \qquad u_2 = \begin{pmatrix} 0.2430 \\ 0.2607 \\ 0.2607 \\ -0.0274 \\ 0.0740 \\ -0.3735 \\ 0.2156 \\ -0.4749 \\ 0.4023 \\ -0.4749 \end{pmatrix},$$

and the singular values are $\Sigma = \mathrm{diag}(2.8546, 1.8823, 1.7321, 1.2603, 0.8483)$. The first four columns in A are strongly coupled via the words *Google*, *matrix*, etc., and

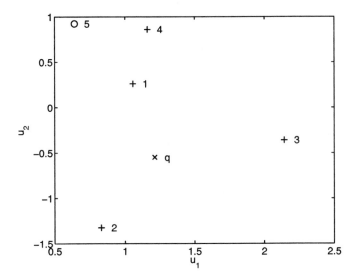

Figure 11.6. *The five documents and the query projected to the coordinate system of the first two left singular vectors.*

those words are the dominating contents of the document collection (cf. the singular values). This shows in the composition of u_1. So even if none of the words in the query are matched by Document 1, that document is so strongly correlated to the dominating direction that it becomes relevant in the reduced representation. ∎

11.4 Clustering

In the case of document collections, it is natural to assume that there are groups of documents with similar contents. If we think of the documents as points in $\mathbb{R}^m$, we may be able to visualize the groups as clusters. Representing each cluster by its mean value, the *centroid*,[26] we can compress the data in terms of the centroids. Thus clustering, using the k-means algorithm, for instance, is another method for low-rank approximation of the term-document matrix. The application of clustering to information retrieval is described in [30, 76, 77].

In analogy to LSI, the matrix $C_k \in \mathbb{R}^{m \times k}$ of (normalized but not orthogonal) centroids can be used as an approximate basis in the "document space." For query matching we then need to determine the coordinates of all the documents in this basis. This can be made by solving the matrix least squares problem,

$$\min_{\hat{G}_k} \| A - C_k \hat{G}_k \|_F.$$

However, it is more convenient first to orthogonalize the columns of C, i.e., compute

---

[26]Closely related to the *concept vector* [30].

its thin QR decomposition,

$$C_k = P_k R, \qquad P_k \in \mathbb{R}^{m \times k}, \qquad R \in \mathbb{R}^{k \times k},$$

and solve

$$\min_{G_k} \| A - P_k G_k \|_F. \tag{11.5}$$

Writing each column of $A - P_k G_k$ separately, we see that this matrix least squares problem is equivalent to n independent standard least squares problems

$$\min_{g_j} \| a_j - P_k g_j \|_2, \qquad j = 1, \ldots, n,$$

where g_j is column j in G_k. Since P_k has orthonormal columns, we get $g_j = P_k^T a_j$, and the solution of (11.5) becomes

$$G_k = P_k^T A.$$

For matching of a query q we compute the product

$$q^T A \approx q^T P_k G_k = (P_k^T q)^T G_k = q_k^T G_k,$$

where $q_k = P_k^T q$. Thus, the cosines in the low-dimensional approximation are

$$\frac{q_k^T g_j}{\| q_k \|_2 \| g_j \|_2}.$$

Example 11.9. We did query matching for Q9 of the Medline collection. Before computing the clustering we normalized the columns to equal Euclidean length. We approximated the matrix using the orthonormalized centroids from a clustering into 50 clusters. The recall-precision diagram is given in Figure 11.7. We see that for high values of recall, the centroid method is as good as the LSI method with double the rank; see Figure 11.4.

For rank 50 the approximation error in the centroid method,

$$\| A - P_k G_k \|_F / \| A \|_F \approx 0.9,$$

is even higher than for LSI of rank 100.

The improved performance can be explained in a similar way as for LSI. Being the "average document" of a cluster, the centroid captures the main links between the dominant documents in the cluster. By expressing all documents in terms of the centroids, the dominant links are emphasized. ■

When we tested all 30 queries in the Medline collection, we found that the centroid method with rank equal to 50 has a similar performance as LSI with rank 100: there are some queries where the full vector space model is considerably better, but there are also some for which the centroid method is much better.

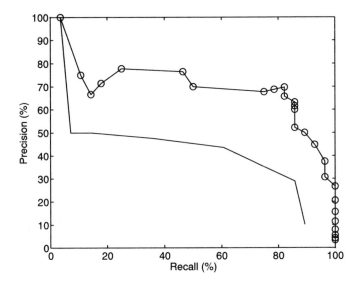

Figure 11.7. *Query matching for Q9. Recall versus precision for the full vector space model (solid line) and the rank 50 centroid approximation (solid line and circles).*

11.5 Nonnegative Matrix Factorization

Assume that we have computed an approximate nonnegative matrix factorization of the term-document matrix,

$$A \approx WH, \qquad W \geq 0, \quad H \geq 0,$$

where $W \in \mathbb{R}^{m \times k}$ and $H \in \mathbb{R}^{k \times n}$. Column j of H holds the coordinates of document j in the approximate, nonorthogonal basis consisting of the columns of W. We want to first determine the representation of the query vector q in the same basis by solving the least squares problem $\min_{\hat{q}} \|q - W\hat{q}\|_2$. Then, in this basis, we compute the angles between the query and all the document vectors. Given the thin QR decomposition of W,

$$W = QR, \qquad P \in \mathbb{R}^{m \times k}, \quad R \in \mathbb{R}^{k \times k},$$

the query in the reduced basis is

$$\hat{q} = R^{-1} Q^T q,$$

and the cosine for document j is

$$\frac{\hat{q}^T h_j}{\|\hat{q}\|_2 \, \|h_j\|_2}.$$

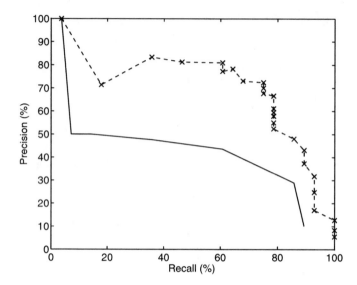

Figure 11.8. *Query matching for Q9. Recall versus precision for the full vector space model (solid line) and the rank 50 nonnegative matrix approximation (dashed line and ×'s).*

Example 11.10. We computed a rank-50 approximation of the Medline term-document matrix using 100 iterations of the multiplicative algorithm described in Section 9.2. The relative approximation error $\|A - WH\|_F/\|A\|_F$ was approximately 0.89. The recall-precision curve for query Q9 is given in Figure 11.8.

11.6   LGK Bidiagonalization

So far in this chapter we have described three methods for improving the vector space method for information retrieval by representing the term-document matrix A by a low-rank approximation, based on SVD, clustering, and nonnegative matrix factorization. These three methods have a common weakness: it is costly to update the low-rank approximation when new documents are added or deleted. In Chapter 7 we described a method for computing a low-rank approximation of A in connection with a least squares problem, using the right-hand side as a starting vector in an LGK bidiagonalization. Here we will apply this methodology to the text mining problem in such a way that a new low-rank approximation will be computed for each query. Therefore there is no extra computational cost when the document collection is changed. On the other hand, the amount of work for each query matching becomes higher. This section is inspired by [16].

Given a query vector q we apply the recursive LGK bidiagonalization algorithm (or PLS).

LGK bidiagonalization for a query q

---

1. $\beta_1 p_1 = q$, $z_0 = 0$

2. **for** $i = 1 : k$

    $\alpha_i z_i = A^T p_i - \beta_i z_{i-1}$

    $\beta_{i+1} p_{i+1} = A z_i - \alpha_i p_i$

3. **end**

The coefficients α_{i-1} and β_i are determined so that $\|p_i\| = \|z_i\| = 1$.

The vectors p_i and z_i are collected in the matrices $P_{k+1} = \begin{pmatrix} p_1 & \cdots & p_{k+1} \end{pmatrix}$ and $Z_k = \begin{pmatrix} z_1 & \cdots & z_k \end{pmatrix}$. After k steps of this procedure we have generated a rank-k approximation of A; see (7.16). We summarize the derivation in the following proposition.

Proposition 11.11. *Let $AZ_k = P_{k+1}B_{k+1}$ be the result of k steps of the LGK recursion, and let*

$$B_{k+1} = Q_{k+1} \begin{pmatrix} \widehat{B}_k \\ 0 \end{pmatrix}$$

be the QR decomposition of the bidiagonal matrix B_{k+1}. Then we have a rank-k approximation

$$A \approx W_k Y_k^T, \tag{11.6}$$

where

$$W_k = P_{k+1} Q_{k+1} \begin{pmatrix} I_k \\ 0 \end{pmatrix}, \qquad Y_k = Z_k \widehat{B}_k^T.$$

It is possible to use the low-rank approximation (11.6) for query matching in much the same way as the SVD low-rank approximation is used in LSI. However, it turns out [16] that better performance is obtained if the following method is used.

The column vectors of W_k are an orthogonal, approximate basis for documents that are close to the query q. Instead of computing the coordinates of the columns of A in terms of this basis, we now choose to compute the projection of the query in terms of this basis:

$$\tilde{q} = W_k W_k^T q \in \mathbb{R}^m.$$

We then use the cosine measure

$$\cos(\tilde{\theta}_j) = \frac{\tilde{q}^T a_j}{\|\tilde{q}\|_2 \, \|a_j\|_2}, \tag{11.7}$$

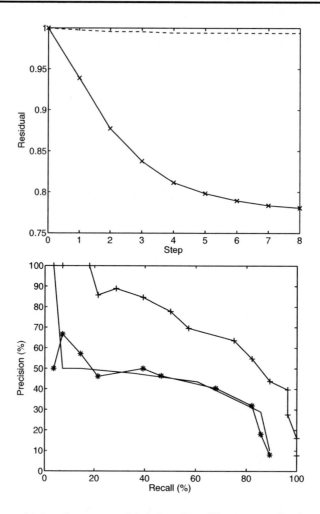

Figure 11.9. *Query matching for Q9. The top graph shows the relative residual as a function of the number of steps in the LGK bidiagonalization (solid line and ×'s). As a comparison, the residual in terms of the basis of the first singular vectors (principal component regression) is given (dashed line). In the bottom graph we give recall versus precision for the full vector space model (solid line) and for bidiagonalization with two steps (solid line and +'s), and eight steps (solid line and *'s).*

i.e., we compute the cosines of the angles between the projected query and the original documents.

Example 11.12. We ran LGK bidiagonalization with Q9 as a starting vector. It turns out that the relative residual decreases rather slowly to slightly below 0.8; see Figure 11.9. Still, after two steps the method already gives results that are much better than the full vector space model. It is also seen that eight steps of bidiagonalization give worse results. ∎

Example 11.12 indicates that the low-rank approximation obtained by LGK bidiagonalization has similar properties in terms of noise reduction as do LSI and the centroid-based method. It is striking that when the query vector is used to influence the first basis vectors, a much lower rank (in this case, 2) gives retrieval results that are about as good. On the other hand, when the number of steps increases, the precision becomes worse and approaches that of the full vector space model. This is natural, since gradually the low-rank approximation becomes better, and after around eight steps it represents almost all the information in the term-document matrix that is relevant to the query, in the sense of the full vector space model.

To determine how many steps of the recursion should be performed, one can monitor the least squares residual:

$$\min_y \|AZ_k y - q\|_2^2 = \min_y \|B_{k+1} y - \beta_1 e_1\|_2^2 = \min_y \|\widehat{B}_k y - Q_{k+1}^T \beta_1 e_1\|_2^2$$
$$= \min_y \|\widehat{B}_k y - \gamma^{(k)}\|_2^2 + |\gamma_k|^2 = |\gamma_k|^2,$$

where

$$\begin{pmatrix} \gamma^{(k)} \\ \gamma_k \end{pmatrix} = \begin{pmatrix} \gamma_0 \\ \gamma_1 \\ \vdots \\ \gamma_k \end{pmatrix} = Q_{k+1}^T \begin{pmatrix} \beta_1 \\ 0 \\ \vdots \\ 0 \end{pmatrix};$$

cf. (7.14). When the norm of the residual stops to decrease substantially, then we can assume that the query is represented as well as is possible by a linear combination of documents. Then we can expect the performance to be about the same as that of the full vector space model. Consequently, to have better performance than the full vector space model, one should stop well before the residual curve starts to level off.

11.7 Average Performance

Experiments to compare different methods for information retrieval should be performed on several test collections.[27] In addition, one should use not only one single query but a sequence of queries.

Example 11.13. We tested the 30 queries in the Medline collection and computed average precision-recall curves for the five methods presented in this chapter. To compute the average precision over the methods to be compared, it is necessary to

---

[27]Test collections and other useful information about text mining can be found at http://trec.nist.gov/, which is the Web site of the Text Retrieval Conference (TREC). See also http://www.cs.utk.edu/~lsi/corpa.html.

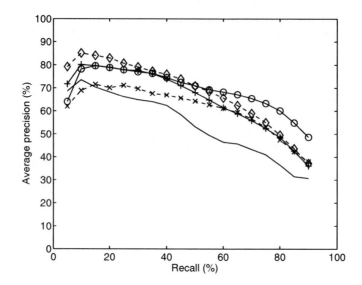

Figure 11.10. *Query matching for all 30 queries in the Medline collection. The methods used are the full vector space method (solid line), LSI of rank 100 (dashed line and diamonds), centroid approximation of rank 50 (solid line and circles), nonnegative matrix factorization of rank 50 (dashed line and ×'s), and two steps of LGK bidiagonalization (solid line and +'s).*

evaluate it at specified values of the recall, 5, 10, 15, ..., 90%, say. We obtained these by linear interpolation.

The results are illustrated in Figure 11.10. It is seen that LSI of rank 100, centroid-based approximation of rank 50, nonnegative matrix factorization, and two steps of LGK bidiagonalization all give considerably better average precision than the full vector space model. ■

From Example 11.13 we see that for the Medline test collection, the methods based on low-rank approximation of the term-document matrix all perform better than the full vector space model. Naturally, the price to be paid is more computation. In the case of LSI, centroid approximation, and nonnegative matrix factorization, the extra computations can be made offline, i.e., separate from the query matching. If documents are added to the collection, then the approximation must be recomputed, which may be costly. The method based on LGK bidiagonalization, on the other hand, performs the extra computation in connection with the query matching. Therefore, it can be used efficiently in situations where the term-document matrix is subject to frequent changes.

Similar results are obtained for other test collections; see, e.g., [11]. However, the structure of the text documents plays an role. For instance, in [52] it is shown that the performance of LSI is considerably better for medical abstracts than for articles from *TIME* magazine.

Chapter 12

Page Ranking for a Web Search Engine

When a search is made on the Internet using a search engine, there is first a traditional text processing part, where the aim is to find all the Web pages containing the words of the query. Due to the massive size of the Web, the number of hits is likely to be much too large to be of use. Therefore, some measure of quality is needed to filter out pages that are assumed to be less interesting.

When one uses a Web search engine it is typical that the search phrase is underspecified.

Example 12.1. A Google[28] search conducted on September 29, 2005, using the search phrase *university*, gave as a result links to the following well-known universities: *Harvard, Stanford, Cambridge, Yale, Cornell, Oxford.* The total number of Web pages relevant to the search phrase was more than 2 billion. ∎

Obviously Google uses an algorithm for ranking all the Web pages that agrees rather well with a common-sense quality measure. Somewhat surprisingly, the ranking procedure is based not on human judgment but on the link structure of the Web. Loosely speaking, Google assigns a high rank to a Web page if it has inlinks from other pages that have a high rank. We will see that this self-referencing statement can be formulated mathematically as an eigenvalue equation for a certain matrix.

12.1   Pagerank

It is of course impossible to define a generally valid measure of relevance that would be acceptable for all users of a search engine. Google uses the concept of *pagerank* as a quality measure of Web pages. It is based on the assumption that the number of links to and from a page give information about the importance of a page. We will give a description of pagerank based primarily on [74] and [33]. Concerning Google, see [19].

---

[28]http://www.google.com/.

147

Let all Web pages be ordered from 1 to n, and let i be a particular Web page. Then O_i will denote the set of pages that i is linked to, the *outlinks*. The number of outlinks is denoted $N_i = |O_i|$. The set of *inlinks*, denoted I_i, are the pages that have an outlink to i.

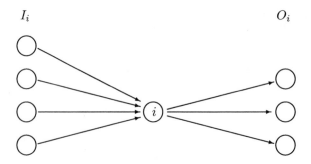

In general, a page i can be considered as more important the more inlinks it has. However, a ranking system based only on the number of inlinks is easy to manipulate:[29] when you design a Web page i that (e.g., for commercial reasons) you would like to be seen by as many users as possible, you could simply create a large number of (informationless and unimportant) pages that have outlinks to i. To discourage this, one defines the rank of i so that if a highly ranked page j has an outlink to i, this adds to the importance of i in the following way: the rank of page i is a weighted sum of the ranks of the pages that have outlinks to i. The weighting is such that the rank of a page j is divided evenly among its outlinks. Translating this into mathematics, we get

$$r_i = \sum_{j \in I_i} \frac{r_j}{N_j}. \tag{12.1}$$

This preliminary definition is recursive, so pageranks cannot be computed directly. Instead a fixed-point iteration might be used. Guess an initial ranking vector r^0. Then iterate

$$r_i^{(k+1)} = \sum_{j \in I_i} \frac{r_j^{(k)}}{N_j}, \quad k = 0, 1, \ldots. \tag{12.2}$$

There are a few problems with such an iteration: if a page has no outlinks, then in the iteration process it accumulates rank only via its inlinks, but this rank is never distributed further. Therefore it is not clear if the iteration converges. We will come back to this problem later.

More insight is gained if we reformulate (12.1) as an eigenvalue problem for a matrix representing the graph of the Internet. Let Q be a square matrix of dimension n. Define

$$Q_{ij} = \begin{cases} 1/N_j & \text{if there is a link from } j \text{ to } i, \\ 0 & \text{otherwise.} \end{cases}$$

---

[29]For an example of attempts to fool a search engine, see [96] and [59, Chapter 5].

This means that row i has nonzero elements in the positions that correspond to inlinks of i. Similarly, column j has nonzero elements equal to $1/N_j$ in the positions that correspond to the outlinks of j, and, provided that the page has outlinks, the sum of all the elements in column j is equal to one. In the following symbolic picture of the matrix Q, nonzero elements are denoted $*$:

$$
j
$$

$$
i \quad \begin{pmatrix} & & & * & & \\ & & & 0 & & \\ & & & \vdots & & \\ 0 & * & \cdots & * & * & \cdots \\ & & & \vdots & & \\ & & & 0 & & \\ & & & * & & \end{pmatrix} \quad \leftarrow \quad \text{inlinks}
$$

$$
\uparrow
$$
$$
\text{outlinks}
$$

Example 12.2. The following link graph illustrates a set of Web pages with outlinks and inlinks:

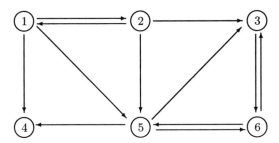

The corresponding matrix becomes

$$
Q = \begin{pmatrix}
0 & \frac{1}{3} & 0 & 0 & 0 & 0 \\
\frac{1}{3} & 0 & 0 & 0 & 0 & 0 \\
0 & \frac{1}{3} & 0 & 0 & \frac{1}{3} & \frac{1}{2} \\
\frac{1}{3} & 0 & 0 & 0 & \frac{1}{3} & 0 \\
\frac{1}{3} & \frac{1}{3} & 0 & 0 & 0 & \frac{1}{2} \\
0 & 0 & 1 & 0 & \frac{1}{3} & 0
\end{pmatrix}.
$$

Since page 4 has no outlinks, the corresponding column is equal to zero. ∎

Obviously, the definition (12.1) is equivalent to the scalar product of row i and the vector r, which holds the ranks of all pages. We can write the equation in matrix form,

$$\lambda r = Qr, \qquad \lambda = 1, \tag{12.3}$$

i.e., r is an *eigenvector* of Q with *eigenvalue* $\lambda = 1$. It is now easily seen that the iteration (12.2) is equivalent to

$$r^{(k+1)} = Qr^{(k)}, \qquad k = 0, 1, \ldots,$$

which is the *power method* for computing the eigenvector. However, at this point it is not clear that pagerank is well defined, as we do not know if there exists an eigenvalue equal to 1. It turns out that the theory of Markov chains is useful in the analysis.

12.2   Random Walk and Markov Chains

There is a random walk interpretation of the pagerank concept. Assume that a surfer visiting a Web page chooses the next page among the outlinks with equal probability. Then the random walk induces a Markov chain (see, e.g., [70]). *A Markov chain is a random process in which the next state is determined completely from the present state; the process has no memory.* The transition matrix of the Markov chain is Q^T. (Note that we use a slightly different notation than is common in the theory of stochastic processes.)

The random surfer should never get stuck. In other words, our random walk model should have no pages without outlinks. (Such a page corresponds to a zero column in Q.) Therefore the model is modified so that zero columns are replaced with a constant value in all positions. This means that there is equal probability to go to any other Internet page. Define the vectors

$$d_j = \left\{ \begin{array}{ll} 1 & \text{if } N_j = 0, \\ 0 & \text{otherwise}, \end{array} \right.$$

for $j = 1, \ldots, n$, and

$$e = \begin{pmatrix} 1 \\ 1 \\ \vdots \\ 1 \end{pmatrix} \in \mathbb{R}^n. \tag{12.4}$$

The modified matrix is defined

$$P = Q + \frac{1}{n} e d^T. \tag{12.5}$$

With this modification the matrix P is a proper *column-stochastic matrix*: It has nonnegative elements, and the elements of each column sum up to 1. The preceding statement can be reformulated as follows.

Proposition 12.3. *A column-stochastic matrix P satisfies*

$$e^T P = e^T, \tag{12.6}$$

where e is defined by (12.4).

Example 12.4. The matrix in the previous example is modified to

$$P = \begin{pmatrix} 0 & \frac{1}{3} & 0 & \frac{1}{6} & 0 & 0 \\ \frac{1}{3} & 0 & 0 & \frac{1}{6} & 0 & 0 \\ 0 & \frac{1}{3} & 0 & \frac{1}{6} & \frac{1}{3} & \frac{1}{2} \\ \frac{1}{3} & 0 & 0 & \frac{1}{6} & \frac{1}{3} & 0 \\ \frac{1}{3} & \frac{1}{3} & 0 & \frac{1}{6} & 0 & \frac{1}{2} \\ 0 & 0 & 1 & \frac{1}{6} & \frac{1}{3} & 0 \end{pmatrix}. \qquad \blacksquare$$

In analogy to (12.3), we would like to define the pagerank vector as a *unique* eigenvector of P with eigenvalue 1,

$$Pr = r.$$

The eigenvector of the transition matrix corresponds to a stationary probability distribution for the Markov chain. The element in position i, r_i, is the probability that after a large number of steps, the random walker is at Web page i. However, the existence of a unique eigenvalue with eigenvalue 1 is still not guaranteed. To ensure uniqueness, the matrix must be *irreducible*; cf. [53].

Definition 12.5. *A square matrix A is called* reducible *if there is a permutation matrix P such that*

$$PAP^T = \begin{pmatrix} X & Y \\ 0 & Z \end{pmatrix}, \tag{12.7}$$

where X and Z are both square. Otherwise the matrix is called irreducible.

Example 12.6. To illustrate the concept of reducibility, we give an example of a link graph that corresponds to a *reducible* matrix:

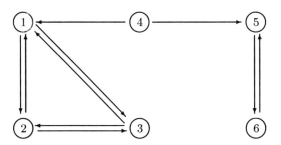

A random walker who has entered the left part of the link graph will never get out of it, and similarly will get stuck in the right part. The corresponding matrix is

$$
P = \begin{pmatrix}
0 & \frac{1}{2} & \frac{1}{2} & \frac{1}{2} & 0 & 0 \\
\frac{1}{2} & 0 & \frac{1}{2} & 0 & 0 & 0 \\
\frac{1}{2} & \frac{1}{2} & 0 & 0 & 0 & 0 \\
0 & 0 & 0 & 0 & 0 & 0 \\
0 & 0 & 0 & \frac{1}{2} & 0 & 1 \\
0 & 0 & 0 & 0 & 1 & 0
\end{pmatrix}, \tag{12.8}
$$

which is of the form (12.7). Actually, this matrix has two eigenvalues equal to 1 and one equal to -1; see Example 12.10. ∎

The directed graph corresponding to an irreducible matrix is *strongly connected*: given any two nodes (N_i, N_j), in the graph, there exists a path leading from N_i to N_j.

The uniqueness of the largest eigenvalue of an irreducible, positive matrix is guaranteed by the *Perron–Frobenius theorem*; we state it for the special case treated here. The inequality $A > 0$ is understood as all the elements of A being strictly positive. By *dominant eigenvalue* we mean the largest eigenvalue in magnitude, which we denote λ_1.

Theorem 12.7. *Let A be an irreducible column-stochastic matrix. The dominant eigenvalue λ_1 is equal to 1. There is a unique corresponding eigenvector r satisfying $r > 0$, and $\|r\|_1 = 1$; this is the only eigenvector that is nonnegative. If $A > 0$, then $|\lambda_i| < 1$, $i = 2, 3, \ldots, n$.*

Proof. Because A is column stochastic, we have $e^T A = e^T$, which means that 1 is an eigenvalue of A. The rest of the statement can be proved using the Perron–Frobenius theory [70, Chapter 8]. □

Given the size of the Internet, we can be sure that the link matrix P is reducible, which means that the pagerank eigenvector of P is not well defined. To ensure irreducibility, i.e., to make it impossible for the random walker to get trapped in a subgraph, one adds, artificially, a link from every Web page to all the others. In matrix terms, this can be made by taking a convex combination of P and a rank-1 matrix,

$$
A = \alpha P + (1 - \alpha)\frac{1}{n}ee^T, \tag{12.9}
$$

for some α satisfying $0 \leq \alpha \leq 1$. It is easy to see that the matrix A is column-stochastic:

$$
e^T A = \alpha e^T P + (1 - \alpha)\frac{1}{n}e^T ee^T = \alpha e^T + (1 - \alpha)e^T = e^T.
$$

The random walk interpretation of the additional rank-1 term is that in each time step the surfer visiting a page will jump to a random page with probability $1 - \alpha$ (sometimes referred to as *teleportation*).

We now see that the pagerank vector for the matrix A is well defined.

Proposition 12.8. *The column-stochastic matrix A defined in (12.9) is irreducible (since $A > 0$) and has the dominant eigenvalue $\lambda_1 = 1$. The corresponding eigenvector r satisfies $r > 0$.*

For the convergence of the numerical eigenvalue algorithm, it is essential to know how the eigenvalues of P are changed by the rank-1 modification (12.9).

Theorem 12.9. *Assume that the eigenvalues of the column-stochastic matrix P are $\{1, \lambda_2, \lambda_3 \ldots, \lambda_n\}$. Then the eigenvalues of $A = \alpha P + (1 - \alpha)\frac{1}{n}ee^T$ are $\{1, \alpha\lambda_2, \alpha\lambda_3, \ldots, \alpha\lambda_n\}$.*

Proof. Define $\hat{e}$ to be e normalized to Euclidean length 1, and let $U_1 \in \mathbb{R}^{n \times (n-1)}$ be such that $U = (\hat{e} \quad U_1)$ is orthogonal. Then, since $\hat{e}^T P = \hat{e}^T$,

$$U^T P U = \begin{pmatrix} \hat{e}^T P \\ U_1^T P \end{pmatrix} (\hat{e} \quad U_1) = \begin{pmatrix} \hat{e}^T \\ U_1^T P \end{pmatrix} (\hat{e} \quad U_1)$$

$$= \begin{pmatrix} \hat{e}^T \hat{e} & \hat{e}^T U_1 \\ U_1^T P \hat{e} & U_1^T P^T U_1 \end{pmatrix} = \begin{pmatrix} 1 & 0 \\ w & T \end{pmatrix}, \tag{12.10}$$

where $w = U_1^T P \hat{e}$ and $T = U_1^T P^T U_1$. Since we have made a similarity transformation, the matrix T has the eigenvalues $\lambda_2, \lambda_3, \ldots, \lambda_n$. Define $v = \frac{1}{n}e$. Then we have

$$U^T v = \begin{pmatrix} 1/\sqrt{n}\, e^T v \\ U_1^T v \end{pmatrix} = \begin{pmatrix} 1/\sqrt{n} \\ U_1^T v \end{pmatrix}.$$

Therefore,

$$U^T A U = U^T (\alpha P + (1 - \alpha)v e^T)U = \alpha \begin{pmatrix} 1 & 0 \\ w & T \end{pmatrix} + (1 - \alpha) \begin{pmatrix} 1/\sqrt{n} \\ U_1^T v \end{pmatrix} (\sqrt{n} \quad 0)$$

$$= \alpha \begin{pmatrix} 1 & 0 \\ w & T \end{pmatrix} + (1 - \alpha) \begin{pmatrix} 1 & 0 \\ \sqrt{n}\, U_1^T v & 0 \end{pmatrix} =: \begin{pmatrix} 1 & 0 \\ w_1 & \alpha T \end{pmatrix}.$$

The statement now follows immediately. $\square$

Theorem 12.9 implies that even if P has a multiple eigenvalue equal to 1, which is actually the case for the Google matrix, the second largest eigenvalue in magnitude of A is always equal to α.

Example 12.10. We compute the eigenvalues and eigenvectors of the matrix $A = \alpha P + (1 - \alpha)\frac{1}{n}ee^T$ with P from (12.8) and $\alpha = 0.85$. The MATLAB code

```
LP=eig(P)';
e=ones(6,1);
A=0.85*P + 0.15/6*e*e';
[R,L]=eig(A)
```

gives the following result:

```
LP = -0.5    1.0    -0.5     1.0    -1.0      0

R = 0.447   -0.365  -0.354   0.000   0.817    0.101
    0.430   -0.365   0.354  -0.000  -0.408   -0.752
    0.430   -0.365   0.354   0.000  -0.408    0.651
    0.057   -0.000  -0.707   0.000   0.000   -0.000
    0.469    0.548  -0.000  -0.707   0.000    0.000
    0.456    0.548   0.354   0.707  -0.000   -0.000

diag(L) = 1.0 0.85 -0.0 -0.85 -0.425 -0.425
```

It is seen that the first eigenvector (which corresponds to the eigenvalue 1), is the only nonnegative one, as stated in Theorem 12.7.   ■

Instead of the modification (12.9) we can define

$$A = \alpha P + (1 - \alpha)ve^T,$$

where v is a nonnegative vector with $\| v \|_1 = 1$ that can be chosen to make the search biased toward certain kinds of Web pages. Therefore, it is sometimes referred to as a *personalization vector* [74, 48]. The vector v can also be used for avoiding manipulation by so-called link farms [57, 59].

12.3   The Power Method for Pagerank Computation

We want to solve the eigenvalue problem

$$Ar = r,$$

where r is normalized $\| r \|_1 = 1$. In this section we denote the sought eigenvector by t_1. Dealing with stochastic matrices and vectors that are probability distributions, it is natural to use the 1-norm for vectors (Section 2.3). Due to the sparsity and the dimension of A (of the order billions), it is out of the question to compute the eigenvector using any of the standard methods described in Chapter 15 for dense matrices, as those methods are based on applying orthogonal transformations to the matrix. The only viable method so far is the *power method*.

Assume that an initial approximation $r^{(0)}$ is given. The power method is given in the following algorithm.

The power method for $Ar = \lambda r$

for $k = 1, 2, \ldots$ until convergence

$\quad q^{(k)} = Ar^{(k-1)}$

$\quad r^{(k)} = q^{(k)}/\| q^{(k)} \|_1$

The purpose of normalizing the vector (making it have 1-norm equal to 1) is to avoid having the vector become either very large or very small and thus unrepresentable in the floating point system. We will see later that normalization is not necessary in the pagerank computation. In this context there is no need to compute an eigenvalue approximation, as the sought eigenvalue is known to be equal to one.

The convergence of the power method depends on the distribution of eigenvalues. To make the presentation simpler, we assume that A is diagonalizable, i.e., there exists a nonsingular matrix T of eigenvectors, $T^{-1}AT = \text{diag}(\lambda_1, \ldots, \lambda_n)$. The eigenvalues λ_i are ordered $1 = \lambda_1 > |\lambda_2| \geq \cdots \geq |\lambda_n|$. Expand the initial approximation $r^{(0)}$ in terms of the eigenvectors,

$$r^{(0)} = c_1 t_1 + c_2 t_2 + \cdots + c_n t_n,$$

where $c_1 \neq 0$ is assumed[30] and $r = t_1$ is the sought eigenvector. Then we have

$$A^k r^{(0)} = c_1 A^k t_1 + c_2 A^k t_2 + \cdots + c_n A^k t_n$$

$$= c_1 \lambda_1^k t_1 + c_2 \lambda_2^k t_2 + \cdots + c_n \lambda_n^k t_n = c_1 t_1 + \sum_{j=2}^{n} c_j \lambda_j^k t_j.$$

Obviously, since for $j = 2, 3, \ldots$ we have $|\lambda_j| < 1$, the second term tends to zero and the power method converges to the eigenvector $r = t_1$. The rate of convergence is determined by $|\lambda_2|$. If this is close to 1, then the iteration is very slow. Fortunately this is not the case for the Google matrix; see Theorem 12.9 and below.

A stopping criterion for the power iteration can be formulated in terms of the residual vector for the eigenvalue problem. Let $\hat{\lambda}$ be the computed approximation of the eigenvalue and $\hat{r}$ the corresponding approximate eigenvector. Then it can be shown [94], [4, p. 229] that the optimal error matrix E, for which

$$(A + E)\hat{r} = \hat{\lambda}\hat{r},$$

exactly, satisfies

$$\| E \|_2 = \| s \|_2,$$

where $s = A\hat{r} - \hat{\lambda}\hat{r}$. This means that if the residual $\|s\|_2$ is small, then the computed approximate eigenvector $\hat{r}$ is the exact eigenvector of a matrix $A + E$ that is close

---

[30]This assumption can be expected to be satisfied in floating point arithmetic, if not at the first iteration, then after the second, due to round-off.

to A. Since in the pagerank computations we are dealing with a positive matrix, whose columns all add up to one, it is natural to use the 1-norm instead [55]. As the 1-norm and the Euclidean norm are equivalent (cf. (2.6)), this does not make much difference.

In the usual formulation of the power method the vector is normalized to avoid underflow or overflow. We now show that this is not necessary when the matrix is column stochastic.

Proposition 12.11. *Assume that the vector z satisfies $\| z \|_1 = e^T z = 1$ and that the matrix A is column stochastic. Then*

$$\| Az \|_1 = 1. \tag{12.11}$$

Proof. Put $y = Az$. Then

$$\| y \|_1 = e^T y = e^T Az = e^T z = 1$$

since A is column stochastic $(e^T A = e^T)$.   □

In view of the huge dimensions of the Google matrix, it is nontrivial to compute the matrix-vector product $y = Az$, where $A = \alpha P + (1 - \alpha)\frac{1}{n}ee^T$. Recall that P was constructed from the actual link matrix Q as

$$P = Q + \frac{1}{n}ed^T,$$

where the row vector d has an element 1 in all those positions that correspond to Web pages with no outlinks (see (12.5)). This means that to form P, we insert a large number of full vectors into Q, each of the same dimension as the total number of Web pages. Consequently, we cannot afford to store P explicitly. Let us look at the multiplication $y = Az$ in more detail:

$$y = \alpha \left(Q + \frac{1}{n}ed^T\right) z + \frac{(1 - \alpha)}{n}e(e^T z) = \alpha Qz + \beta\frac{1}{n}e, \tag{12.12}$$

where

$$\beta = \alpha d^T z + (1 - \alpha)e^T z.$$

We do not need to compute β from this equation. Instead we can use (12.11) in combination with (12.12):

$$1 = e^T(\alpha Qz) + \beta e^T \left(\frac{1}{n}e\right) = e^T(\alpha Qz) + \beta.$$

Thus, we have $\beta = 1 - \| \alpha Qz \|_1$. An extra bonus is that we do not use the vector d at all, i.e., we need not know which pages lack outlinks.

The following MATLAB code implements the matrix vector multiplication:

```
yhat=alpha*Q*z;
beta=1-norm(yhat,1);
y=yhat+beta*v;
residual=norm(y-z,1);
```

Here $v = (1/n)\,e$, or a personalized teleportation vector; see p. 154. To save memory, we should even avoid using the extra vector **yhat** and replace it with **y**.

From Theorem 12.9 we know that the second eigenvalue of the Google matrix satisfies $\lambda_2 = \alpha$. A typical value of α is 0.85. Approximately $k = 57$ iterations are needed to make the factor 0.85^k equal to 10^{-4}. This is reported [57] to be close to the number of iterations used by Google.

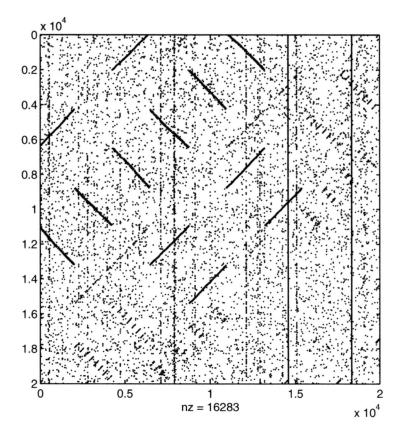

Figure 12.1. *A* 20000×20000 *submatrix of the stanford.edu matrix.*

Example 12.12. As an example we used the matrix P obtained from the domain stanford.edu.[31] The number of pages is 281903, and the total number of links is 2312497. Part of the matrix is displayed in Figure 12.1. We computed the pagerank

---

[31] http://www.stanford.edu/~sdkamvar/research.html.

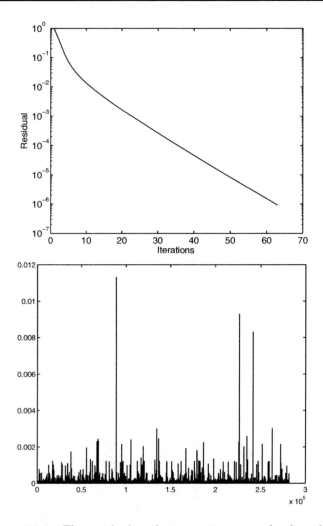

Figure 12.2. *The residual in the power iterations (top) and the pagerank vector (bottom) for the stanford.edu matrix.*

vector using the power method with $\alpha = 0.85$ and iterated 63 times until the 1-norm of the residual was smaller than 10^{-6}. The residual and the final pagerank vector are illustrated in Figure 12.2.   ∎

Because one pagerank calculation can take several days, several enhancements of the iteration procedure have been proposed. In [53] an adaptive method is described that checks the convergence of the components of the pagerank vector and avoids performing the power iteration for those components. Up to 30% speed-up has been reported. The block structure of the Web is used in [54], and speed-ups of a factor of 2 have been reported. An acceleration method based on Aitken extrapolation is described in [55]. Aggregation methods are discussed in several papers by Langville and Meyer and in [51].

When computing the pagerank for a subset of the Internet, say, one particular domain, the matrix P may be of a dimension for which one can use methods other than the power method, e.g., the Arnoldi method; see [40] and Section 15.8.3. It may even be sufficient to use the MATLAB function `eigs`, which computes a small number of eigenvalues and the corresponding eigenvectors of a sparse matrix using an Arnoldi method with restarts.

A variant of pagerank is proposed in [44]. Further properties of the pagerank matrix are given in [84].

12.4 HITS

Another method based on the link structure of the Web was introduced at the same time as pagerank [56]. It is called HITS (Hypertext Induced Topic Search) and is based on the concepts of *authorities* and *hubs*. An authority is a Web page with many inlinks, and a hub has many outlinks. The basic idea is that *good hubs point to good authorities and good authorities are pointed to by good hubs*. Each Web page is assigned both a hub score y and an authority score x.

Let L be the adjacency matrix of the directed Web graph. Then two equations are given that mathematically define the relation between the two scores, based on the basic idea:

$$x = L^T y, \qquad y = Lx. \tag{12.13}$$

The algorithm for computing the scores is the power method, which converges to the left and right singular vectors corresponding to the largest singular value of L. In the implementation of HITS, the adjacency matrix not of the whole Web but of all the pages relevant to the query is used.

There is now an extensive literature on pagerank, HITS, and other ranking methods. For overviews, see [7, 58, 59]. A combination of HITS and pagerank has been proposed in [65].

Obviously, the ideas underlying pagerank and HITS are not restricted to Web applications but can be applied to other network analyses. A variant of the HITS method was recently used in a study of Supreme Court precedent [36]. HITS is generalized in [17], which also treats synonym extraction. In [72], generank, which is based on the pagerank concept, is used for the analysis of microarray experiments.

Chapter 13

Automatic Key Word and Key Sentence Extraction

Due to the explosion of the amount of textual information available, there is a need to develop automatic procedures for text summarization. A typical situation is when a Web search engine presents a small amount of text from each document that matches a certain query. Another relevant area is the summarization of news articles.

Automatic text summarization is an active research field with connections to several other areas, such as information retrieval, natural language processing, and machine learning. Informally, the goal of text summarization is to *extract content from a text document and present the most important content to the user in a condensed form and in a manner sensitive to the user's or application's need* [67]. In this chapter we will have a considerably less ambitious goal: we will present a method for automatically extracting key words and key sentences from a text. There will be connections to the vector space model in information retrieval and to the concept of pagerank. We will also use nonnegative matrix factorization. The presentation is based on [114]. Text summarization using QR decomposition is described in [26, 83].

13.1 Saliency Score

Consider a text from which we want to extract key words and key sentences. As an example we will take Chapter 12 from this book. As one of the preprocessing steps, one should perform stemming so that the same word stem with different endings is represented by one token only. Stop words (cf. Chapter 11) occur frequently in texts, but since they do not distinguish between different sentences, they should be removed. Similarly, if the text carries special symbols, e.g., mathematics or mark-up language tags (HTML, LaTeX), it may be necessary to remove those.

Since we want to compare word frequencies in different sentences, we must consider each sentence as a separate document (in the terminology of information retrieval). After the preprocessing has been done, we parse the text, using the same type of parser as in information retrieval. This way a term-document matrix is prepared, which in this chapter we will refer to as a *term-sentence* matrix. Thus we have a matrix $A \in \mathbb{R}^{m \times n}$, where m denotes the number of different terms and n the number of sentences. The element a_{ij} is defined as the frequency[32] of term i in sentence j.

The column vector $(a_{1j}\, a_{2j}\, \ldots\, a_{mj})^T$ is nonzero in the positions corresponding to the terms occurring in sentence j. Similarly, the row vector $(a_{i1}\, a_{i2}\, \ldots\, a_{in})$ is nonzero in the positions corresponding to sentences containing term i.

The basis of the procedure in [114] is the simultaneous but separate *ranking* of the terms and the sentences. Thus, term i is given a nonnegative *saliency score*, denoted u_i. The higher the saliency score, the more important the term. The saliency score of sentence j is denoted v_j.

The assignment of saliency scores is made based on the *mutual reinforcement principle* [114]:

> A term should have a high saliency score if it appears in many sentences with high saliency scores. A sentence should have a high saliency score if it contains many words with high saliency scores.

More precisely, we assert that the saliency score of term i is proportional to the sum of the scores of the sentences where it appears; in addition, each term is weighted by the corresponding matrix element,

$$u_i \propto \sum_{j=1}^{n} a_{ij} v_j, \qquad i = 1, 2, \ldots, m.$$

Similarly, the saliency score of sentence j is defined to be proportional to the scores of its words, weighted by the corresponding a_{ij},

$$v_j =\propto \sum_{i=1}^{m} a_{ij} u_i, \qquad j = 1, 2, \ldots, n.$$

Collecting the saliency scores in two vectors $u \in \mathbb{R}^m$ and $v \in \mathbb{R}^n$, these two equations can be written as

$$\sigma_u u = A v, \tag{13.1}$$

$$\sigma_v v = A^T u, \tag{13.2}$$

where σ_u and σ_v are proportionality constants. In fact, the constants must be equal. Inserting one equation into the other, we get

$$\sigma_u\, u = \frac{1}{\sigma_v} A A^T u,$$

$$\sigma_v\, v = \frac{1}{\sigma_u} A^T A v,$$

---

[32]Naturally, a term and document weighting scheme (see [12]) should be used.

which shows that u and v are eigenvectors of AA^T and $A^T A$, respectively, with the same eigenvalue. It follows that u and v are singular vectors corresponding to the same singular value.[33]

If we choose the largest singular value, then we are guaranteed that the components of u and v are nonnegative.[34]

In summary, the saliency scores of the terms are defined as the components of u_1, and the saliency scores of the sentences are the components of v_1.

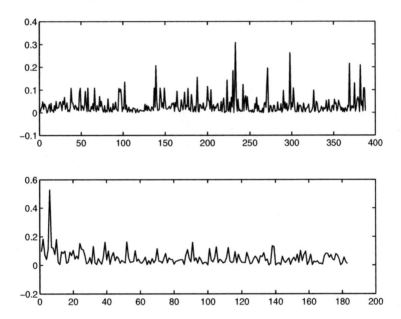

Figure 13.1. *Saliency scores for Chapter* 12: *term scores (top) and sentence scores (bottom).*

Example 13.1. We created a term-sentence matrix based on Chapter 12. Since the text is written using LaTeX, we first had to remove all LaTeX typesetting commands. This was done using a lexical scanner called detex.[35] Then the text was stemmed and stop words were removed. A term-sentence matrix A was constructed using the text parser TMG [113]: there turned out to be 388 terms in 183 sentences. The first singular vectors were computed in MATLAB, [u,s,v]=svds(A,1). (The matrix is sparse, so we used the SVD function for sparse matrices.) The singular vectors are plotted in Figure 13.1.

By locating the 10 largest components of u_1 and using the dictionary produced by the text parser, we found that the following words, ordered by importance, are the most important in the chapter:

---

[33]This can be demonstrated easily using the SVD of A.

[34]The matrix A has nonnegative elements; therefore the first principal component u_1 (see Section 6.4) must have nonnegative components. The corresponding holds for v_1.

[35]http://www.cs.purdue.edu/homes/trinkle/detex/.

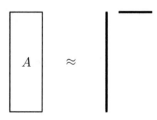

Figure 13.2. *Symbolic illustration of a rank-1 approximation:* $A \approx \sigma_1 u_1 v_1^T$.

page, search, university, web, Google, rank, outlink, link, number, equal

The following are the six most important sentences, in order:

1. A Google search conducted on September 29, 2005, using the search phrase *university*, gave as a result links to the following well-known universities: *Harvard, Stanford, Cambridge, Yale, Cornell, Oxford*.

2. When a search is made on the Internet using a search engine, there is first a traditional text processing part, where the aim is to find all the Web pages containing the words of the query.

3. Loosely speaking, Google assign a high rank to a Web page if it has inlinks from other pages that have a high rank.

4. Assume that a surfer visiting a Web page chooses the next page from among the outlinks with equal probability.

5. Similarly, column j has nonzero elements equal to N_j in those positions that correspond to the outlinks of j, and, provided that the page has outlinks, the sum of all the elements in column j is equal to one.

6. The random walk interpretation of the additional rank-1 term is that in each time step the surfer visiting a page will jump to a random page with probability $1 - \alpha$ (sometimes referred to as *teleportation*).

It is apparent that this method prefers long sentences. On the other hand, these sentences are undeniably key sentences for the text.   ∎

The method described above can also be thought of as a rank-1 approximation of the term-sentence matrix A, illustrated symbolically in Figure 13.2.

In this interpretation, the vector u_1 is a basis vector for the subspace spanned by the columns of A, and the row vector $\sigma_1 v_1^T$ holds the coordinates of the columns of A in terms of this basis. Now we see that the method based on saliency scores has a drawback: if there are, say, two "top sentences" that contain the same high-saliency terms, then their coordinates will be approximately the same, and both sentences will be extracted as key sentences. This is unnecessary, since they are very similar. We will next see that this can be avoided if we base the key sentence extraction on a rank-k approximation.

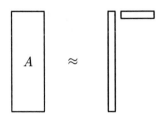

Figure 13.3. *Symbolic illustration of low-rank approximation: $A \approx CD$.*

13.2 Key Sentence Extraction from a Rank-k Approximation

Assume that we have computed a good rank-k approximation of the term-sentence matrix,

$$A \approx CD, \qquad C \in \mathbb{R}^{m \times k}, \quad D \in \mathbb{R}^{k \times n}, \tag{13.3}$$

illustrated in Figure 13.3. This approximation can be be based on the SVD, clustering [114], or nonnegative matrix factorization. The dimension k is chosen greater than or equal to the number of key sentences that we want to extract. C is a rank-k matrix of basis vectors, and each column of D holds the coordinates of the corresponding column in A in terms of the basis vectors.

Now recall that *the basis vectors in C represent the most important directions in the "sentence space,"* the column space. However, the low-rank approximation does not immediately give an indication of which are the most important sentences. Those sentences can be found if we first determine the column of A that is the "heaviest" in terms of the basis, i.e., the column in D with the largest 2-norm. This defines one new basis vector. Then we proceed by determining the column of D that is the heaviest in terms of the remaining $k - 1$ basis vectors, and so on.

To derive the method, we note that in the approximate equality (13.3) we may introduce any nonsingular matrix T and its inverse between C and D, and we may multiply the relation with any permutation P from the right, without changing the relation:

$$AP \approx CDP = (CT)(T^{-1}DP),$$

where $T \in \mathbb{R}^{k \times k}$.

Starting from the approximation (13.3), we first find the column of largest norm in D and permute it by P_1 to the first column; at the same time we move the corresponding column of A to the first position. Then we determine a Householder transformation Q_1 that zeros the elements in the first column below the element in position $(1, 1)$ and apply the transformation to both C and D:

$$AP_1 \approx (CQ_1)(Q_1^T DP_1).$$

In fact, this is the first step in the QR decomposition with column pivoting of D. We continue the discussion in terms of an example with $m = 6$, $n = 5$, and $k = 3$.

To illustrate that the procedure deals with the problem of having two or more very similar important sentences (cf. p. 164), we have also assumed that column 4 of D had almost the same coordinates as the column that was moved to the first position. After the first step the matrices have the structure

$$(CQ_1)(Q_1^T DP_1) = \begin{pmatrix} \times & \times & \times \\ \times & \times & \times \\ \times & \times & \times \\ \times & \times & \times \\ \times & \times & \times \\ \times & \times & \times \\ \times & \times & \times \end{pmatrix} \begin{pmatrix} \kappa_1 & \times & \times & \times & \times \\ 0 & \times & \times & \epsilon_1 & \times \\ 0 & \times & \times & \epsilon_2 & \times \end{pmatrix},$$

where κ_1 is the Euclidean length of the first column of DP_1. Since column 4 was similar to the one that is now in position 1, it has small entries in rows 2 and 3. Then we introduce the diagonal matrix

$$T_1 = \begin{pmatrix} \kappa_1 & 0 & 0 \\ 0 & 1 & 0 \\ 0 & 0 & 1 \end{pmatrix}$$

between the factors:

$$C_1 D_1 := (CQ_1 T_1)(T_1^{-1} Q_1^T DP_1) = \begin{pmatrix} * & \times & \times \\ * & \times & \times \\ * & \times & \times \\ * & \times & \times \\ * & \times & \times \\ * & \times & \times \\ * & \times & \times \end{pmatrix} \begin{pmatrix} 1 & * & * & * & * \\ 0 & \times & \times & \epsilon_1 & \times \\ 0 & \times & \times & \epsilon_2 & \times \end{pmatrix}.$$

This changes only column 1 of the left factor and column 1 of the right factor (marked with $*$). From the relation

$$AP_1 \approx C_1 D_1,$$

we now see that the first column in AP_1 is approximately equal to the first column in C_1. Remembering that the columns of the original matrix C are the dominating directions in the matrix A, *we have now identified the "dominating column" of A.*

Before continuing, we make the following observation. If one column of D is similar to the first one (column 4 in the example), then it will now have small elements below the first row, and it will not play a role in the selection of the second most dominating document. Therefore, *if there are two or more important sentences with more or less the same key words, only one of then will be selected.*

Next we determine the second most dominating column of A. To this end we compute the norms of the columns of D_1, excluding the first row (because that row holds the coordinates in terms of the first column of C_1). The column with the largest norm is moved to position 2 and reduced by a Householder transformation in a similar manner as above. After this step we have

$$C_2 D_2 := (C_1 Q_2 T_2)(T_2^{-1} Q_2^T D_1 P_2) = \begin{pmatrix} * & * & \times \\ * & * & \times \\ * & * & \times \\ * & * & \times \\ * & * & \times \\ * & * & \times \\ * & * & \times \end{pmatrix} \begin{pmatrix} 1 & * & * & * & * \\ 0 & 1 & * & \epsilon_1 & * \\ 0 & 0 & \times & \epsilon_2 & \times \end{pmatrix}.$$

Therefore the second column of

$$A P_1 P_2 \approx C_2 D_2$$

holds the second most dominating column.

Continuing the process, the final result is

$$AP \approx C_k D_k, \qquad D_k = \begin{pmatrix} R & S \end{pmatrix},$$

where R is upper triangular and P is a product of permutations. Now the first k columns of AP hold the dominating columns of the matrix, and the rank-k approximations of these columns are in C_k. This becomes even clearer if we write

$$AP \approx C_k R R^{-1} D_k = \widehat{C} \begin{pmatrix} I & \widehat{S} \end{pmatrix}, \tag{13.4}$$

where $\widehat{C} = C_k R$ and $\widehat{S} = R^{-1} S$. Since

$$\widehat{C} = C Q_1 T_1 Q_2 T_2 \cdots Q_k T_k R$$

is a rotated and scaled version of the original C (i.e., the columns of C and $\widehat{C}$ span the same subspace in $\mathbb{R}^m$), it still holds the dominating directions of A. Assume that $a_{i_1}, a_{i_2}, \ldots, a_{i_k}$ are the first k columns of AP. Then (13.4) is equivalent to

$$a_{i_j} \approx \hat{c}_j, \qquad j = 1, 2, \ldots, k.$$

This means that *the dominating directions, which are given by the columns of $\widehat{C}$, have been directly associated with k columns in A.*

The algorithm described above is equivalent to computing the QR decomposition with column pivoting (see Section 6.9.1),

$$DP = Q \begin{pmatrix} R & S \end{pmatrix},$$

where Q is orthogonal and R is upper triangular. Note that if we are interested only in finding the top k sentences, we need not apply any transformations to the matrix of basis vectors, and the algorithm for finding the top k sentences can be implemented in MATLAB as follows:

```
% C * D is a rank k approximation of A
[Q,RS,P]=qr(D);
p=[1:n]*P;
pk=p(1:k);      % Indices of the first k columns of AP
```

Example 13.2. We computed a nonnegative matrix factorization of the term-sentence matrix of Example 13.1 using the multiplicative algorithm of Section 9.2. Then we determined the six top sentences using the method described above. The sentences 1, 2, 3, and 5 in Example 13.1 were selected, and in addition the following two:

1. Due to the sparsity and the dimension of A (of the order billions), it is out of the question to compute the eigenvector using any of the standard methods described in Chapter 15 for dense matrices, as those methods are based on applying orthogonal transformations to the matrix.

2. In [53] an adaptive method is described that checks the convergence of the components of the pagerank vector and avoids performing the power iteration for those components.

The same results were obtained when the low-rank approximation was computed using the SVD. ∎

Chapter 14

Face Recognition Using Tensor SVD

Human beings are very skillful at recognizing faces even when the facial expression, the illumination, the viewing angle, etc., vary. To develop automatic procedures for face recognition that are robust with respect to varying conditions is a challenging research problem that has been investigated using several different approaches. Principal component analysis (i.e., SVD) is a popular technique that often goes by the name "eigenfaces" [23, 88, 100]. However, this method is best when all pictures are taken under similar conditions, and it does not perform well when several environment factors are varied. More general bilinear models also have been investigated; see, e.g., [95].

Recently [102, 103, 104, 105], methods for multilinear analysis of image ensembles were studied. In particular, the face recognition problem was considered using a tensor model, the TensorFaces approach. By letting the modes of the tensor represent a different viewing condition, e.g., illumination or facial expression, it became possible to improve the precision of the recognition algorithm compared to the PCA method.

In this chapter we will describe a tensor method for face recognition, related to TensorFaces. Since we are dealing with images, which are often stored as $m \times n$ arrays, with m and n of the order 100–500, the computations for each face to be identified are quite heavy. We will discuss how the tensor SVD (HOSVD) can also be used for dimensionality reduction to reduce the flop count.

14.1 Tensor Representation

Assume that we have a collection of images of n_p persons, where each image is an $m_{i_1} \times m_{i_2}$ array with $m_{i_1} m_{i_2} = n_i$. We will assume that the columns of the images are stacked so that each image is represented by a vector in $\mathbb{R}^{n_i}$. Further assume that each person has been photographed with n_e different facial expressions.[36] Often one can have $n_i \geq 5000$, and usually n_i is considerably larger than n_e and n_p. The

---

[36]For simplicity here we refer to different illuminations, etc., as expressions.

collection of images is stored as a tensor,

$$\mathcal{A} \in \mathbb{R}^{n_i \times n_e \times n_p}. \tag{14.1}$$

We refer to the different modes as the image mode, the expression mode, and the person mode, respectively.

If, for instance we also had photos of each person with different illumination, viewing angles, etc., then we could represent the image collection by a tensor of higher degree [104]. For simplicity, here we consider only the case of a 3-mode tensor. The generalization to higher order tensors is straightforward.

Example 14.1. We preprocessed images of 10 persons from the Yale Face Database by cropping and decimating each image to 112×78 pixels stored in a vector of length 8736. Five images are illustrated in Figure 14.1.

Figure 14.1. *Person 1 with five different expressions (from the Yale Face Database).*

Each person is photographed with a total of 11 different expressions.   ∎

The ordering of the modes is arbitrary, of course; for definiteness and for illustration purposes we will assume the ordering of (14.1). However, to (somewhat) emphasize the ordering arbitrariness, we will use the notation $\times_e$ for multiplication of the tensor by matrix along the expression mode, and similarly for the other modes. We now assume that $n_i \gg n_e n_p$ and write the *thin HOSVD* (see Theorem 8.3 and (8.9)),

$$\mathcal{A} = \mathcal{S} \times_i F \times_e G \times_p H, \tag{14.2}$$

where $\mathcal{S} \in \mathbb{R}^{n_e n_p \times n_e \times n_p}$ is the core tensor, $F \in \mathbb{R}^{n_i \times n_e n_p}$ has orthonormal columns, and $G \in \mathbb{R}^{n_e \times n_e}$ and $H \in \mathbb{R}^{n_p \times n_p}$ are orthogonal.

Example 14.2. We computed the HOSVD of the tensor of face images of 10 persons, each with 10 different expressions. The singular values are plotted in Figure 14.2. All 10 singular values in the expression and person modes are significant, which means that it should be relatively easy to distinguish between expressions and persons.   ∎

The HOSVD can be interpreted in different ways depending on what it is to be used for. We first illustrate the relation

$$\mathcal{A} = \mathcal{D} \times_e G \times_p H,$$

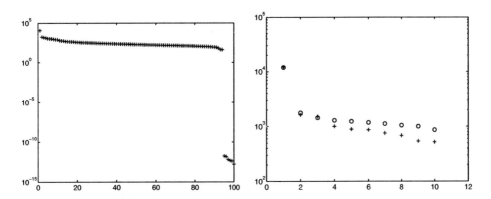

Figure 14.2. *The singular values in the image mode (left), the expression mode (right, +), and the person mode (right, circles).*

where $\mathcal{D} = \mathcal{S} \times_i F$:

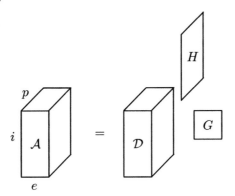

At this point, let us recapitulate the definition of tensor-matrix multiplication (Section 8.2). For definiteness we consider 2-mode, i.e., here e-mode, multiplication:

$$(\mathcal{D} \times_e G)(i_1, j, i_3) = \sum_{k=1}^{n_e} g_{j,k} \, d_{i_1,k,i_3}.$$

We see that fixing a particular value of the expression parameter, i.e., putting $j = e_0$, say, corresponds to using only the e_0th row of G. By doing the analogous choice in the person mode, we get

$$\mathcal{A}(:, e_0, p_0) = \mathcal{D} \times_e g_{e_0} \times_p h_{p_0}, \tag{14.3}$$

where g_{e_0} denotes the e_0th row vector of G and h_{p_0} the p_0th row vector of H. We illustrate (14.3) in the following figure:

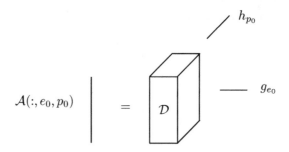

We summarize this in words:

The image of person p_0 in expression e_0 can be synthesized by multiplication of the tensor $\mathcal{D}$ by h_{p_0} and g_{e_0} in their respective modes. Thus person p_0 is uniquely characterized by the row vector h_{p_0} and expression e_0 is uniquely characterized by g_{e_0}, via the bilinear form

$$\mathcal{D} \times_e g \times_p h.$$

Example 14.3. The MATLAB code

```
a=tmul(tmul(D,Ue(4,:),2),Up(6,:),3);
```

gives person 6 in expression 4 (happy); see Figure 14.3. Recall that the function `tmul(A,X,i)` multiplies the tensor `A` by the matrix `X` in mode `i`. ∎

Figure 14.3. *Person 6 in expression 4 (happy).*

14.2 Face Recognition

We will now consider the classification problem as follows:

Given an image of an unknown person, represented by a vector in $\mathbb{R}^{n_i}$, determine which of the n_p persons it represents, or decide that the unknown person is not in the database.

For the classification we write the HOSVD (14.2) in the following form:

$$\mathcal{A} = \mathcal{C} \times_p H, \qquad \mathcal{C} = \mathcal{S} \times_i F \times_e G. \tag{14.4}$$

For a particular expression e we have

$$\mathcal{A}(:, e, :) = \mathcal{C}(:, e, :) \times_p H. \tag{14.5}$$

Obviously we can identify the tensors $\mathcal{A}(:, e, :)$ and $\mathcal{C}(:, e, :)$ with matrices, which we denote A_e and C_e. Therefore, for all the expressions, we have linear relations

$$A_e = C_e H^T, \qquad e = 1, 2, \ldots, n_e. \tag{14.6}$$

Note that the same (orthogonal) matrix H occurs in all n_e relations. With $H^T = \begin{pmatrix} h_1 & \ldots & h_{n_p} \end{pmatrix}$, column p of (14.6) can be written

$$a_p^{(e)} = C_e h_p. \tag{14.7}$$

We can interpret (14.6) and (14.7) as follows:

> Column p of A_e contains the image of person p in expression e. The columns of C_e are *basis vectors for expression e*, and row p of H, i.e., h_p, holds the *coordinates* of the image of person p in this basis. Furthermore, *the same h_p holds the coordinates of the images of person p in all expression bases*.

Next assume that $z \in \mathbb{R}^{n_i}$ is an image of an unknown person in an unknown expression (out of the n_e) and that we want to classify it. We refer to z as a test image. Obviously, if it is an image of person p in expression e, then the coordinates of z in that basis are equal to h_p. Thus we can classify z by computing its coordinates in all the expression bases and checking, for each expression, whether the coordinates of z coincide (or almost coincide) with the elements of any row of H.

The coordinates of z in expression basis e can be found by solving the least squares problem

$$\min_{\alpha_e} \| C_e \alpha_e - z \|_2. \tag{14.8}$$

The algorithm is summarized below:

Classification algorithm (preliminary version)

% z is a test image.

for $e = 1, 2, \ldots, n_e$

    Solve $\min_{\alpha_e} \| C_e \alpha_e - z \|_2$.

    for $p = 1, 2, \ldots, n_p$

        If $\| \alpha_e - h_p \|_2 < \text{tol}$, then classify as person p and **stop**.

    end

end

The amount of work in this algorithm is high: for each test image z we must solve n_e least squares problems (14.8) with $C_e \in \mathbb{R}^{n_i \times n_p}$.

However, recall from (14.4) that $\mathcal{C} = \mathcal{S} \times_i F \times_e G$, which implies

$$C_e = FB_e,$$

where $B_e \in \mathbb{R}^{n_e n_p \times n_p}$ is the matrix identified with $(\mathcal{S} \times_e G)(:, e, :)$. Note that $F \in \mathbb{R}^{n_i \times n_e n_p}$; we assume that n_i is considerably larger than $n_e n_p$. Then, for the analysis only, enlarge the matrix so that it becomes square and orthogonal:

$$\hat{F} = \begin{pmatrix} F & F^\perp \end{pmatrix}, \qquad \hat{F}^T \hat{F} = I.$$

Now insert $\hat{F}^T$ inside the norm:

$$\| C_e \alpha_e - z \|_2^2 = \| \hat{F}^T (FB_e \alpha_e - z) \|_2 = \left\| \begin{pmatrix} B_e \alpha_e - F^T z \\ -(F^\perp)^T z \end{pmatrix} \right\|_2^2$$
$$= \| B_e \alpha_e - F^T z \|_2^2 + \| (F^\perp)^T z \|_2^2.$$

It follows that we can solve the n_e least squares problems by first computing $F^T z$ and then solving

$$\min_{\alpha_e} \| B_e \alpha_e - F^T z \|_2, \qquad e = 1, 2, \ldots, n_e. \tag{14.9}$$

The matrix B_e has dimension $n_e n_p \times n_p$, so it is much cheaper to solve (14.9) than (14.8). It is also possible to precompute a QR decomposition of each matrix B_e to further reduce the work. Thus we arrive at the following algorithm.

Classification algorithm

Preprocessing step. Compute and save the thin QR decompositions of all the B_e matrices, $B_e = Q_e R_e$, $e = 1, 2, \ldots, n_e$.

% z is a test image.

Compute $\hat{z} = F^T z$.

for $e = 1, 2, \ldots, n_e$

    Solve $R_e \alpha_e = Q_e^T \hat{z}$ for α_e.

    for $p = 1, 2, \ldots, n_p$

        If $\| \alpha_e - h_p \|_2 < \text{tol}$, then classify as person p and **stop**.

    end

end

In a typical application it is likely that even if the test image is an image of a person in the database, it is taken with another expression that is not represented in the database. However, the above algorithm works well in such cases, as reported in [104].

Example 14.4. For each of the 10 persons in the Yale database, there is an image of the person winking. We took these as test images and computed the closest image in the database, essentially by using the algorithm above. In all cases the correct person was identified; see Figure 14.4. ■

Figure 14.4. *The upper row shows the images to be classified, the bottom row the corresponding closest image in the database.*

14.3   Face Recognition with HOSVD Compression

Due to the ordering properties of the core, with respect to the different modes (Theorem 8.3), we may be able to truncate the core in such a way that the truncated HOSVD is still a good approximation of $\mathcal{A}$. Define $F_k = F(:, 1 : k)$ for some value of k that we assume is much smaller than n_i but larger than n_p. Then, for the analysis only, enlarge the matrix so that it becomes square and orthogonal:

$$\widehat{F} = (F_k \; \widetilde{F}_\perp), \qquad \widehat{F}^T \widehat{F} = I.$$

Then truncate the core tensor similarly, i.e., put

$$\widehat{\mathcal{C}} = (\mathcal{S} \times_e G)(1 : k, :, :) \times_i F_k. \tag{14.10}$$

It follows from Theorem 8.3, and the fact that the multiplication by G in the e-mode does not affect the HOSVD ordering properties in the i-mode, that

$$\|\widehat{\mathcal{C}} - \mathcal{C}\|_F^2 = \sum_{\nu=k+1}^{n_i} \sigma_\nu^{(i)}.$$

Therefore, if the rate of decay of the image mode singular values is fast enough, it should be possible to obtain good recognition precision, despite the compression. So if we use $\widehat{\mathcal{C}}$ in the algorithm of the preceding section, we will have to solve least squares problems

$$\min_{\alpha_e} \| \widehat{C}_e \alpha_e - z \|_2$$

with the obvious definition of $\widehat{C}_e$. Now, from (14.10) we have $\widehat{C}_e = F_k \widehat{B}_e$, where $\widehat{B}_e \in \mathbb{R}^{k \times n_p}$. Multiplying by $\widehat{F}$ inside the norm sign we get

$$\| \widehat{C}_e \alpha_e - z \|_2^2 = \| \widehat{B}_e \alpha_e - F_k^T z \|_2^2 + \| \widetilde{F}_\perp^T z \|_2^2.$$

In this "compressed" variant of the recognition algorithm, the operation $\hat{z} = F^T z$ is replaced with $\hat{z}_k = F_k^T z$, and also the least squares problems in the loop are smaller.

Example 14.5. We used the same data as in the previous example but truncated the orthogonal basis in the image mode to rank k. With $k = 10$, all the test images were correctly classified, but with $k = 5$, 2 of 10 images were incorrectly classified. Thus a substantial rank reduction (from 100 to 10) was possible in this example without sacrificing classification accuracy.   ■

In our illustrating example, the numbers of persons and different expressions are so small that it is not necessary to further compress the data. However, in a realistic application, to classify images in a reasonable time, one can truncate the core tensor in the expression and person modes and thus solve much smaller least squares problems than in the uncompressed case.

Part III

Computing the Matrix Decompositions

Chapter 15

Computing Eigenvalues
and Singular Values

In MATLAB and other modern programming environments, eigenvalues and singular values are obtained using high-level functions, e.g., `eig(A)` and `svd(A)`. These functions implement algorithms from the LAPACK subroutine library [1]. To give an orientation about what is behind such high-level functions, in this chapter we briefly describe some methods for computing eigenvalues and singular values of dense matrices and large sparse matrices. For more extensive treatments, see e.g., [4, 42, 79].

The functions `eig` and `svd` are used for dense matrices, i.e., matrices where most of the elements are nonzero. Eigenvalue algorithms for a dense matrix have two phases:

1. Reduction of the matrix to compact form: tridiagonal in the symmetric case and Hessenberg in the nonsymmetric case. This phase consists of a finite sequence of orthogonal transformations.

2. Iterative reduction to diagonal form (symmetric case) or triangular form (nonsymmetric case). This is done using the QR algorithm.

For large, sparse matrices it is usually not possible (or even interesting) to compute all the eigenvalues. Here there are special methods that take advantage of the sparsity. Singular values are computed using variations of the eigenvalue algorithms.

As background material we give some theoretical results concerning perturbation theory for the eigenvalue problem. In addition, we briefly describe the power method for computing eigenvalues and its cousin inverse iteration.

In linear algebra textbooks the eigenvalue problem for the matrix $A \in \mathbb{R}^{n \times n}$ is often introduced as the solution of the polynomial equation

$$\det(A - \lambda I) = 0.$$

In the computational solution of general problems, this approach is useless for two reasons: (1) for matrices of interesting dimensions it is too costly to compute the determinant, and (2) even if the determinant and the polynomial could be computed, the eigenvalues are extremely sensitive to perturbations in the coefficients of the polynomial. Instead, the basic tool in the numerical computation of eigenvalues are *orthogonal similarity transformations*. Let V be an orthogonal matrix. Then make the transformation (which corresponds to a change of basis)

$$A \longrightarrow V^T A V. \tag{15.1}$$

It is obvious that the eigenvalues are preserved under this transformation:

$$Ax = \lambda x \quad \Leftrightarrow \quad V^T A V y = \lambda y, \tag{15.2}$$

where $y = V^T x$.

15.1   Perturbation Theory

The QR algorithm for computing eigenvalues is based on orthogonal similarity transformations (15.1), and it computes a sequence of transformations such that the final result is diagonal (in the case of symmetric A) or triangular (for nonsymmetric A). Since the algorithm is iterative, it is necessary to decide when a floating point number is small enough to be considered as zero numerically. To have a sound theoretical basis for this decision, one must know how sensitive the eigenvalues and eigenvectors are to small perturbations of the data, i.e., the coefficients of the matrix.

Knowledge about the sensitivity of eigenvalues and singular values is useful also for a more fundamental reason: often matrix elements are measured values and subject to errors. Sensitivity theory gives information about how much we can trust eigenvalues, etc., in such situations.

In this section we give a couple of perturbation results, without proofs,[37] first for a symmetric matrix $A \in \mathbb{R}^{n \times n}$. Assume that eigenvalues of $n \times n$ matrices are ordered

$$\lambda_1 \geq \lambda_2 \geq \cdots \geq \lambda_n.$$

We consider a perturbed matrix $A + E$ and ask how far the eigenvalues and eigenvectors of $A + E$ are from those of A.

Example 15.1. Let

$$A = \begin{pmatrix} 2 & 1 & 0 & 0 \\ 1 & 2 & 0.5 & 0 \\ 0 & 0.5 & 2 & 0 \\ 0 & 0 & 0 & 1 \end{pmatrix}, \qquad A + E = \begin{pmatrix} 2 & 1 & 0 & 0 \\ 1 & 2 & 0.5 & 0 \\ 0 & 0.5 & 2 & 10^{-15} \\ 0 & 0 & 10^{-15} & 1 \end{pmatrix}.$$

This is a typical situation in the QR algorithm for tridiagonal matrices: by a sequence of orthogonal similarity transformations, a tridiagonal matrix is made to converge toward a diagonal matrix. When are we then allowed to consider a small off-diagonal floating point number as zero? How much can the eigenvalues of A and $A + E$ deviate?   ∎

---

[37] For proofs, see, e.g., [42, Chapters 7, 8].

Theorem 15.2. *Let $A \in \mathbb{R}^{n \times n}$ and $A + E$ be symmetric matrices. Then*

$$\lambda_k(A) + \lambda_n(E) \leq \lambda_k(A + E) \leq \lambda_k(A) + \lambda_1(E), \qquad k = 1, 2, \ldots, n,$$

and

$$|\lambda_k(A + E) - \lambda_k(A)| \leq \|E\|_2, \qquad k = 1, 2, \ldots, n.$$

From the theorem we see that, loosely speaking, if we perturb the matrix elements by ϵ, then the eigenvalues are also perturbed by $O(\epsilon)$. For instance, in Example 15.1 the matrix E has the eigenvalues $\pm 10^{-15}$ and $\|E\|_2 = 10^{-15}$. Therefore the eigenvalues of the two matrices differ by 10^{-15} at the most.

The sensitivity of the eigenvectors depends on the separation of eigenvalues.

Theorem 15.3. *Let $[\lambda, q]$ be an eigenvalue-eigenvector pair of the symmetric matrix A, and assume that the eigenvalue is simple. Form the orthogonal matrix $Q = \begin{pmatrix} q & Q_1 \end{pmatrix}$ and partition the matrices $Q^T A Q$ and $Q^T E Q$,*

$$Q^T A Q = \begin{pmatrix} \lambda & 0 \\ 0 & A_2 \end{pmatrix}, \qquad Q^T E Q = \begin{pmatrix} \epsilon & e^T \\ e & E_2 \end{pmatrix}.$$

Define

$$d = \min_{\lambda_i(A) \neq \lambda} |\lambda - \lambda_i(A)|$$

and assume that $\| E \|_2 \leq d/4$. Then there exists an eigenvector $\hat{q}$ of $A + E$ such that the distance between q and $\hat{q}$, measured as the sine of the angle between the vectors, is bounded:

$$\sin(\theta(q, \hat{q})) \leq \frac{4 \| e \|_2}{d}.$$

The theorem is meaningful only if the eigenvalue is simple. It shows that eigenvectors corresponding to close eigenvalues can be sensitive to perturbations and are therefore more difficult to compute to high accuracy.

Example 15.4. The eigenvalues of the matrix A in Example 15.1 are

$$0.8820, \ 1.0000, \ 2.0000, \ 3.1180.$$

The deviation between the eigenvectors of A and $A + E$ corresponding to the smallest eigenvalue can be estimated by

$$\frac{4\|e\|_2}{|0.8820 - 1|} \approx 1.07 \cdot 10^{-14}.$$

Since the eigenvalues are well separated, the eigenvectors of this matrix are rather insensitive to perturbations in the data. ∎

To formulate perturbation results for nonsymmetric matrices, we first introduce the concept of an *upper quasi-triangular matrix*: $R \in \mathbb{R}^{n \times n}$ is called upper quasi-triangular if it has the form

$$
R = \begin{pmatrix}
R_{11} & R_{12} & \cdots & R_{1m} \\
0 & R_{22} & \cdots & R_{2m} \\
\vdots & \vdots & \ddots & \vdots \\
0 & 0 & \cdots & R_{mm}
\end{pmatrix},
$$

where each R_{ii} is either a scalar or a 2×2 matrix having complex conjugate eigenvalues. The eigenvalues of R are equal to the eigenvalues of the diagonal blocks R_{ii} (which means that if R_{ii} is a scalar, then it is an eigenvalue of R).

Theorem 15.5 (real Schur decomposition[38]). *For any (symmetric or nonsymmetric) matrix $A \in \mathbb{R}^{n \times n}$ there exists an orthogonal matrix U such that*

$$
U^T A U = R, \tag{15.3}
$$

where R is upper quasi-triangular.

Partition U and R:

$$
U = \begin{pmatrix} U_k & \widehat{U} \end{pmatrix}, \qquad R = \begin{pmatrix} R_k & S \\ 0 & \widehat{R} \end{pmatrix},
$$

where $U_k \in \mathbb{R}^{n \times k}$ and $R_k \in \mathbb{R}^{k \times k}$. Then from (15.3) we get

$$
A U_k = U_k R_k, \tag{15.4}
$$

which implies $\mathcal{R}(A U_k) \subset \mathcal{R}(U_k)$, where $\mathcal{R}(U_k)$ denotes the range of U_k. Therefore U_k is called an *invariant subspace* or an *eigenspace* of A, and the decomposition (15.4) is called a *partial Schur decomposition*.

If A is symmetric, then R is diagonal, and the Schur decomposition is the same as the *eigenvalue decomposition* $U^T A U = D$, where D is diagonal. If A is nonsymmetric, then some or all of its eigenvalues may be complex.

Example 15.6. The Schur decomposition is a standard function in MATLAB. If the matrix is real, then R is upper quasi-triangular:

```
>> A=randn(3)
A = -0.4326     0.2877     1.1892
    -1.6656    -1.1465    -0.0376
     0.1253     1.1909     0.3273

>> [U,R]=schur(A)
U = 0.2827     0.2924     0.9136
    0.8191    -0.5691    -0.0713
   -0.4991    -0.7685     0.4004
```

---

[38]There is complex version of the decomposition, where U is unitary and R is complex and upper triangular.

```
R = -1.6984      0.2644     -1.2548
         0       0.2233      0.7223
         0      -1.4713      0.2233
```

If we compute the eigenvalue decomposition, we get

```
>> [X,D]=eig(A)

X =  0.2827          0.4094 - 0.3992i    0.4094 + 0.3992i
     0.8191         -0.0950 + 0.5569i   -0.0950 - 0.5569i
    -0.4991          0.5948              0.5948


D = -1.6984              0                   0
         0       0.2233+1.0309i              0
         0               0           0.2233-1.0309i
```

The eigenvectors of a nonsymmetric matrix are not orthogonal. ∎

The sensitivity of the eigenvalues of a nonsymmetric matrix depends on the norm of the strictly upper triangular part of R in the Schur decomposition. For convenience we here formulate the result using the complex version of the decomposition.[39]

Theorem 15.7. *Let $U^H AU = R = D + N$ be the complex Schur decomposition of A, where U is unitary, R is upper triangular, and D is diagonal, and let τ denote an eigenvalue of a perturbed matrix $A + E$. Further, let p be the smallest integer such that $N^p = 0$. Then*

$$\min_{\lambda_i(A)} |\lambda_i(A) - \tau| \le \max(\eta, \eta^{1/p}),$$

where

$$\eta = \| E \|_2 \sum_{k=0}^{p-1} \| N \|_2^k.$$

The theorem shows that the eigenvalues of a highly nonsymmetric matrix can be considerably more sensitive to perturbations than the eigenvalues of a symmetric matrix; cf. Theorem 15.2.

Example 15.8. The matrices

$$A = \begin{pmatrix} 2 & 0 & 10^3 \\ 0 & 2 & 0 \\ 0 & 0 & 2 \end{pmatrix}, \qquad B = A + \begin{pmatrix} 0 & 0 & 0 \\ 0 & 0 & 0 \\ 10^{-10} & 0 & 0 \end{pmatrix}$$

have the eigenvalues

---

[39]The notation U^H means transposed and conjugated.

$$2,\ 2,\ 2,$$

and

$$2.00031622776602,\ 1.99968377223398,\ 2.00000000000000,$$

respectively. The relevant quantity for the perturbation is $\eta^{1/2} \approx 3.164 \cdot 10^{-04}$. ∎

The nonsymmetric version of Theorem 15.3 is similar: again the angle between the eigenvectors depends on the separation of the eigenvalues. We give a simplified statement below, where we disregard the possibility of a complex eigenvalue.

Theorem 15.9. *Let $[\lambda, q]$ be an eigenvalue-eigenvector pair of A, and assume that the eigenvalue is simple. Form the orthogonal matrix $Q = \begin{pmatrix} q & Q_1 \end{pmatrix}$ and partition the matrices $Q^T A Q$ and $Q^T E Q$:*

$$Q^T A Q = \begin{pmatrix} \lambda & v^T \\ 0 & A_2 \end{pmatrix}, \qquad Q^T E Q = \begin{pmatrix} \epsilon & e^T \\ \delta & E_2 \end{pmatrix}.$$

Define

$$d = \sigma_{min}(A_2 - \lambda I),$$

and assume $d > 0$. If the perturbation E is small enough, then there exists an eigenvector $\hat{q}$ of $A + E$ such that the distance between q and $\hat{q}$ measured as the sine of the angle between the vectors is bounded by

$$\sin(\theta(q, \hat{q})) \leq \frac{4 \, \| \, \delta \, \|_2}{d}.$$

The theorem says essentially that if we perturb A by ϵ, then the eigenvector is perturbed by ϵ/d.

Example 15.10. Let the tridiagonal matrix be defined as

$$A_n = \begin{pmatrix} 2 & -1.1 & & & \\ -0.9 & 2 & -1.1 & & \\ & \ddots & \ddots & \ddots & \\ & & -0.9 & 2 & -1.1 \\ & & & -0.9 & 2 \end{pmatrix} \in \mathbb{R}^{n \times n}.$$

For $n = 100$, its smallest eigenvalue is 0.01098771, approximately. The following MATLAB script computes the quantity d in Theorem 15.9:

```
% xn is the eigenvector corresponding to
% the smallest eigenvalue
[Q,r]=qr(xn);
H=Q'*A*Q; lam=H(1,1);
A2=H(2:n,2:n);
d=min(svd(A2-lam*eye(size(A2))));
```

We get $d = 1.6207 \cdot 10^{-4}$. Therefore, if we perturb the matrix by 10^{-10}, say, this may change the eigenvector by a factor $4 \cdot 10^{-6}$, approximately. ∎

15.2   The Power Method and Inverse Iteration

The power method is a classical iterative method for computing the largest (in magnitude) eigenvalue and the corresponding eigenvector. Its convergence can be very slow, depending on the distribution of eigenvalues. Therefore it should never be used for dense matrices. Usually for sparse matrices one should use a variant of the Lanczos method or the Jacobi–Davidson method; see [4] and Section 15.8.3. However, in some applications the dimension of the problem is so huge that no other method is viable; see Chapter 12.

Despite its limited usefulness for practical problems, the power method is important from a theoretical point of view. In addition, there is a variation of the power method, inverse iteration, that is of great practical importance.

In this section we give a slightly more general formulation of the power method than in Chapter 12 and recall a few of its properties.

The power method for computing the largest eigenvalue

```
% Initial approximation x
for k=1:maxit
  y=A*x;
  lambda=y'*x;
  if norm(y-lambda*x) < tol*abs(lambda)
    break  % stop the iterations
  end
  x=1/norm(y)*y;
end
```

The convergence of the power method depends on the distribution of eigenvalues of the matrix A. Assume that the largest eigenvalue in magnitude is simple and that λ_i are ordered $|\lambda_1| > |\lambda_2| \geq \cdots \geq |\lambda_n|$. The rate of convergence is determined by the ratio $|\lambda_2/\lambda_1|$. If this ratio is close to 1, then the iteration is very slow.

A stopping criterion for the power iteration can be formulated in terms of the residual vector for the eigenvalue problem: if the norm of the residual $r = A\hat{x} - \hat{\lambda}\hat{x}$ is small, then the eigenvalue approximation is good.

Example 15.11. Consider again the tridiagonal matrix

$$A_n = \begin{pmatrix} 2 & -1.1 & & & \\ -0.9 & 2 & -1.1 & & \\ & \ddots & \ddots & \ddots & \\ & & -0.9 & 2 & -1.1 \\ & & & -0.9 & 2 \end{pmatrix} \in \mathbb{R}^{n \times n}.$$

The two largest eigenvalues of A_{20} are 3.9677 and 3.9016, approximately. As initial approximation we chose a random vector. In Figure 15.1 we plot different error measures during the iterations: the relative residual $\| Ax^{(k)} - \lambda^{(k)}x^{(k)} \|/\lambda_1$ ($\lambda^{(k)}$ denotes

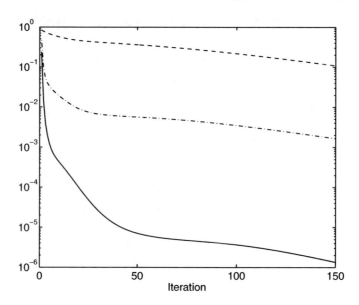

Figure 15.1. *Power iterations for A_{20}. The relative residual $\| Ax^{(k)} - \lambda^{(k)}x^{(k)} \|/\lambda_1$ (solid line), the absolute error in the eigenvalue approximation (dash-dotted line), and the angle (in radians) between the exact eigenvector and the approximation (dashed line).*

the approximation of λ_1 in the kth iteration), the error in the eigenvalue approximation, and the angle between the exact and the approximate eigenvector. After 150 iterations the relative error in the computed approximation of the eigenvalue is 0.0032.

We have $\lambda_2(A_{20})/\lambda_1(A_{20}) = 0.9833$. It follows that

$$0.9833^{150} \approx 0.0802,$$

which indicates that the convergence is quite slow, as seen in Figure 15.1. This is comparable to the reduction of the angle between the exact and the approximate eigenvector during 150 iterations: from 1.2847 radians to 0.0306. ■

If we iterate with A^{-1} in the power method,

$$x^{(k)} = A^{-1}x^{(k-1)},$$

then, since the eigenvalues of A^{-1} are $1/\lambda_i$, the sequence of eigenvalue approximations converges toward $1/\lambda_{min}$, where λ_{min} is the eigenvalue of smallest absolute value. Even better, if we have a good enough approximation of one of the eigenvalues, $\tau \approx \lambda_j$, then the shifted matrix $A - \tau I$ has the smallest eigenvalue $\lambda_j - \tau$. Thus, we can expect very fast convergence in the "inverse power method." This method is called *inverse iteration*.

Inverse iteration

```
% Initial approximation x and eigenvalue approximation tau
[L,U]=lu(A - tau*I);
for k=1:maxit
  y=U\(L\x);
  theta=y'*x;
  if norm(y-theta*x) < tol*abs(theta)
    break  % stop the iteration
  end
  x=1/norm(y)*y;
end
lambda=tau+1/theta; x=1/norm(y)*y;
```

Example 15.12. The smallest eigenvalue of the matrix A_{100} from Example 15.10 is $\lambda_{100} = 0.01098771187192$ to 14 decimals accuracy. If we use the approximation $\lambda_{100} \approx \tau = 0.011$ and apply inverse iteration, we get fast convergence; see Figure 15.2. In this example the convergence factor is

$$\left| \frac{\lambda_{100} - \tau}{\lambda_{99} - \tau} \right| \approx 0.0042748,$$

which means that after four iterations, the error is reduced by a factor of the order $3 \cdot 10^{-10}$. ∎

To be efficient, inverse iteration requires that we have a good approximation of the eigenvalue. In addition, we must be able to solve linear systems $(A - \tau I)y = x$ (for y) cheaply. If A is a band matrix, then the LU decomposition can be obtained easily and in each iteration the system can be solved by forward and back substitution (as in the code above). The same method can be used for other sparse matrices if a sparse LU decomposition can be computed without too much fill-in.

15.3 Similarity Reduction to Tridiagonal Form

The QR algorithm that we will introduce in Section 15.4 is an iterative algorithm, where in each step a QR decomposition is computed. If it is applied to a dense matrix $A \in \mathbb{R}^{n \times n}$, then the cost of a step is $O(n^3)$. This prohibitively high cost can be reduced substantially by first transforming the matrix to compact form, by an orthogonal similarity transformation (15.1),

$$A \longrightarrow V^T A V,$$

for an orthogonal matrix V. We have already seen in (15.2) that the eigenvalues are preserved under this transformation,

$$Ax = \lambda x \quad \Leftrightarrow \quad V^T A V y = \lambda y,$$

where $y = V^T x$.

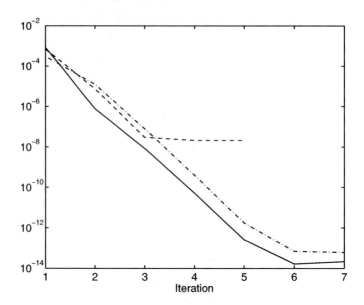

Figure 15.2. *Inverse iterations for A_{100} with $\tau = 0.011$. The relative residual $\| Ax^{(k)} - \lambda^{(k)} x^{(k)} \| / \lambda^{(k)}$ (solid line), the absolute error in the eigenvalue approximation (dash-dotted line), and the angle (in radians) between the exact eigenvector and the approximation (dashed line).*

Let $A \in \mathbb{R}^{n \times n}$ be symmetric. By a sequence of Householder transformations it can be reduced to tridiagonal form. We illustrate the procedure using an example with $n = 6$. First we construct a transformation that zeros the elements in positions 3 through n in the first column when we multiply A from the left:

$$H_1 A = H_1 \begin{pmatrix} \times & \times & \times & \times & \times & \times \\ \times & \times & \times & \times & \times & \times \\ \times & \times & \times & \times & \times & \times \\ \times & \times & \times & \times & \times & \times \\ \times & \times & \times & \times & \times & \times \\ \times & \times & \times & \times & \times & \times \end{pmatrix} = \begin{pmatrix} \times & \times & \times & \times & \times & \times \\ * & * & * & * & * & * \\ 0 & * & * & * & * & * \\ 0 & * & * & * & * & * \\ 0 & * & * & * & * & * \\ 0 & * & * & * & * & * \end{pmatrix}.$$

Elements that are changed in the transformation are denoted by $*$. Note that the elements of the first row are not changed. In an orthogonal similarity transformation we shall multiply by the same matrix transposed from the right. Since in the left multiplication the first row was not touched, the first column will remain unchanged:

$$H_1 A H_1^T = \begin{pmatrix} \times & \times & \times & \times & \times & \times \\ \times & \times & \times & \times & \times & \times \\ 0 & \times & \times & \times & \times & \times \\ 0 & \times & \times & \times & \times & \times \\ 0 & \times & \times & \times & \times & \times \\ 0 & \times & \times & \times & \times & \times \end{pmatrix} H_1^T = \begin{pmatrix} \times & * & 0 & 0 & 0 & 0 \\ \times & * & * & * & * & * \\ 0 & * & * & * & * & * \\ 0 & * & * & * & * & * \\ 0 & * & * & * & * & * \\ 0 & * & * & * & * & * \end{pmatrix}.$$

Due to symmetry, elements 3 through n in the first row will be equal to zero.

In the next step we zero the elements in the second column in positions 4 through n. Since this affects only rows 3 through n and the corresponding columns, this does not destroy the zeros that we created in the first step. The result is

$$H_2 H_1 A H_1^T H_2^T = \begin{pmatrix} \times & \times & 0 & 0 & 0 & 0 \\ \times & \times & * & 0 & 0 & 0 \\ 0 & * & * & * & * & * \\ 0 & 0 & * & * & * & * \\ 0 & 0 & * & * & * & * \\ 0 & 0 & * & * & * & * \end{pmatrix}.$$

After $n - 2$ such similarity transformations the matrix is in tridiagonal form:

$$V^T A V = \begin{pmatrix} \times & \times & 0 & 0 & 0 & 0 \\ \times & \times & \times & 0 & 0 & 0 \\ 0 & \times & \times & \times & 0 & 0 \\ 0 & 0 & \times & \times & \times & 0 \\ 0 & 0 & 0 & \times & \times & \times \\ 0 & 0 & 0 & 0 & \times & \times \end{pmatrix},$$

where $V = H_1^T H_2^T \cdots H_{n-2}^T = H_1 H_2 \cdots H_{n-2}$.

In summary, we have demonstrated how a symmetric matrix can be reduced to tridiagonal form by a sequence of $n - 2$ Householder transformations:

$$A \longrightarrow T = V^T A V, \qquad V = H_1 H_2 \cdots H_{n-2}, \tag{15.5}$$

Since the reduction is done by similarity transformations, the tridiagonal matrix T has the same eigenvalues as A.

The reduction to tridiagonal form requires $4n^3/3$ flops if one takes advantage of symmetry. As in the case of QR decomposition, the Householder transformations can be stored in the subdiagonal part of A. If V is computed explicitly, this takes $4n^3/3$ additional flops.

15.4   The QR Algorithm for a Symmetric Tridiagonal Matrix

We will now give a sketch of the QR algorithm for a symmetric, tridiagonal matrix. We emphasize that our MATLAB codes are greatly simplified and are intended only to demonstrate the basic ideas of the algorithm. The actual software (in LAPACK) contains numerous features for efficiency, robustness, and numerical stability.

The procedure that we describe can be considered as a continuation of the similarity reduction (15.5), but now we reduce the matrix T to diagonal form:

$$T \longrightarrow \Lambda = Q^T T Q, \qquad Q = Q_1 Q_2 \cdots, \tag{15.6}$$

where $\Lambda = \text{diag}(\lambda_1\ \lambda_2\ \ldots, \lambda_n)$. The matrices Q_i will be orthogonal, but here they will be constructed using plane rotations. However, the most important difference between (15.5) and (15.6) is that there does not exist a finite algorithm[40] for computing Λ. We compute a sequence of matrices,

$$T_0 := T, \qquad T_i = Q_i^T T_{i-1} Q_i, \qquad i = 1, 2, \ldots, \qquad (15.7)$$

such that it converges to a diagonal matrix,

$$\lim_{i \to \infty} T_i = \Lambda.$$

We will demonstrate in numerical examples that the convergence is very rapid, so that *in floating point arithmetic the algorithm can actually be considered as finite.* Since all the transformations in (15.7) are similarity transformations, the diagonal elements of Λ are the eigenvalues of T.

We now give a first version of the QR algorithm for a symmetric tridiagonal matrix $T \in \mathbb{R}^{n \times n}$.

QR iteration for symmetric T: Bottom eigenvalue

```
for i=1:maxit    % Provisional simplification
  mu=wilkshift(T(n-1:n,n-1:n));
  [Q,R]=qr(T-mu*I);
  T=R*Q+mu*I
end

function mu=wilkshift(T);
  % Compute the Wilkinson shift
  l=eig(T);
  if abs(l(1)-T(2,2))<abs(l(2)-T(2,2))
    mu=l(1);
  else
    mu=l(2);
  end
```

We see that the QR decomposition of a shifted matrix $QR = T - \tau I$ is computed and that the shift is then added back $T := RQ + \tau I$. The shift is the eigenvalue of the 2×2 submatrix in the lower right corner that is closest to t_{nn}. This is called the *Wilkinson shift*.

We applied the algorithm to the matrix

$$T_6 = \begin{pmatrix} 2 & -1 & 0 & 0 & 0 & 0 \\ -1 & 2 & -1 & 0 & 0 & 0 \\ 0 & -1 & 2 & -1 & 0 & 0 \\ 0 & 0 & -1 & 2 & -1 & 0 \\ 0 & 0 & 0 & -1 & 2 & -1 \\ 0 & 0 & 0 & 0 & -1 & 2 \end{pmatrix}. \qquad (15.8)$$

After the first step the result was (slightly edited for readability)

---

[40]By a finite algorithm, we mean an algorithm for computing the diagonalization of T *in the field of real numbers, i.e., in exact arithmetic,* using a finite number of operations.

$$
T = \begin{matrix}
1.0000 & 0.7071 & 0 & 0 & 0 & 0 \\
0.7071 & 2.0000 & 1.2247 & 0 & 0 & 0 \\
0 & 1.2247 & 2.3333 & -0.9428 & 0 & 0 \\
0 & 0 & -0.9428 & 1.6667 & 0.8660 & 0 \\
0 & 0 & 0 & 0.8660 & 2.0000 & -0.5000 \\
0 & 0 & 0 & 0 & -0.5000 & 3.0000
\end{matrix}
$$

We see first that the triangular structure is preserved and that the off-diagonal elements in the lower right corner have become smaller. We perform three more steps and look more closely at that submatrix:

$$
\begin{matrix}
2.36530292572181 & -0.02609619264716 \\
-0.02609619264716 & 3.24632297453998
\end{matrix}
$$

$$
\begin{matrix}
2.59270689576885 & 0.00000366571479 \\
0.00000366571479 & 3.24697960370634
\end{matrix}
$$

$$
\begin{matrix}
2.77097818052654 & 0.00000000000000 \\
-0.00000000000000 & 3.24697960371747
\end{matrix}
$$

Thus, after four iterations the off-diagonal element has become zero in working precision and therefore we have an eigenvalue in the lower right corner.

When the eigenvalue has been found, we can deflate the problem and continue working with the upper $(n-1) \times (n-1)$ submatrix, which is now

$$
\begin{matrix}
0.4374 & 0.3176 & 0 & 0 & 0 \\
0.3176 & 0.7961 & -0.4395 & 0 & 0 \\
0 & -0.4395 & 1.3198 & 0.2922 & 0 \\
0 & 0 & 0.2922 & 3.4288 & 0.5902 \\
0 & 0 & 0 & 0.5902 & 2.7710
\end{matrix}
$$

We now apply the same algorithm to this matrix. Tracing its lower right submatrix during three subsequent steps, we have

$$
\begin{matrix}
3.74629910763238 & -0.01184028941948 \\
-0.01184028941948 & 2.44513898239641
\end{matrix}
$$

$$
\begin{matrix}
3.68352336882524 & 0.00000009405188 \\
0.00000009405188 & 2.44504186791263
\end{matrix}
$$

$$
\begin{matrix}
3.54823766699472 & 0.00000000000000 \\
-0.00000000000000 & 2.44504186791263
\end{matrix}
$$

After these three iterations we again have an eigenvalue at the lower right corner. The algorithm now proceeds by deflating this eigenvalue and reducing the dimension of the active matrix by one. A preliminary implementation of the algorithm is given below.

QR iteration for symmetric T

```
function [D,it]=qrtrid(T);
  % Compute the eigenvalues of a symmetric tridiagonal
  % matrix using the QR algorithm with explicit
  % Wilkinson shift
  n=size(T,1); it=0;
  for i=n:-1:3
    while abs(T(i-1,i)) > ...
                (abs(T(i,i))+abs(T(i-1,i-1)))*C*eps
      it=it+1;
      mu=wilkshift(T(i-1:i,i-1:i));
      [Q,R]=qr(T(1:i,1:i)-mu*eye(i));
      T=R*Q+mu*eye(i);
    end
    D(i)=T(i,i);
  end
  D(1:2)=eig(T(1:2,1:2))';
```

For a given submatrix T(1:i,1:i) the QR steps are iterated until the stopping criterion

$$\frac{|t_{i-1,i}|}{|t_{i-1,i-1}| + |t_{i,i}|} < C\mu$$

is satisfied, where C is a small constant and μ is the unit round-off. From Theorem 15.2 we see that considering such a tiny element as a numerical zero leads to a very small (and acceptable) perturbation of the eigenvalues. In actual software, a slightly more complicated stopping criterion is used.

When applied to the matrix T_{100} (cf. (15.8)) with the value $C = 5$, 204 QR steps were taken, i.e., approximately 2 steps per eigenvalue. The maximum deviation between the computed eigenvalues and those computed by the MATLAB `eig` function was $2.9 \cdot 10^{-15}$.

It is of course inefficient to compute the QR decomposition of a tridiagonal matrix using the MATLAB function `qr`, which is a Householder-based algorithm. Instead the decomposition should be computed using $n - 1$ plane rotations in $O(n)$ flops. We illustrate the procedure with a small example, where the tridiagonal matrix $T = T^{(0)}$ is 6×6. The first subdiagonal element (from the top) is zeroed by a rotation from the left in the $(1, 2)$ plane, $G_1^T(T^{(0)} - \tau I)$, and then the second subdiagonal is zeroed by a rotation in $(2, 3)$, $G_2^T G_1^T(T^{(0)} - \tau I)$. Symbolically,

$$\begin{pmatrix} \times & \times & & & & \\ \times & \times & \times & & & \\ & \times & \times & \times & & \\ & & \times & \times & \times & \\ & & & \times & \times & \times \\ & & & & \times & \times \end{pmatrix} \longrightarrow \begin{pmatrix} \times & \times & + & & & \\ 0 & \times & \times & + & & \\ & 0 & \times & \times & & \\ & & \times & \times & \times & \\ & & & \times & \times & \times \\ & & & & \times & \times \end{pmatrix}.$$

Note the fill-in (new nonzero elements, denoted $+$) that is created. After $n-1$ steps we have an upper triangular matrix with three nonzero diagonals:

$$R = G_{n-1}^T \cdots G_1^T (T^{(0)} - \tau I) = \begin{pmatrix} \times & \times & + & & & \\ 0 & \times & \times & + & & \\ & 0 & \times & \times & + & \\ & & 0 & \times & \times & + \\ & & & 0 & \times & \times \\ & & & & 0 & \times \end{pmatrix}.$$

We then apply the rotations from the right, $RG_1 \cdots G_{n-1}$, i.e., we start with a transformation involving the first two columns. Then follows a rotation involving the second and third columns. The result after two steps is

$$\begin{pmatrix} \times & \times & \times & & & \\ + & \times & \times & \times & & \\ & + & \times & \times & \times & \\ & & & \times & \times & \times \\ & & & & \times & \times \\ & & & & & \times \end{pmatrix}.$$

We see that the zeroes that we introduced below the diagonal in the transformations from the left are systematically filled in. After $n-1$ steps we have

$$T^{(1)} = RG_1 G_2 \cdots G_{n-1} + \tau I = \begin{pmatrix} \times & \times & \times & & & \\ + & \times & \times & \times & & \\ & + & \times & \times & \times & \\ & & + & \times & \times & \times \\ & & & + & \times & \times \\ & & & & + & \times \end{pmatrix}.$$

But we have made a similarity transformation: with $Q = G_1 G_2 \cdots G_{n-1}$ and using $R = Q^T (T^{(0)} - \tau I)$, we can write

$$T^{(1)} = RQ + \tau I = Q^T (T^{(0)} - \tau I)Q + \tau I = Q^T T^{(0)} Q, \qquad (15.9)$$

so we know that $T^{(1)}$ is symmetric,

$$T^{(1)} = \begin{pmatrix} \times & \times & & & & \\ \times & \times & \times & & & \\ & \times & \times & \times & & \\ & & \times & \times & \times & \\ & & & \times & \times & \times \\ & & & & \times & \times \end{pmatrix}.$$

Thus we have shown the following result.

Proposition 15.13. *The QR step for a tridiagonal matrix*

$$QR = T^{(k)} - \tau_k I, \qquad T^{(k+1)} = RQ + \tau_k I,$$

is a similarity transformation

$$T^{(k+1)} = Q^T T^{(k)} Q, \tag{15.10}$$

and the tridiagonal structure is preserved. The transformation can be computed with plane rotations in $O(n)$ flops.

From (15.9) it may appear as if the shift plays no significant role. However, it determines the value of the orthogonal transformation in the QR step. Actually, the shift strategy is absolutely necessary for the algorithm to be efficient: if no shifts are performed, then the QR algorithm usually converges very slowly, in fact as slowly as the power method; cf. Section 15.2. On the other hand, it can be proved [107] (see, e.g., [93, Chapter 3]) that the shifted QR algorithm has very fast convergence.

Proposition 15.14. *The symmetric QR algorithm with Wilkinson shifts converges cubically toward the eigenvalue decomposition.*

In actual software for the QR algorithm, there are several enhancements of the algorithm that we outlined above. For instance, the algorithm checks all off-diagonals if they are small: when a negligible off-diagonal element is found, then the problem can be split in two. There is also a divide-and-conquer variant of the QR algorithm. For an extensive treatment, see [42, Chapter 8].

15.4.1 Implicit shifts

One important aspect of the QR algorithm is that the shifts can be performed *implicitly*. This is especially useful for the application of the algorithm to the SVD and the nonsymmetric eigenproblem. This variant is based on the *implicit Q theorem*, which we here give in slightly simplified form.

Theorem 15.15. *Let A be symmetric, and assume that Q and V are orthogonal matrices such that $Q^T A Q$ and $V^T A V$ are both tridiagonal. Then, if the first columns of Q and V are equal, $q_1 = v_1$, then Q and V are essentially equal: $q_i = \pm v_i$, $i = 2, 3, \ldots, n$.*

For a proof, see [42, Chapter 8].

A consequence of this theorem is that if we determine and apply the first transformation in the QR decomposition of $T - \tau I$, and if we construct the rest of the transformations in such a way that we finally arrive at a tridiagonal matrix, then we have performed a shifted QR step as in Proposition 15.13. This procedure is implemented as follows.

Let the first plane rotation be determined such that

$$\begin{pmatrix} c & s \\ -s & c \end{pmatrix} \begin{pmatrix} \alpha_1 - \tau \\ \beta_1 \end{pmatrix} = \begin{pmatrix} \times \\ 0 \end{pmatrix}, \tag{15.11}$$

where α_1 and β_1 are the top diagonal and subdiagonal elements of T. Define

$$
G_1^T = \begin{pmatrix} c & s & & & \\ -s & c & & & \\ & & 1 & & \\ & & & \ddots & \\ & & & & 1 \end{pmatrix},
$$

and apply the rotation to T. The multiplication from the left introduces a new nonzero element in the first row, and, correspondingly a new nonzero is introduced in the first column by the multiplication from the right:

$$
G_1^T T G_1 = \begin{pmatrix} \times & \times & + & & & \\ \times & \times & \times & & & \\ + & \times & \times & \times & & \\ & & \times & \times & \times & \\ & & & \times & \times & \times \\ & & & & \times & \times \end{pmatrix},
$$

where $+$ denotes a new nonzero element. We next determine a rotation in the $(2,3)$-plane that annihilates the new nonzero and at the same time introduces a new nonzero further down:

$$
G_2^T G_1^T T G_1 B_2 = \begin{pmatrix} \times & \times & 0 & & & \\ \times & \times & \times & + & & \\ 0 & \times & \times & \times & & \\ & + & \times & \times & \times & \\ & & & \times & \times & \times \\ & & & & \times & \times \end{pmatrix}.
$$

In an analogous manner we "chase the bulge" downward until we have

$$
\begin{pmatrix} \times & \times & & & & \\ \times & \times & \times & & & \\ & \times & \times & \times & & \\ & & \times & \times & \times & + \\ & & & \times & \times & \times \\ & & & + & \times & \times \end{pmatrix},
$$

where by a final rotation we can zero the bulge and at the same time restore the tridiagonal form.

Note that it was only in the determination of the first rotation (15.11) that the shift was used. The rotations were applied only to the *unshifted* tridiagonal matrix. Due to the implicit QR theorem, Theorem 15.15, this is equivalent to a shifted QR step as given in Proposition 15.13.

15.4.2 Eigenvectors

The QR algorithm for computing the eigenvalues of a symmetric matrix (including the reduction to tridiagonal form) requires about $4n^3/3$ flops if only the eigenvalues are computed. Accumulation of the orthogonal transformations to compute the matrix of eigenvectors takes another $9n^3$ flops approximately.

If all n eigenvalues are needed but only a few of the eigenvectors are, then it is cheaper to use inverse iteration (Section 15.2) to compute these eigenvectors, with the computed eigenvalues $\hat{\lambda}_i$ as shifts:

$$(A - \hat{\lambda}_i I)x^{(k)} = x^{(k-1)}, \qquad k = 1, 2, \ldots.$$

The eigenvalues produced by the QR algorithm are so close to the exact eigenvalues (see below) that usually only one step of inverse iteration is needed to get a very good eigenvector, even if the initial guess for the eigenvector is random.

The QR algorithm is ideal from the point of view of numerical stability. There exist an exactly orthogonal matrix Q and a perturbation E such that the computed diagonal matrix of eigenvalues $\hat{D}$ satisfies exactly

$$Q^T(A + E)Q = \hat{D}$$

with $\| E \|_2 \approx \mu \| A \|_2$, where μ is the unit round-off of the floating point system. Then, from Theorem 15.2 we know that a computed eigenvalue $\hat{\lambda}_i$ differs from the exact eigenvalue by a small amount: $\|\hat{\lambda}_i - \lambda_i\|_2 \leq \mu \| A \|_2$.

15.5   Computing the SVD

Since the singular values of a matrix A are the eigenvalues squared of $A^T A$ and AA^T, it is clear that the problem of computing the SVD can be solved using algorithms similar to those of the symmetric eigenvalue problem. However, it is important to avoid forming the matrices $A^T A$ and AA^T, since that would lead to loss of information (cf. the least squares example on p. 54).

Assume that A is $m \times n$ with $m \geq n$. The first step in computing the SVD of a dense matrix A is to reduce it to upper bidiagonal form by Householder transformations from the left and right,

$$A = H \begin{pmatrix} B \\ 0 \end{pmatrix} W^T, \qquad B = \begin{pmatrix} \alpha_1 & \beta_1 & & & \\ & \alpha_2 & \beta_2 & & \\ & & \ddots & \ddots & \\ & & & \alpha_{n-1} & \beta_{n-1} \\ & & & & \alpha_n \end{pmatrix}. \qquad (15.12)$$

For a description of this reduction, see Section 7.2.1. Since we use orthogonal transformations in this reduction, the matrix B has the same singular values as A. Let σ be a singular value of A with singular vectors u and v. Then $Av = \sigma u$ is equivalent to

$$\begin{pmatrix} B \\ 0 \end{pmatrix} \tilde{v} = \sigma \tilde{u}, \qquad \tilde{v} = W^T v, \qquad \tilde{u} = H^T u,$$

from (15.12).

It is easy to see that the matrix $B^T B$ is tridiagonal. The method of choice for computing the singular values of B is the tridiagonal QR algorithm with implicit shifts applied to the matrix $B^T B$, without forming it explicitly.

Let $A \in \mathbb{R}^{m \times n}$, where $m \geq n$. The thin SVD $A = U_1 \Sigma V^T$ (cf. Section 6.1) can be computed in $6mn^2 + 20n^3$ flops.

15.6 The Nonsymmetric Eigenvalue Problem

If we perform the same procedure as in Section 15.3 to a nonsymmetric matrix, then due to nonsymmetry, no elements above the diagonal are zeroed. Thus the final result is a *Hessenberg matrix*:

$$V^T A V = \begin{pmatrix} \times & \times & \times & \times & \times & \times \\ \times & \times & \times & \times & \times & \times \\ 0 & \times & \times & \times & \times & \times \\ 0 & 0 & \times & \times & \times & \times \\ 0 & 0 & 0 & \times & \times & \times \\ 0 & 0 & 0 & 0 & \times & \times \end{pmatrix}.$$

The reduction to Hessenberg form using Householder transformations requires $10n^3/3$ flops.

15.6.1 The QR Algorithm for Nonsymmetric Matrices

The "unrefined" QR algorithm for tridiagonal matrices given in Section 15.4 works equally well for a Hessenberg matrix, and the result is an upper triangular matrix, i.e., the R factor in the Schur decomposition. For efficiency, as in the symmetric case, the QR decomposition in each step of the algorithm is computed using plane rotations, but here the transformation is applied to more elements.

We illustrate the procedure with a small example. Let the matrix $H \in \mathbb{R}^{6 \times 6}$ be upper Hessenberg, and assume that a Wilkinson shift τ has been computed from the bottom right 2×2 matrix. For simplicity we assume that the shift is real. Denote $H^{(0)} := H$. The first subdiagonal element (from the top) in $H - \tau I$ is zeroed by a rotation from the left in the $(1,2)$ plane, $G_1^T(H^{(0)} - \tau I)$, and then the second subdiagonal is zeroed by a rotation in $(2,3)$, $G_2^T G_1^T(H^{(0)} - \tau I)$. Symbolically,

$$\begin{pmatrix} \times & \times & \times & \times & \times & \times \\ \times & \times & \times & \times & \times & \times \\ & \times & \times & \times & \times & \times \\ & & \times & \times & \times & \times \\ & & & \times & \times & \times \\ & & & & \times & \times \end{pmatrix} \longrightarrow \begin{pmatrix} \times & \times & \times & \times & \times & \times \\ 0 & \times & \times & \times & \times & \times \\ & 0 & \times & \times & \times & \times \\ & & \times & \times & \times & \times \\ & & & \times & \times & \times \\ & & & & \times & \times \end{pmatrix}.$$

After $n - 1$ steps we have an upper triangular matrix:

$$R = G_{n-1}^T \cdots G_1^T (H^{(0)} - \tau I) = \begin{pmatrix} \times & \times & \times & \times & \times & \times \\ 0 & \times & \times & \times & \times & \times \\ & 0 & \times & \times & \times & \times \\ & & 0 & \times & \times & \times \\ & & & 0 & \times & \times \\ & & & & 0 & \times \end{pmatrix}.$$

We then apply the rotations from the right, $RG_1 \cdots G_{n-1}$, i.e., we start with a transformation involving the first two columns. Then follows a rotation involving the second and third columns. The result after two steps is

$$\begin{pmatrix} \times & \times & \times & \times & \times & \times \\ + & \times & \times & \times & \times & \times \\ & + & \times & \times & \times & \times \\ & & & \times & \times & \times \\ & & & & \times & \times \\ & & & & & \times \end{pmatrix}.$$

We see that the zeroes that we introduced in the transformations from the left are systematically filled in. After $n - 1$ steps we have

$$H^{(1)} = RG_1 G_2 \cdots G_{n-1} + \tau I = \begin{pmatrix} \times & \times & \times & \times & \times & \times \\ + & \times & \times & \times & \times & \times \\ & + & \times & \times & \times & \times \\ & & + & \times & \times & \times \\ & & & + & \times & \times \\ & & & & + & \times \end{pmatrix}.$$

But we have made a similarity transformation: with $Q = G_1 G_2 \cdots G_{n-1}$ and using $R = Q^T (H^{(0)} - \tau I)$, we can write

$$H^{(1)} = RQ + \tau I = Q^T (H^{(0)} - \tau I)Q + \tau I = Q^T H^{(0)} Q, \qquad (15.13)$$

and we know that $H^{(1)}$ has the same eigenvalues as $H^{(0)}$.

The convergence properties of the nonsymmetric QR algorithm are almost as nice as those of its symmetric counterpart [93, Chapter 2].

Proposition 15.16. *The nonsymmetric QR algorithm with Wilkinson shifts converges quadratically toward the Schur decomposition.*

As in the symmetric case there are numerous refinements of the algorithm sketched above; see, e.g., [42, Chapter 7], [93, Chapter 2]. In particular, one usually uses implicit double shifts to avoid complex arithmetic.

Given the eigenvalues, selected eigenvectors can be computed by inverse iteration with the upper Hessenberg matrix and the computed eigenvalues as shifts.

15.7 Sparse Matrices

In many applications, a very small proportion of the elements of a matrix are nonzero. Then the matrix is called *sparse*. It is quite common that less than 1% of the matrix elements are nonzero.

In the numerical solution of an eigenvalue problem for a sparse matrix, usually an iterative method is employed. This is because the transformations to compact form described in Section 15.3 would completely destroy the sparsity, which leads to excessive storage requirements. In addition, the computational complexity of the reduction to compact form is often much too high.

In Sections 15.2 and 15.8 we describe a couple of methods for solving numerically the eigenvalue (and singular value) problem for a large sparse matrix. Here we give a brief description of one possible method for storing a sparse matrix.

To take advantage of sparseness of the matrix, only the nonzero elements should be stored. We describe briefly one storage scheme for sparse matrices, *compressed row storage*.

Example 15.17. Let

$$A = \begin{pmatrix} 0.6667 & 0 & 0 & 0.2887 \\ 0 & 0.7071 & 0.4082 & 0.2887 \\ 0.3333 & 0 & 0.4082 & 0.2887 \\ 0.6667 & 0 & 0 & 0 \end{pmatrix}.$$

In compressed row storage, the nonzero entries are stored in a vector, here called `val` (we round the elements in the table to save space here), along with the corresponding column indices in a vector `colind` of equal length:

val	0.67	0.29	0.71	0.41	0.29	0.33	0.41	0.29	0.67
colind	1	4	2	3	4	1	3	4	1
rowptr	1	3	6	9	10				

The vector `rowptr` points to the positions in `val` that are occupied by the first element in each row. ∎

The compressed row storage scheme is convenient for multiplying $y = Ax$. The extra entry in the `rowptr` vector that points to the (nonexistent) position after the end of the `val` vector is used to make the code for multiplying $y = Ax$ simple.

Multiplication $y = Ax$ for sparse A

```
function y=Ax(val,colind,rowptr,x)
  % Compute y = A * x, with A in compressed row storage
  m=length(rowptr)-1;
  for i=1:m
    a=val(rowptr(i):rowptr(i+1)-1);
    y(i)=a*x(colind(rowptr(i):rowptr(i+1)-1));
  end
  y=y';
```

It can be seen that compressed row storage is inconvenient for multiplying $y = A^T z$. However, there is an analogous *compressed column storage* scheme that, naturally, is well suited for this.

Compressed row (column) storage for sparse matrices is relevant in programming languages like Fortran and C, where the programmer must handle the sparse storage explicitly [27]. MATLAB has a built-in storage scheme for sparse matrices, with overloaded matrix operations. For instance, for a sparse matrix A, the MATLAB statement y=A*x implements sparse matrix-vector multiplication, and internally MATLAB executes a code analogous to the one above.

In a particular application, different sparse matrix storage schemes can influence the performance of matrix operations, depending on the structure of the matrix. In [39], a comparison is made of sparse matrix algorithms for information retrieval.

15.8   The Arnoldi and Lanczos Methods

The QR method can be used to compute the eigenvalue and singular value decompositions of medium-size matrices. (What a medium-size matrix is depends on the available computing power.) Often in data mining and pattern recognition the matrices are very large and sparse. However, the eigenvalue, singular value, and Schur decompositions of sparse matrices are usually dense: almost all elements are nonzero.

Example 15.18. The Schur decomposition of the link graph matrix in Example 1.3,

$$
P = \begin{pmatrix}
0 & \frac{1}{3} & 0 & 0 & 0 & 0 \\
\frac{1}{3} & 0 & 0 & 0 & 0 & 0 \\
0 & \frac{1}{3} & 0 & 0 & \frac{1}{3} & \frac{1}{2} \\
\frac{1}{3} & 0 & 0 & 0 & \frac{1}{3} & 0 \\
\frac{1}{3} & \frac{1}{3} & 0 & 0 & 0 & \frac{1}{2} \\
0 & 0 & 1 & 0 & \frac{1}{3} & 0
\end{pmatrix},
$$

was computed in MATLAB: [U,R]=schur(A), with the result

```
U =
    -0.0000   -0.4680   -0.0722   -0.0530    0.8792   -0.0000
    -0.0000   -0.4680   -0.0722   -0.3576   -0.2766   -0.7559
    -0.5394    0.0161    0.3910    0.6378    0.0791   -0.3780
    -0.1434   -0.6458   -0.3765    0.3934   -0.3509    0.3780
    -0.3960   -0.2741    0.6232   -0.4708   -0.1231    0.3780
    -0.7292    0.2639   -0.5537   -0.2934    0.0773   -0.0000
```

```
R =
     0.9207      0.2239     -0.2840      0.0148     -0.1078      0.3334
          0      0.3333      0.1495      0.3746     -0.3139      0.0371
          0           0     -0.6361     -0.5327     -0.0181     -0.0960
          0           0           0     -0.3333     -0.1850      0.1751
          0           0           0           0     -0.2846     -0.2642
          0           0           0           0           0      0.0000
```

We see that almost all elements of the orthogonal matrix are nonzero. ∎

Therefore, since the storage requirements become prohibitive, it is usually out of the question to use the QR method. Instead one uses methods that do not transform the matrix itself but rather use it as an operator, i.e., to compute matrix vector products $y = Ax$. We have already described one such method in Section 15.2, the power method, which can be used to compute the largest eigenvalue and the corresponding eigenvector. Essentially, in the power method we compute a sequence of vectors, $Ax_0, A^2x_0, A^3x_0, \ldots$, that converges toward the eigenvector. However, as soon as we have computed one new power, i.e., we have gone from $y_{k-1} = A^{k-1}x$ to $y_k = A^k x$, we throw away y_{k-1} and all the information that was contained in the earlier approximations of the eigenvector.

The idea in a Krylov subspace method is to use the information in the sequence of vectors $x_0, Ax_0, A^2x_0, \ldots, A^{k-1}$, organized in a subspace, the *Krylov subspace*,

$$\mathcal{K}_k(A, x_0) = \text{span}\{x_0, Ax_0, A^2x_0, \ldots, A^{k-1}x_0\},$$

and to extract as good an approximation of the eigenvector as possible from this subspace. In Chapter 7 we have already described the Lanczos bidiagonalization method, which is a Krylov subspace method that can be used for solving approximately least squares problems. In Section 15.8.3 we will show that it can also be used for computing an approximation of some of the singular values and vectors of a matrix. But first we present the Arnoldi method and its application to the problem of computing a partial Schur decomposition of a large and sparse matrix.

15.8.1   The Arnoldi Method and the Schur Decomposition

Assume that $A \in \mathbb{R}^{n \times n}$ is large, sparse, and nonsymmetric and that we want to compute the Schur decomposition (Theorem 15.5) $A = URU^T$, where U is orthogonal and R is upper triangular. Our derivation of the Arnoldi method will be analogous to that in Chapter 7 of the LGK bidiagonalization method. Thus we will start from the existence of an orthogonal similarity reduction to upper Hessenberg form (here $n = 6$):

$$V^T A V = H = \begin{pmatrix} \times & \times & \times & \times & \times & \times \\ \times & \times & \times & \times & \times & \times \\ 0 & \times & \times & \times & \times & \times \\ 0 & 0 & \times & \times & \times & \times \\ 0 & 0 & 0 & \times & \times & \times \\ 0 & 0 & 0 & 0 & \times & \times \end{pmatrix}. \tag{15.14}$$

In principle this can be computed using Householder transformations as in Section 15.3, but since A is sparse, this would cause the fill-in of the zero elements. Instead we will show that columns of V and H can be computed in a recursive way, using only matrix-vector products (like in the LGK bidiagonalization method).

Rewriting (15.14) in the form

$$AV = \begin{pmatrix} Av_1 & Av_2 & \dots & Av_j & \cdots \end{pmatrix} \qquad (15.15)$$

$$= \begin{pmatrix} v_1 & v_2 & \dots & v_j & v_{j+1} & \cdots \end{pmatrix} \begin{pmatrix} h_{11} & h_{12} & \cdots & h_{1j} & \cdots \\ h_{21} & h_{22} & \cdots & h_{2j} & \cdots \\ & h_{32} & \cdots & h_{3j} & \cdots \\ & & \ddots & \vdots & \\ & & & h_{j+1,j} & \\ & & & & \ddots \end{pmatrix} \qquad (15.16)$$

and reading off the columns one by one, we see that the first is

$$Av_1 = h_{11}v_1 + h_{21}v_2,$$

and it can be written in the form

$$h_{21}v_2 = Av_1 - h_{11}v_1.$$

Therefore, since v_1 and v_2 are orthogonal, we have $h_{11} = v_1^T A v_1$, and h_{21} is determined from the requirement that v_2 has Euclidean length 1. Similarly, the jth column of (15.15)–(15.16) is

$$Av_j = \sum_{i=1}^{j} h_{ij}v_i + h_{j+1,j}v_{j+1},$$

which can be written

$$h_{j+1,j}v_{j+1} = Av_j - \sum_{i=1}^{j} h_{ij}v_i. \qquad (15.17)$$

Now, with $v_1, v_2, \dots, v_j$ given, we can compute v_{j+1} from (15.17) if we prescribe that it is orthogonal to the previous vectors. This gives the equations

$$h_{ij} = v_i^T A v_j, \qquad i = 1, 2, \dots, j.$$

The element $h_{j+1,j}$ is obtained from the requirement that v_{j+1} has length 1.

Thus we can compute the columns of V and H using the following recursion:

Arnoldi method

1. Starting vector v_1, satisfying $\|v_1\|_2 = 1$.

2. **for** $j = 1, 2, \ldots$

   (a) $h_{ij} = v_i^T A v_j, \quad i = 1, 2, \ldots, j.$

   (b) $v = A v_j - \sum_{i=1}^{j} h_{ij} v_i.$

   (c) $h_{j+1,j} = \|v\|_2.$

   (d) $v_{j+1} = (1/h_{j+1,j})\, v.$

3. **end**

Obviously, in step j only one matrix-vector product $A v_j$ is needed.

For a large sparse matrix it is out of the question, mainly for storage reasons, to perform many steps in the recursion. Assume that k steps have been performed, where $k \ll n$, and define

$$V_k = \begin{pmatrix} v_1 & v_2 & \cdots & v_k \end{pmatrix}, \qquad H_k = \begin{pmatrix} h_{11} & h_{12} & \cdots & h_{1k-1} & h_{1k} \\ h_{21} & h_{22} & \cdots & h_{2k-1} & h_{2k} \\ & h_{32} & \cdots & h_{3k-1} & h_{3k} \\ & & \ddots & \vdots & \vdots \\ & & & h_{k,k-1} & h_{kk} \end{pmatrix} \in \mathbb{R}^{k \times k}.$$

We can now write the first k steps of the recursion in matrix form:

$$A V_k = V_k H_k + h_{k+1,k} v_{k+1} e_k^T, \tag{15.18}$$

where $e_k^T = \begin{pmatrix} 0 & 0 & \ldots & 0 & 1 \end{pmatrix} \in \mathbb{R}^{1 \times k}$. This is called the *Arnoldi decomposition*.

After k steps of the recursion we have performed k matrix-vector multiplications. The following proposition shows that we have retained all the information produced during those steps (in contrast to the power method).

Proposition 15.19. *The vectors* $v_1, v_2, \ldots, v_k$ *are an orthonormal basis in the Krylov subspace* $\mathcal{K}(A, v_1) = \text{span}\{v_1, A v_1, \ldots, A^{k-1} v_1\}$.

Proof. The orthogonality of the vectors follows by construction (or is verified by direct computation). The second part can be proved by induction. $\quad \square$

The question now arises of how well we can approximate eigenvalues and eigenvectors from the Krylov subspace. Note that if Z_k were an eigenspace (see (15.4)), then we would have $A Z_k = Z_k M$ for some matrix $M \in \mathbb{R}^{k \times k}$. Therefore, to see how much V_k deviates from being an eigenspace, we can check how large the residual $A V_k - V_k M$ is for some matrix M. Luckily, there is a recipe for choosing the optimal M for any given V_k.

Theorem 15.20. *Let $V_k \in \mathbb{R}^{n \times k}$ have orthonormal columns, and define $R(M) = AV_k - V_k M$, where $M \in \mathbb{R}^{k \times k}$. Then*

$$\min_M \|R(M)\|_F = \min_M \|AV_k - V_k M\|_F$$

has the solution $M = V_k^T A V_k$.

Proof. See, e.g., [93, Theorem 4.2.6].   □

From the Arnoldi decomposition (15.18) we immediately get the optimal matrix

$$M = V_k^T (V_k H_k + h_{k+1,k} v_{k+1} e_k^T) = H_k,$$

because v_{k+1} is orthogonal to the previous vectors. It follows, again from the Arnoldi decomposition, that the optimal residual is given by

$$\min_M \|R(M)\|_F = \|AV_k - V_k H_k\|_F = |h_{k+1,k}|,$$

so the residual norm comes for free in the Arnoldi recursion.

Assuming that V_k is a good enough approximation of an eigenspace, how can we compute an approximate partial Schur decomposition $AU_k = U_k R_k$? Let

$$H_k = Z_k \widehat{R}_k Z_k^T$$

be the Schur decomposition of H_k. Then, from $AV_k \approx V_k H_k$ we get the approximate partial Schur decomposition of

$$A\widehat{U}_k \approx \widehat{U}_k \widehat{R}_k, \qquad \widehat{U}_k = V_k Z_k.$$

It follows that the eigenvalues of $\widehat{R}_k$ are approximations of the eigenvalues of A.

Example 15.21. We computed the largest eigenvalue of the matrix A_{100} defined in Example 15.10 using the power method and the Arnoldi method. The errors in the approximation of the eigenvalue are given in Figure 15.3. It is seen that the Krylov subspace holds much more information about the eigenvalue than is carried by the only vector in the power method.   ■

The basic Arnoldi method sketched above has two problems, both of which can be dealt with efficiently:

- In exact arithmetic the v_j vectors are orthogonal, but in floating point arithmetic orthogonality is lost as the iterations proceed. Orthogonality is repaired by explicitly *reorthogonalizing the vectors*. This can be done in every step of the algorithm or selectively, when nonorthogonality has been detected.

- The amount of work and the storage requirements increase as the iterations proceed, and one may run out of memory before sufficiently good approximations have been computed. This can be remedied by restarting the Arnoldi

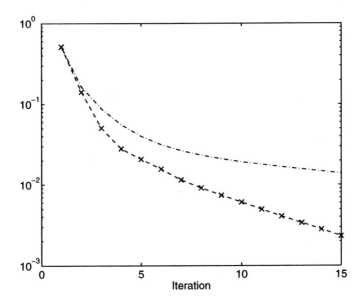

Figure 15.3. *The power and Arnoldi methods for computing the largest eigenvalue of A_{100}. The relative error in the eigenvalue approximation for the power method (dash-dotted line) and the Arnoldi method (dash-$\times$ line).*

procedure. A method has been developed that, given an Arnoldi decomposition of dimension k reduces it to an Arnoldi decomposition of smaller dimension k_0, and in this reduction purges unwanted eigenvalues. This *implicitly restarted Arnoldi method* [64] has been implemented in the MATLAB function eigs.

15.8.2 Lanczos Tridiagonalization

If the Arnoldi procedure is applied to a symmetric matrix A, then, due to symmetry, the upper Hessenberg matrix H_k becomes tridiagonal. A more economical symmetric version of the algorithm can be derived, starting from an orthogonal tridiagonalization (15.5) of A, which we write in the form

$$AV = \begin{pmatrix} Av_1 & Av_2 & \dots & Av_n \end{pmatrix} = VT$$

$$= \begin{pmatrix} v_1 & v_2 & \dots & v_n \end{pmatrix} \begin{pmatrix} \alpha_1 & \beta_1 & & & & \\ \beta_1 & \alpha_2 & \beta_2 & & & \\ & \beta_2 & \alpha_3 & \beta_3 & & \\ & & \ddots & \ddots & \ddots & \\ & & & \beta_{n-2} & \alpha_{n-1} & \beta_{n-1} \\ & & & & \beta_{n-1} & \alpha_n \end{pmatrix}.$$

By identifying column j on the left- and right-hand sides and rearranging the equation, we get

$$\beta_j v_{j+1} = A v_j - \alpha_j v_j - \beta_{j-1} v_{j-1},$$

and we can use this in a recursive reformulation of the equation $AV = VT$. The coefficients α_j and β_j are determined from the requirements that the vectors are orthogonal and normalized. Below we give a basic version of the *Lanczos tridiagonalization method* that generates a Lanczos decomposition,

$$AV_k = V_k T_k + \beta_k v_{k+1} e_k^T,$$

where T_k consists of the k first rows and columns of T.

Lanczos tridiagonalization

---

1. Put $\beta_0 = 0$ and $v_0 = 0$, and choose a starting vector v_1, satisfying $\|v_1\|_2 = 1$.

2. **for** $j = 1, 2, \ldots$

   (a) $\alpha_j = v_j^T A v_j$.

   (b) $v = A v_j - \alpha_j v_j - \beta_{j-1} v_{j-1}$.

   (c) $\beta_j = \|v\|_2$.

   (d) $v_{j+1} = (1/\beta_j)\, v$.

3. **end**

Again, in the recursion the matrix, A is not transformed but is used only in matrix-vector multiplications, and in each iteration only one matrix-vector product need be computed. This basic Lanczos tridiagonalization procedure suffers from the same deficiencies as the basic Arnoldi procedure, and the problems can be solved using the same methods.

The MATLAB function `eigs` checks if the matrix is symmetric, and if this is the case, then the implicitly restarted Lanczos tridiagonalization method is used.

15.8.3   Computing a Sparse SVD

The LGK bidiagonalization method was originally formulated [41] for the computation of the SVD. It can be used for computing a partial bidiagonalization (7.11),

$$AZ_k = P_{k+1} B_{k+1},$$

where B_{k+1} is bidiagonal, and the columns of Z_k and P_{k+1} are orthonormal. Based on this decomposition, approximations of the singular values and the singular vectors can be computed in a similar way as using the tridiagonalization in the preceding section. In fact, it can be proved (see, e.g., [4, Chapter 6.3.3]) that the LGK bidiagonalization procedure is equivalent to applying Lanczos tridiagonalization to the symmetric matrix

$$\begin{pmatrix} 0 & A \\ A^T & 0 \end{pmatrix},$$
(15.19)

with a particular starting vector, and therefore implicit restarts can be applied.

The MATLAB function svds implements the Lanczos tridiagonalization method for the matrix (15.19), with implicit restarts.

15.9 Software

A rather common mistake in many areas of computing is to underestimate the costs of developing software. Therefore, it would be very unwise not to take advantage of existing software, especially when it is developed by world experts and is available free of charge.

15.9.1 LAPACK

LAPACK is a linear algebra package that can be accessed and downloaded from Netlib at http://www.netlib.org/lapack/.

We quote from the Web page description:

LAPACK is written in Fortran 77 and provides routines for solving systems of simultaneous linear equations, least-squares solutions of linear systems of equations, eigenvalue problems, and singular value problems. The associated matrix factorizations (LU, Cholesky, QR, SVD, Schur, generalized Schur) are also provided, as are related computations such as reordering of the Schur factorizations and estimating condition numbers. Dense and banded matrices are handled, but not general sparse matrices. In all areas, similar functionality is provided for real and complex matrices, in both single and double precision.

LAPACK routines are written so that as much as possible of the computation is performed by calls to the Basic Linear Algebra Subprograms (BLAS).... Highly efficient machine-specific implementations of the BLAS are available for many modern high-performance computers.... Alternatively, the user can download ATLAS to automatically generate an optimized BLAS library for the architecture.

The basic dense matrix functions in MATLAB are built on LAPACK.

Alternative language interfaces to LAPACK (or translations/conversions of LAPACK) are available in Fortran 95, C, C++, and Java.

ScaLAPACK, a parallel version of LAPACK, is also available from Netlib at http://www.netlib.org/scalapack/. This package is designed for message passing parallel computers and can be used on any system that supports MPI.

15.9.2   Software for Sparse Matrices

As mentioned earlier, the eigenvalue and singular value functions in MATLAB are based on the Lanczos and Arnoldi methods with implicit restarts [64]. These algorithms are taken from ARPACK at http://www.caam.rice.edu/software/ARPACK/.

From the Web page:

> The package is designed to compute a few eigenvalues and corresponding eigenvectors of a general n by n matrix A. It is most appropriate for large sparse or structured matrices A where structured means that a matrix-vector product w ← Av requires order n rather than the usual order n^2 floating point operations.

An overview of algorithms and software for eigenvalue and singular value computations can be found in the book [4].

Additional software for dense and sparse matrix computations can be found at http://www.netlib.org/linalg/.

15.9.3   Programming Environments

We used MATLAB in this book as a vehicle for describing algorithms. Among other commercially available software systems, we would like to mention Mathematica, and statistics packages like SAS® and SPSS®,[41] which have facilities for matrix computations and data and text mining.

---

[41] http://www.wolfram.com/, http://www.sas.com/, and http://www.spss.com/.

Bibliography

[1] E. Anderson, Z. Bai, C. Bischof, L. S. Blackford, J. Demmel, J. Dongarra, J. Du Croz, A. Greenbaum, S. Hammarling, A. McKenney, and D. C. Sorensen. *LAPACK Users' Guide*, 3rd ed. SIAM, Philadelphia, 1999.

[2] ANSI/IEEE 754. *Binary Floating Point Arithmetic*. IEEE, New York, 1985.

[3] R. Baeza-Yates and B. Ribeiro-Neto. *Modern Information Retrieval*. ACM Press, Addison-Wesley, New York, 1999.

[4] Z. Bai, J. Demmel, J. Dongarra, A. Ruhe, and H. van der Vorst, eds. *Templates for the Solution of Algebraic Eigenvalue Problems: A Practical Guide*. SIAM, Philadelphia, 2000.

[5] R. Barrett, M. Berry, T. F. Chan, J. Demmel, J. Donato, J. Dongarra, V. Eijkhout, R. Pozo, C. Romine, and H. van der Vorst. *Templates for the Solution of Linear Systems: Building Blocks for Iterative Methods*. SIAM, Philadelphia, 1994.

[6] B. Bergeron. *Bioinformatics Computing*. Prentice–Hall, New York, 2002.

[7] P. Berkin. A survey on PageRank computing. *Internet Math.*, 2:73–120, 2005.

[8] M. Berry and M. Browne. Email surveillance using non-negative matrix factorization. *Comput. Math. Organization Theory*, 11:249–264, 2005.

[9] M. W. Berry, S. T. Dumais, and G. W. O'Brien. Using linear algebra for intelligent information retrieval. *SIAM Rev.*, 37:573–595, 1995.

[10] M. J. A. Berry and G. Linoff. *Mastering Data Mining. The Art and Science of Customer Relationship Management*. John Wiley, New York, 2000.

[11] M. W. Berry, ed. *Computational Information Retrieval*. SIAM, Philadelphia, 2001.

[12] M. W. Berry and M. Browne. *Understanding Search Engines. Mathematical Modeling and Text Retrieval*, 2nd ed. SIAM, Philadelphia, 2005.

[13] M. W. Berry, M. Browne, A. Langville, V. P. Pauca, and R. J. Plemmons. *Algorithms and Applications for Approximate Nonnegative Matrix Factorization.* Technical report, Department of Computer Science, University of Tennessee, 2006.

[14] Å. Björck. *Numerical Methods for Least Squares Problems.* SIAM, Philadelphia, 1996.

[15] Å. Björck. The calculation of least squares problems. *Acta Numer.*, 13:1–51, 2004.

[16] K. Blom and A. Ruhe. A Krylov subspace method for information retrieval. *SIAM J. Matrix Anal. Appl.*, 26:566–582, 2005.

[17] V. D. Blondel, A. Gajardo, M. Heymans, P. Senellart, and P. Van Dooren. A measure of similarity between graph vertices: Applications to synonym extraction and web searching. *SIAM Rev.*, 46:647–666, 2004.

[18] C. Boutsidis and E. Gallopoulos. *On SVD-Based Initialization for Nonnegative Matrix Factorization.* Technical Report HPCLAB-SCG-6/08-05, University of Patras, Patras, Greece, 2005.

[19] S. Brin and L. Page. The anatomy of a large-scale hypertextual web search engine. *Comput. Networks ISDN Syst.*, 30:107–117, 1998.

[20] J.-P. Brunet, P. Tamayo, T. R. Golub, and J. P. Mesirov. Metagenes and molecular pattern discovery using matrix factorization. *PNAS*, 101:4164–4169, 2004.

[21] M. C. Burl, L. Asker, P. Smyth, U. Fayyad, P. Perona, L. Crumpler, and J. Aubele. Learning to recognize volcanoes on Venus. *Machine Learning*, 30:165–195, 1998.

[22] P. A. Businger and G. H. Golub. Linear least squares solutions by Householder transformations. *Numer. Math.*, 7:269–276, 1965.

[23] R. Chelappa, C. L. Wilson, and S. Sirohey. Human and machine recognition of faces: A survey. *Proc. IEEE*, 83:705–740, 1995.

[24] N. Christianini and J. Shawe-Taylor. *An Introduction to Support Vector Machines.* Cambridge University Press, London, 2000.

[25] K. J. Cios, W. Pedrycz, and R. W. Swiniarski. *Data Mining. Methods for Knowledge Discovery.* Kluwer, Boston, 1998.

[26] J. M. Conroy, J. D. Schlesinger, D. P. O'Leary, and J. Goldstein. Back to basics: CLASSY 2006. In *DUC 02 Conference Proceedings*, 2006. Available at http://duc.nist.gov/pubs.html.

[27] T. A. Davis. *Direct Methods for Sparse Linear Systems.* Fundamentals of Algorithms 2. SIAM, Philadelphia, 2006.

[28] S. Deerwester, S. Dumais, G. Furnas, T. Landauer, and R. Harsman. Indexing by latent semantic analysis. *J. Amer. Soc. Inform. Sci.*, 41:391–407, 1990.

[29] J. W. Demmel. *Applied Numerical Linear Algebra*. SIAM, Philadelphia, 1997.

[30] I. S. Dhillon and D. S. Modha. Concept decompositions for large sparse text data using clustering. *Machine Learning*, 42:143–175, 2001.

[31] R. O. Duda, P. E. Hart, and D. G. Storck. *Pattern Classification*, 2nd ed. Wiley-Interscience, New York, 2001.

[32] L. Eldén. Partial least squares vs. Lanczos bidiagonalization I: Analysis of a projection method for multiple regression. *Comput. Statist. Data Anal.*, 46:11–31, 2004.

[33] L. Eldén. Numerical linear algebra in data mining. *Acta Numer.*, 15:327–384, 2006.

[34] L. Eldén, L. Wittmeyer-Koch, and H. Bruun Nielsen. *Introduction to Numerical Computation—Analysis and MATLAB Illustrations*. Studentlitteratur, Lund, 2004.

[35] U. M. Fayyad, G. Piatetsky-Shapiro, P. Smyth, and R. Uthurusamy, eds. *Advances in Knowledge Discovery and Data Mining*. AAAI Press/The MIT Press, Menlo Park, CA, 1996.

[36] J. H. Fowler and S. Jeon. *The Authority of Supreme Court Precedent: A Network Analysis*. Technical report, Department of Political Science, University of California, Davis, 2005.

[37] Y. Gao and G. Church. Improving molecular cancer class discovery through sparse non-negative matrix factorization. *Bioinform.*, 21:3970–3975, 2005.

[38] J. T. Giles, L. Wo, and M. W. Berry. GTP (General Text Parser) software for text mining. In *Statistical Data Mining and Knowledge Discovery*, H. Bozdogan, ed., CRC Press, Boca Raton, FL, 2003, pp. 455–471.

[39] N. Goharian, A. Jain, and Q. Sun. Comparative analysis of sparse matrix algorithms for information retrieval. *J. System. Cybernet. Inform.*, 1, 2003.

[40] G. H. Golub and C. Greif. An Arnoldi-type algorithm for computing pagerank. *BIT*, 46:759–771, 2006.

[41] G. Golub and W. Kahan. Calculating the singular values and pseudo-inverse of a matrix. *SIAM J. Numer. Anal. Ser. B*, 2:205–224, 1965.

[42] G. H. Golub and C. F. Van Loan. *Matrix Computations*, 3rd ed. Johns Hopkins Press, Baltimore, 1996.

[43] D. Grossman and O. Frieder. *Information Retrieval: Algorithms and Heuristics*. Kluwer, Boston, 1998.

[44] Z. Gyöngyi, H. Garcia-Molina, and J. Pedersen. Combating web spam with TrustRank. In *Proc., 30th International Conference on Very Large Databases*, Morgan Kaufmann, 2004, pp. 576–587.

[45] J. Han and M. Kamber. *Data Mining: Concepts and Techniques*. Morgan Kaufmann, San Francisco, 2001.

[46] D. Hand, H. Mannila, and P. Smyth. *Principles of Data Mining*. MIT Press, Cambridge, MA, 2001.

[47] T. Hastie, R. Tibshirani, and J. Friedman. *The Elements of Statistical Learning. Data Mining, Inference and Prediction*. Springer, New York, 2001.

[48] T. H. Haveliwala and S. D. Kamvar. *An Analytical Comparison of Approaches to Personalizing PageRank*. Technical report, Computer Science Department, Stanford University, Stanford, CA, 2003.

[49] M. Hegland. Data mining techniques. *Acta Numer.*, 10:313–355, 2001.

[50] N. J. Higham. *Accuracy and Stability of Numerical Algorithms*, 2nd ed. SIAM, Philadelphia, 2002.

[51] I. C. F. Ipsen and S. Kirkland. Convergence analysis of a PageRank updating algorithm by Langville and Meyer. *SIAM J. Matrix Anal. Appl.*, 27:952–967, 2006.

[52] E. R. Jessup and J. H. Martin. Taking a new look at the latent semantic analysis approach to information retrieval. In *Computational Information Retrieval*, M. W. Berry, ed., SIAM, Philadelphia, 2001, pp. 121–144.

[53] S. D. Kamvar, T. H. Haveliwala, and G. H. Golub. Adaptive methods for the computation of pagerank. *Linear Algebra Appl.*, 386:51–65, 2003.

[54] S. D. Kamvar, T. H. Haveliwala, C. D. Manning, and G. H. Golub. *Exploiting the Block Structure of the Web for Computing PageRank*. Technical report, Computer Science Department, Stanford University, Stanford, CA, 2003.

[55] S. D. Kamvar, T. H. Haveliwala, C. D. Manning, and G. H. Golub. Extrapolation methods for accelerating PageRank computations. In *Proc., 12th International World Wide Web Conference*, Budapest, 2003, pp. 261–270.

[56] J. M. Kleinberg. Authoritative sources in a hyperlinked environment. *J. Assoc. Comput. Mach.*, 46:604–632, 1999.

[57] A. N. Langville and C. D. Meyer. Deeper inside PageRank. *Internet Math.*, 1:335–380, 2005.

[58] A. N. Langville and C. D. Meyer. A survey of eigenvector methods for web information retrieval. *SIAM Rev.*, 47:135–161, 2005.

[59] A. N. Langville and C. D. Meyer. *Google's PageRank and Beyond: The Science of Search Engine Rankings*. Princeton University Press, Princeton, NJ, 2006.

[60] L. De Lathauwer, B. De Moor, and J. Vandewalle. A multilinear singular value decomposition. *SIAM J. Matrix Anal. Appl.*, 21:1253–1278, 2000.

[61] C. L. Lawson and R. J. Hanson. *Solving Least Squares Problems*. Classics in Appl. Math. 15. SIAM, Philadelphia, 1995. Revised republication of work first published in 1974 by Prentice–Hall.

[62] Y. LeCun, L. Bottou, Y. Bengio, and P. Haffner. Gradient-based learning applied to document recognition. *Proc. IEEE*, 86:2278–2324, Nov. 1998.

[63] D. Lee and H. Seung. Learning the parts of objects by non-negative matrix factorization. *Nature*, 401:788–791, Oct. 1999.

[64] R. B. Lehoucq, D. C. Sorensen, and C. Yang. *ARPACK Users' Guide: Solution of Large-Scale Eigenvalue Problems with Implicitly Restarted Arnoldi Methods*. SIAM, Philadelphia, 1998.

[65] R. Lempel and S. Moran. Salsa: The stochastic approach for link-structure analysis. *ACM Trans. Inform. Syst.*, 19:131–160, 2001.

[66] O. Mangasarian and W. Wolberg. Cancer diagnosis via linear programming. *SIAM News*, 23:1,18, 1990.

[67] I. Mani. *Automatic Summarization*. John Benjamins, Amsterdam, 2001.

[68] *Matlab User's Guide*. Mathworks, Inc., Natick, MA, 1996.

[69] J. Mena. *Data Mining Your Website*. Digital Press, Boston, 1999.

[70] C. D. Meyer. *Matrix Analysis and Applied Linear Algebra*. SIAM, Philadelphia, 2000.

[71] C. Moler. The world's largest matrix computation. *Matlab News and Notes*, Oct. 2002, pp. 12–13.

[72] J. L. Morrison, R. Breitling, D. J. Higham, and D. R. Gilbert. Generank: Using search engine technology for the analysis of microarray experiment. *BMC Bioinform.*, 6:233, 2005.

[73] P. Paatero and U. Tapper. Positive matrix factorization: A non-negative factor model with optimal utilization of error estimates of data values. *Environmetrics*, 5:111–126, 1994.

[74] L. Page, S. Brin, R. Motwani, and T. Winograd. *The PageRank Citation Ranking: Bringing Order to the Web*. Stanford Digital Library Working Papers, Stanford, CA, 1998.

[75] C. C. Paige and M. Saunders. LSQR: An algorithm for sparse linear equations and sparse least squares. *ACM Trans. Math. Software*, 8:43–71, 1982.

[76] H. Park, M. Jeon, and J. Ben Rosen. Lower dimensional representation of text data in vector space based information retrieval. In *Computational Information Retrieval*, M. W. Berry, ed., SIAM, Philadelphia, 2001, pp. 3–23.

[77] H. Park, M. Jeon, and J. B. Rosen. Lower dimensional representation of text data based on centroids and least squares. *BIT*, 43:427–448, 2003.

[78] V. P. Pauca, J. Piper, and R. Plemmons. Nonnegative matrix factorization for spectral data analysis. *Linear Algebra Appl.*, 416:29–47, 2006.

[79] Y. Saad. *Numerical Methods for Large Eigenvalue Problems*. Manchester University Press, Manchester, UK, 1992.

[80] Y. Saad. *Iterative Methods for Sparse Linear Systems*, 2nd ed. SIAM, Philadelphia, 2003.

[81] G. Salton, C. Yang, and A. Wong. A vector-space model for automatic indexing. *Comm. Assoc. Comput. Mach.*, 18:613–620, 1975.

[82] B. Savas. *Analyses and Test of Handwritten Digit Algorithms*. Master's thesis, Mathematics Department, Linköping University, 2002.

[83] J. D. Schlesinger, J. M. Conroy, M. E. Okurowski, H. T. Wilson, D. P. O'Leary, A. Taylor, and J. Hobbs. Understanding machine performance in the context of human performance for multi-document summarization. In *DUC 02 Conference Proceedings*, 2002. Available at http://duc.nist.gov/pubs.html.

[84] S. Serra-Capizzano. Jordan canonical form of the Google matrix: A potential contribution to the PageRank computation. *SIAM J. Matrix Anal. Appl.*, 27:305–312, 2005.

[85] F. Shahnaz, M. Berry, P. Pauca, and R. Plemmons. Document clustering using nonnegative matrix factorization. *J. Inform. Proc. Management*, 42:373–386, 2006.

[86] P. Simard, Y. Le Cun, and J. S. Denker. Efficient pattern recognition using a new transformation distance. In *Advances in Neural Information Processing Systems* 5, J. D. Cowan, S. J. Hanson, and C. L. Giles, eds., Morgan Kaufmann, San Francisco, 1993, pp. 50–58.

[87] P. Y. Simard, Y.A. Le Cun, J. S. Denker, and B. Victorri. Transformation invariance in pattern recognition—tangent distance and tangent propagation. *Internat. J. Imaging System Tech.*, 11:181–194, 2001.

[88] L. Sirovich and M. Kirby. Low dimensional procedures for the characterization of human faces. *J. Optical Soc. Amer. A*, 4:519–524, 1987.

[89] M. Sjöström and S. Wold. SIMCA: A pattern recognition method based on principal component models. In *Pattern Recognition in Practice*, E. S. Gelsema and L. N. Kanal, eds., North-Holland, Amsterdam, 1980, pp. 351–359.

[90] P. Smaragdis and J. Brown. Non-negative matrix factorization for polyphonic music transcription. In *Proc., IEEE Workshop on Applications of Signal Processing to Audio and Acoustics*, 2003, pp. 177–180.

[91] A. Smilde, R. Bro, and P. Geladi. *Multi-way Analysis: Applications in the Chemical Sciences*. John Wiley, New York, 2004.

[92] G. W. Stewart. *Matrix Algorithms: Basic Decompositions*. SIAM, Philadelphia, 1998.

[93] G. W. Stewart. *Matrix Algorithms Volume II: Eigensystems*. SIAM, Philadelphia, 2001.

[94] G. W. Stewart and J.-G. Sun. *Matrix Perturbation Theory*. Academic Press, Boston, 1990.

[95] J. B. Tenenbaum and W. T. Freeman. Separating style and content with bilinear models. *Neural Comput.*, 12:1247–1283, 2000.

[96] M. Totty and M. Mangalindan. As Google becomes Web's gatekeeper, sites fight to get in. *Wall Street Journal*, 39, Feb. 26, 2003.

[97] L. N. Trefethen and D. B. Bau, III. *Numerical Linear Algebra*. SIAM, Philadelphia, 1997.

[98] L. R. Tucker. The extension of factor analysis to three-dimensional matrices. In *Contributions to Mathematical Psychology*, H. Gulliksen and N. Frederiksen, eds., Holt, Rinehart and Winston, New York, 1964, pp. 109–127.

[99] L. R. Tucker. Some mathematical notes on three-mode factor analysis. *Psychometrika*, 31:279–311, 1966.

[100] M. A. Turk and A. P. Pentland. Eigenfaces for recognition. *J. Cognitive Neurosci.*, 3:71–86, 1991.

[101] G. van den Bergen. *Collision Detection in Interactive 3D Environments*. Morgan Kaufmann, San Francisco, 2004.

[102] M. A. O. Vasilescu. Human motion signatures: Analysis, synthesis, recognition. In *Proc., International Conference on Pattern Recognition (ICPR '02)*, Quebec City, Canada, 2002.

[103] M. A. O. Vasilescu and D. Terzopoulos. Multilinear analysis of image ensembles: Tensorfaces. In *Proc., 7th European Conference on Computer Vision (ECCV '02)*, Copenhagen, Denmark, Lecture Notes in Computer Science 2350, Springer-Verlag, New York, 2002, pp. 447–460.

[104] M. A. O. Vasilescu and D. Terzopoulos. Multilinear image analysis for facial recognition. In *Proc., International Conference on Pattern Recognition (ICPR '02)*, Quebec City, Canada, 2002, pp. 511–514.

[105] M. A. O. Vasilescu and D. Terzopoulos. Multilinear subspace analysis of image ensembles. In *Proc., IEEE Conference on Computer Vision and Pattern Recognition (CVPR '03)*, Madison, WI, 2003, pp. 93–99.

[106] P. Å. Wedin. Perturbation theory for pseudoinverses. *BIT*, 13:344–354, 1973.

[107] J. H. Wilkinson. Global convergene of tridiagonal qr algorithm with origin shifts. *Linear Algebra Appl.*, 1:409–420, 1968.

[108] I. H. Witten and E. Frank. *Data Mining. Practical Machine Learning Tools and Techniques with Java Implementations*. Morgan Kaufmann, San Francisco, 2000.

[109] H. Wold. Soft modeling by latent variables: The nonlinear iterative partial least squares approach. In *Perspectives in Probability and Statistics, Papers in Honour of M. S. Bartlett*, J. Gani, ed., Academic Press, London, 1975.

[110] S. Wold, A. Ruhe, H. Wold, and W. J. Dunn, III. The collinearity problem in linear regression. The partial least squares (PLS) approach to generalized inverses. *SIAM J. Sci. Stat. Comput.*, 5:735–743, 1984.

[111] S. Wold, M. Sjöström, and L. Eriksson. PLS-regression: A basic tool of chemometrics. *Chemometrics Intell. Lab. Systems*, 58:109–130, 2001.

[112] S. Wolfram. *The Mathematica Book*, 4th ed. Cambridge University Press, London, 1999.

[113] D. Zeimpekis and E. Gallopoulos. Design of a MATLAB toolbox for term-document matrix generation. In *Proc., Workshop on Clustering High Dimensional Data and Its Applications*, I. S. Dhillon, J. Kogan, and J. Ghosh, eds., Newport Beach, CA, 2005, pp. 38–48.

[114] H. Zha. Generic summarization and keyphrase extraction using mutual reinforcement principle and sentence clustering. In *Proc., 25th Annual International ACM SIGIR Conference on Research and Development in Information Retrieval*, Tampere, Finland, 2002, pp. 113–120.

Index

volcanos on Venus, 3

Web page, 4
Web search engine, *see* search engine
weighting
        document, 132, 162
        term, 132, 162
Wilkinson shift, 190

XML, 132

Yale Face Database, 170

zip code, 113